Teaching Alone, Teaching Together

Teaching Alone, Teaching Together

Transforming the Structure of Teams for Teaching

James L. Bess and Associates

JOSSEY-BASS
A Wiley Company
San Francisco

Jossey-Bass books and products are available through most bookstores. To contact Jossey-Bass directly, call (888) 378-2537, fax to (800) 605-2665, or visit our website at www.josseybass.com.

Substantial discounts on bulk quantities of Jossey-Bass books are available to corporations, professional associations, and other organizations. For details and discount information, contact the special sales department at Jossey-Bass.

 Manufactured in the United States of America on Lyons Falls Turin Book. This paper is acid-free and 100 percent totally chlorine-free.

Library of Congress Cataloging-in-Publication Data

Bess, James L.
Teaching alone, teaching together : transforming the structure of teams for teaching / James L. Bess and associates.—1st ed.
p. cm. — (The Jossey-Bass higher and adult education series)
Includes bibliographical references and index.
ISBN 0-7879-4798-9 (alk. paper)
1. College teaching—United States. 2. Team learning approach in education—United States. 3.   Teaching teams—United States. 4. Group work in education—United States. I. Title. II. Series

LB2331 .B48 2000
378.1'228—dc21   99-050828

FIRST EDITION
HB Printing 10 9 8 7 6 5 4 3 2 1

The Jossey-Bass
Higher and Adult Education Series

Contents

Figures and Exhibits

Preface

Marshall McLuhan (1964) in *Understanding Media* notes that the introduction of new technologies turns previous technologies into art forms. "Film," he says, "is not really a single medium like song or the written word, but a collective art form with different individuals directing color, lighting, sound, acting, speaking. The press, radio and TV, and the comics are also art forms dependent upon entire teams and hierarchies of skill in corporate action" (p. 292). So also may this be true for the profession of teaching in colleges and universities. Although teaching has traditionally been dominated by the single faculty member alone in his or her classroom, as higher education is increasingly bombarded with external demands for more effectiveness in undergraduate education and with the infusion of innovations in methods and the introduction of new technologies, a fresh look at the traditional modes of organization for teaching is called for—especially one that would involve the talent and input of many persons instead of the one faculty member per course that is the prevailing common technology for teaching. In this new view, for example, to teach a "course," many different individuals—each with special task or methods competencies—might well be joined in a collective or corporate enterprise which is rich and alive with the human interaction that can produce an educational "art form" in the McLuhan mode. Teaching is, after all, not just a mechanical production, but the result of communal human effort and creative imagination that is directed at many different objectives and responsive to many different antecedent, contemporaneous, and anticipated stimuli.

This book represents some radically new and admittedly somewhat speculative ideas about a new way of organizing teaching in colleges and universities. It offers no ready-made panacea to the teaching dilemmas of the modern college or university, but it does address the basic question of the nature of the organization of faculty needed for teaching that will better utilize faculty competencies and will more effectively integrate the disparate elements that now constitute the diverse set of teaching acts in which faculty engage. The approach will be seen to represent a quite new and different perspective on how teaching personnel in colleges and universities can be put to work most effectively to achieve the objectives of teaching. In particular, the book is concerned with the requisite special expertise and competencies, psychological dispositions, and interactions of faculty used in the more traditional modes that have been employed in the past as well as the technological advances that have taken place and those that are on the horizon.

As I discuss in detail in Chapter One, the thesis that will be pursued is that it is possible to design an institutionally efficient mode of organization of faculty whose skills, dispositions, and sources of professional and life satisfaction are intentionally significantly *different* from one another. The following chapters will demonstrate more precisely what these faculty characteristics are and how to make the differences among faculty complementary, indeed, symbiotic, in the service of excellent teaching. Newly conceived and designed "teams" of faculty will work together to produce higher-quality student outcomes. Equally important, the faculty will, collectively and separately, find greater satisfaction and fulfillment in their work and in this work setting.

Aims of the Book

This, then, is a book about the *organization* of teaching—about the connections among the tasks of teaching and among the teachers themselves and about faculty motivation and commitment. Its purpose is to suggest a new mode of revivifying faculty interest in teaching by creating a mode of concerted action that is both more efficient for the college or university and more motivating for the faculty.

There are several other related purposes. The first is to develop a "scientific" understanding of the basis of college teaching. This is not to imply that teaching can be reduced to its component parts and then integrated as a scientific venture only (Gage, 1978). Although the authors of each of the chapters unravel and dissect the separate roles of teaching, they do not depersonalize them, nor do they remove their artistic or aesthetic or creative character.

A second objective is to present a new, or at least a reconstituted, paradigm of teaching—one that returns to the notion of a community of teachers and learners. As noted above, good teaching requires not only diverse skills but also a culture of commitment and dedication to teaching and students that can best be generated through continual communication of evolving aims, problems, ideas, issues, failures, hopes, and achievements (Vygotsky, 1978).

Further, the isolation of teaching has deprived teachers of the benefits and joys of collaborative behaviors. As sociologist Émile Durkheim reminded us, modern social systems are linked by virtue of the division of labor through an "organic solidarity," not a "mechanical" one. He notes: "It is the division of labor that is increasingly filling the role that once fell to the common consciousness" (1933, p. 173). In the presence of differences among workers, the interdependence of their work must bind them in cooperative effort. In our view, the organization of small congeries of faculty joined in challenging common efforts over periods of time is likely to generate a new spirit of mutuality and collective and individual commitment that is not provided by the insular, independent efforts characteristic of most current instructional activity. It will also spawn an organizational context for teaching that provides sustained, observable, timely, and meaningful psychological rewards for teaching—an elusive, nebulous, if not absent, condition in the present system. But this innovative enterprise must be thoughtfully organized, and faculty participants must be unequivocally focused on the task and joined psychologically. This book endeavors to describe a structure for teaching in higher education that not only accomplishes the goals of teaching but also continually renews the energies and commitment of faculty.

Plan of the Book

The subject matter domains central to our concept comprise primarily the *processes* or *methods* of teaching and the modes of integrating them. For purposes of diagnosis and analysis, teaching methods can be considered counterparts to the technological procedures in a manufacturing enterprise, in that they constitute the known workable techniques for accomplishing the tasks. There is some good reason, of course, to be cautious about the use of the word *methods* in connection with teaching, given the long and controversial history of debates in schools of education over elementary and secondary school teacher preparation.

While the processes or methods of teaching are susceptible to a virtual infinite regress of microanalyses of the major components of teaching (for example, down to "optimum hand and body movements"), we have identified just seven major domains for our emphasis. Carefully reviewed in the chapters that follow, they are *pedagogy, research, lecturing, leading discussions, mentoring, curricular-cocurricular integration,* and *assessment.* (Because of space limitations, not all of the major teaching subroles are included.)

Chapter One lays out the commonly cited current problems of teaching. These include teaching effectiveness in the presence of old and new teaching technologies and the motivation of faculty when they are pressured to perform in diverse teaching and non-teaching roles in which they have neither interest nor talent. This chapter introduces the major subroles of teaching and suggests the requisite skills and psychological dispositions that are needed to play them. It lays out the basic thesis of the book, namely, that for teaching to be effective, it is necessary to break down the usual omnibus role into component parts and to assign those parts to different individuals who are both skilled and psychologically disposed to find satisfaction in performing these more narrowly circumscribed parts. Finally, the chapter introduces the idea of a new form of organization for teaching that involves the formation of multiple within-discipline teams of faculty members.

Chapter Two considers the subject of pedagogy, or the design of learning experiences for students. Janet Donald introduces the general and specific domains of pedagogy, including curricular knowledge, content knowledge, knowledge of learners, knowledge of contexts, and knowledge of educational ends. The impact of each of these domains on pedagogy and ultimately on teaching effectiveness may be attenuated by their diffuseness and complexity, the breadth of the knowledge base and skills of students, the decline in attention to individualized learning, and the impersonality of large campuses. The expertise required for pedagogy is thus both diverse and prodigious, requiring substantial mediating and integrating skills.

Chapter Three is directed at the research function. Disciplinary and methodological knowledge is both difficult and time consuming to come by, yet it is the foundation of teaching. The first section of this chapter, by John Braxton and Marietta Del Favero, argues that the incumbent in the role of researcher, in consultation with team colleagues, uniquely defines the domain of inquiry for a course, or unit of instruction. The work of the researcher involves spending a great deal of time exploring information sources through library, electronic, and other means. In the positivistic mode, the researcher engages with realms of knowledge in impersonal, rational, and logical ways, with the aim of producing *objective knowledge* that can be useful to the team. The faculty member who likes this kind of activity takes great pleasure in the juxtaposition of ideas, in discovery, and in logic, organization, integration, and synthesis.

Lecturing is the subject of Chapter Four. The author, Alenoush Saroyan, focuses first on the task attributes needed for effective lecturing, especially when the lecture is not conceived as simple information transfer. One set of these might include skills at presentation—at sensing audience cues, at visual and auditory dynamics, at storytelling, at mystery mood creation, at unraveling conundrums, and at denouement. The skills required for this role are similar to those needed by performers on stage in a theater (though to be sure, mere entertainment is not sufficient). In the second part of the chapter, Saroyan focuses on "the individual lecturer and personal characteristics that either foster or hinder competency in delivering good lectures." The argument includes factors such as personality, beliefs, and social and contextual constraints.

In Chapter Five, about leading discussion groups, Richard Tiberius and Jane Tipping examine the goals of such teaching-learning settings, the problems presented by diverse students with different learning style preferences, the intervention strategies that are needed to deal with them, and the special competencies and psychological orientations of the faculty who will find satisfaction in this role. The authors draw from three literatures in this discussion—the field of teaching practice, the field of cognitive science, and the theories of learning "that emphasize the cognitive, social, and cultural contexts." The skills needed for this team player involve developing formal and informal leadership, understanding group culture and group norms, and communicating effectively. The faculty member occupying this role will find pleasure in the human interactions of the group, from the melding of a diverse set of individuals into an effective learning group, and from the perception of student insights achieved and understanding demonstrated.

If these two chapters—on lecturing and conducting discussions—are concerned with more traditional classroom learning experiences, the next three chapters take up forms of teaching in related learning settings—in the teacher-student mentoring interaction; in the cocurricular environments in which students test out through experience their curricular learnings and from which they bring new problems to be solved intellectually; and in the formative and summative evaluation activities in which students reflect on what they have learned, discover their misapprehensions, and reconstitute knowledge to make it personally meaningful and relevant.

Chapter Six, the faculty-as-mentor chapter, defines and describes the profile of the complete mentor. Mentoring goes beyond the role of adviser, say the authors, Michael Galbraith and Patricia Maslin-Ostrowski. They discuss how true mentoring is a complex process that supports a mutual enhancement of critically reflective and independent thinking. The ultimate goal of mentoring is to assist students in becoming autonomous, self-directed learners. The authors go on to describe the desired attributes of the good mentor and mentee, as well as to explore the various roles and phases of mentorship, such as techniques of listening and interacting. It is unrealistic to believe that all professors are capable of being effective mentors and for that matter that all students are effective mentees. In addition, mentoring is not a short-term relationship. It does not fit the higher education model of taking a series of courses with different professors. Yet if one is engaged in mentoring, one is very much engaged in teaching. The faculty member practicing this role well will find great pleasure in seeing students discover their new identities, both personal and career, and in helping students find avenues to pursue their interests in outside venues.

The cocurriculum used to be called "extracurriculum," thus assigning it to a subordinate position in the academic hierarchy.

In Chapter Seven, Thomas Grace elevates this domain of learning to its proper parallel position in the collegiate learning environment. He argues that integrating the curricular and cocurricular experiences of students is increasingly being recognized as the key to enhancing the educational process. This newly designed team member role bridges the gap between the academic and student affairs functions and includes the design of strategies that complement and reinforce learning in both sectors. The curriculum-cocurriculum integrator also links faculty with other services to students, such as remedial or library support staffs. Psychologically, this person takes pleasure in integrating knowledge from different fields, organizing it in unique ways, and "translating" it for faculty and student use through different technologies or in different learning contexts—for example, books and other instructional media, classrooms, student residence halls, and student recreational areas.

Evaluation of student performance has many functions. Its certification role, however, has unfortunately dominated its other cognitive and affective growth-inducing roles. In Chapter Eight, Bruce Speck notes that any assessment system must "consider assessment methods that will promote both institutional mission and individual professors' concerns without invalidating the generalizability of assessment results to the larger context of higher education as a whole." Issues of the relationship of knowledge generation, transmission, and application to classroom teaching are considered as are formulas for making the evaluations. Speck recognizes how the ambiguity of goals in higher education affects the decisions about evaluation methods. Echoing the theme of the previous chapter, the author here suggests that evaluation must take into account how the overall and specific formal and informal input from the collegiate environment affects cognitive learning and affective growth and development. The faculty member occupying this role is still different psychologically from those in other roles. The faculty member as assessor finds pleasure in diagnosing, analyzing, and making critical judgments about teaching-learning situations, but also enjoys the interpersonally sensitive transmission of these findings to others.

In the penultimate chapter in the book, I address the organizational question of how to carve up the territory of teaching into manageable instructional segments and how to integrate the professionals who have been selected to play the disparate roles—how they must interact and relate to one another as partners in a shared enterprise. This chapter borrows heavily from the literature on team effectiveness in organizations. Issues of autonomy, ambiguity, conflict, and norms and social integration are taken up here. A matrix organizational alternative is proposed to address the need for efficient delivery of teaching by these newly designed teams.

Finally, in Chapter Ten, I offer a recapitulation and reintegration of the critical themes discussed in the book. Anticipating some criticisms of readers, I address such issues as ethnicity, gender, and age in team composition; diversity of student learning styles; the differences in the structure of knowledge in the disciplines; the shift from traditional loose coupling among faculty to a more tightly connected work setting; the variety of goals and objectives across institutions of higher education; the changed nature of "expertise" in academia; and the coming shape of the academic profession.

Disclaimers

Because the subject of teaching is exceedingly broad and the literature voluminous, it is important to state at the outset what this book is not intended to do. It is cast in the mode of "middle-range" theory—that is, it pretends neither to address or deal with the highest level of theoretical abstractions in the field of teaching and learning nor to offer "how-to" pragmatics. Even though some reviewers of drafts of the manuscript for the book recommended more practical examples of how the proposed new structure would work, the authors decided that it would be premature to engage expansively in such suppositions. Doing so might invite readers more to question the examples than to consider the broader conceptual issues that we wish to present.

Further, there are a number of issues related to teaching that this book does not consider, primarily because they represent complex problems that need much fuller attention than can be covered in this already complicated area of the organization of teaching. For example, as Jacques Ellul (1964) has noted, alleged technological imperatives (such as changes in the organizational structure for teaching to meet newly conceived task connections) have important immediate and remote repercussions on the "culture" of an organization. They inculcate their own ideologies and associated organizational practices as well as seductive justifications for their continued use. Though the nature of the changes in academic culture (within institutions and nationally) that would accompany these proposed changes in teaching in higher education is partially considered in subsequent chapters, here we beg the question, leaving to research and later publications the specifics of that new culture and its impact.

Similarly, we are cognizant of the fact that methods of teaching have been largely ignored in graduate school or teaching assistant training. Though there seems to be some evidence of renewed attention around the country to faculty development for new teachers, the subjects of recruitment and graduate education are not extensively considered here.

Though a number of critical related subjects are introduced with considerable sophistication in the various chapters, we do not attempt exhaustively to explore them either theoretically or practically. For example, the goals of American higher education are often hidden, in conflict, or ambiguous on many college campuses. But this subject is broader than the focus of this book. Philosophies of education that underpin both the goals of higher education and the objectives of teaching are also not explored in depth. In addition, although conceptual "models" of effective teaching are utilized, no attempt is made to develop new ones. Student motivation is a subject of considerable research and publication, but its social science foundations are not explicitly addressed here. Nor is learning theory. An important domain in contemporary writing about students is their psychosocial and moral development. Again, we make assumptions that these are (or should be) an aim of colleges and universities, but we do not attempt to reformulate these theories nor to develop new ones. The dynamics of group process are critical to teaching and learning, especially in small classes, but the emphasis in this book is not to expand that domain theoretically, except as it helps inform the team approach advocated. Curriculum is another area not addressed. With new technologies and teaching media flooding the campuses, it is almost impossible not to explore their implications, but our purpose is not to extend knowledge in that domain. Finally, the impact of college on students, so fundamental to all that takes place in colleges and universities, is a rich theoretical and practical mine to be excavated—but not here.

On the other hand, we do recognize the critical place of services that are intimately related to teaching but whose professional workers may not need to be quite so frequently or directly involved in the planning of a teaching-learning experience or in the daily conduct of it. Among these service personnel are those in libraries, computer centers, remedial writing centers, instructional resource centers, career planning offices, and bookstores.

Rewards of Teaching

There are some who will claim that it is the very diversity of the teaching tasks in which faculty engage that provides incentives and sustains the motivation to teach. Though, to be sure, task variety has been shown to be important in motivation when that variety requires commitment and dedication to uninteresting activities, the worker neither performs them well nor finds satisfaction in the performance. Moreover, the less desirable tasks are distractions from engagement in preferred and more enjoyable roles. As explained in detail in Chapter One, the premise of this book is that it is possible to structure academic roles and tasks so that most (though not all) faculty can be engaged largely in activities that they do well and in which they find enjoyment, leaving to others the performance of different tasks in which those others find pleasure.

There are also some who observe that one of the greatest sources of satisfaction in teaching is through the opportunities to express and meet needs for generativity, especially in more mature years. Faculty members (like most human beings) find one source of fulfillment in being of service to others, particularly in sharing their wisdom with younger or less sophisticated individuals. In this book, for faculty a broad set of adult human needs is assumed to be met through teaching. In particular, the authors believe that faculty needs for security, affiliation, achievement, challenge, and ego can be met through identification with a small group and through the accomplishments of that group. With particular respect to generativity needs, it is felt that teams, just as families, can find both direct and vicarious fulfillment through the growth and development of young persons with whom some, but not necessarily all, of the team members are directly involved.

As the chapters unfold, the richness and diversity of the two sets of human beings involved in teaching—faculty and students—will be seen as a persistent theme. We attempt to understand and plan for ways of integrating disparate faculty in a mutual effort to address the needs of a diverse student body. Thus, two groups—one temporary and the other more long-lived—are intertwined in a learning and growth-inducing activity. Different kinds of students come together in artificially created classroom settings, and their needs are met by different kinds of faculty, who meet to share their discrete wisdom and experience with the students. Surely, it is argued in these chapters, the formation of teams of faculty will result in greater wisdom and accumulated skills and competencies that can better address the manifold needs, interests, and values of their students than any one faculty member. And surely, each team member will be happier performing tasks that he or she is most competent to perform and in which there is more interest. And finally, most surely, faculty who are enveloped in a true collaborative community of teaching and learning will find greater joy and fulfillment than in present circumstances.

James L. Bess
New York, New York
January 2000

References

Durkheim, E. (1933). *The division of labor in society*. (G. Simpson, trans.) New York: Free Press.

Ellul, J. (1964). *The technological society* (2nd ed.). New York: Norton.

Gage, N. L. (1978). *The scientific basis of the art of teaching*. New York: Teachers College Press.

McLuhan, M. (1964). *Understanding media*. New York: McGraw-Hill.

Vygotsky, L. S. (1978). *Mind in Society: The development of higher psychological processes*. (M. Cole, Ed.). (p. xvii). Cambridge, MA: Harvard University Press.

Acknowledgments

The authors of this book gratefully acknowledge the assistance of many whose sharp and insightful critiques of early drafts helped clarify and tighten the theses presented. Among these persons, we thank especially Arthur Chickering, Maryellen Weimer, Marilla Svinicki, and Jossey-Bass editor, Gale Erlandson. Needless to say, we, not they, are responsible for the final product.

The Editor

JAMES L. BESS is professor of higher education at New York University. He earned his bachelor of arts degree (1956) in economics at Cornell University, his master of business administration degree (1960) at Harvard University, his master of arts degree (1965) in social foundations at New York University, and his doctorate (1971) in higher education at the University of California at Berkeley. Before joining the teaching staff at New York University, he taught at Teachers College Columbia University, served as director of institutional research at the State University of New York at Stony Brook, as program associate in the School of Continuing Education at New York University, and as financial analyst at Harper and Row, Publishers.

Bess's research activities have been spread over several fields, ranging from the psychological development of students to organizational assessment, organizational design, leadership, comparative higher education, and faculty motivation to teach. His most recent previous book was *Teaching Well and Liking It* (1997). Recent articles on faculty roles and on faculty contracts have appeared in the *Review of Higher Education* and the *Journal of Higher Education*, respectively. His current research, funded by the TIAA-CREF, seeks to identify and understand college seniors who are likely to be excellent college teachers but who decline to enter the field.

Bess has been active in various professional organizations, including the Association for the Study of Higher Education and the American Educational Research Association. He has spent a number of years studying higher education in other countries (Japan, Belarus) and is the recipient of numerous grants, including one from the Fund for the Improvement of Postsecondary Education. He consults regularly with colleges and universities around the world.

The Contributors

JOHN M. BRAXTON is associate professor of education and coordinator of the Higher Education Administration Program in the Department of Leadership and Organizations at Peabody College, Vanderbilt University. He earned his bachelor of arts degree (1967) in psychology from Gettysburg College, his master of arts degree (1968) in college student personnel administration from Colgate University, and his doctorate (1980) in higher education from the Pennsylvania State University. His research interests center on the sociology of the academic profession, the college student experience, and academic course-level processes. He has published over forty refereed journal articles and book chapters on topics related to these areas of research interest. His current scholarly interests include scientific misconduct, the normative structure of undergraduate college teaching, and research and theory development pertaining to college student departure. Recent articles and book chapters on these topics have appeared in the *Journal of Higher Education, Research in Higher Education, Science, Technology and Human Values,* and *Higher Education: Handbook of Theory and Research.* He is the editor of *Faculty Teaching and Research: Is There a Conflict?* and *Perspectives on Scholarly Misconduct in the Sciences.* He is also the author, with Alan E. Bayer, of *Faculty Misconduct in Collegiate Teaching.*

Braxton serves as consulting editor for the *Journal of Higher Education* and for *Research in Higher Education* and is a member of the national review panel for the ASHE-ERIC Higher Education Report series. He also serves as general editor for the Vanderbilt Issues in Higher Education book series published by the Vanderbilt University Press.

MARIETTA DEL FAVERO is a doctoral candidate in higher education administration at Vanderbilt University. She received a master of business administration degree from San Diego State University (1993) and a bachelor's degree in sociology from Newcomb College of Tulane University (1969). In 1998–99, she was selected to represent Peabody College as one of eight master teaching fellows at Vanderbilt, where she presented workshops and consulted with graduate students from all disciplines on teaching development and improvement. Her experience in university administration spans all three segments of postsecondary education in California. Immediately prior to her doctoral work, she served as assistant dean for administration in the University of California Irvine's Graduate School of Management. Del Favero holds memberships in the Association for the Study of Higher Education, the American Educational Research Association, the American Association for Higher Education, and the Southern Sociological Society. Her research interests include academic unit leadership, faculty work and the academic profession, and faculty-administrator relationships.

JANET G. DONALD is professor and director of the Graduate Program in Cognition and Instruction in the Department of Educational and Counselling Psychology at McGill University and is the former director of the Centre for University Teaching and Learning. She received her bachelor of arts degree (1962) and her master of arts degree (1963) in psychology from the University of Western Ontario, and her doctoral degree in educational theory (1968) from the University of Toronto. Her recent research has focused on the quality of postsecondary learning and teaching, particularly on fostering higher-order learning. She is also investigating disciplinary differences in knowledge acquisition and methods of inquiry in higher education, and postsecondary students' conceptualizations of learning and the effect of direct interventions on them. Her most recent book is *Improving the Environment for Learning: Academic Leaders Talk About What Works* (1997), in which she discusses optimal practices for improving student learning. Her articles and book chapters examine disciplinary differences in knowledge validation, the role of higher education centers in improving the academy, the evaluation of undergraduate education, and professors' and students' conceptualizations of learning in physics, engineering, and psychology. Donald won the Distinguished Researcher Award of the Canadian Society for the Study of Higher Education in 1994, its Distinguished Member Award in 1998, and the McKeachie Career Award from the American Educational Research Association in 1999.

MICHAEL W. GALBRAITH is professor of adult education in the Department of Educational Leadership at Florida Atlantic University in Boca Raton. He received his doctor of education degree (1984) from Oklahoma State University in adult education and gerontology, and his master of education degree in gerontology and social theory (1981) and bachelor of education degree in social studies (1973) from the University of Toledo. Before coming to Florida Atlantic University, Galbraith was on the faculties of Temple University and the University of Missouri-Columbia. Galbraith's main research activities have focused on adult learning, teaching adults, administration of community-based organizations, rural education, educational gerontology, and mentoring. His books include *Adult Learning Methods* (second edition) (1998), *Administering Successful Programs for Adults* (1997), *Mentoring: New Challenges and Visions* (1995), *Confronting Controversies in Challenging Times* (1992), *Facilitating Adult Learning* (1991), *Education Through Community Organizations* (1990), and *Adult Learning Methods* (1990). He has authored or coauthored more than eighty refereed journal articles associated with his research interests. Galbraith serves on the editorial boards of three national and international refereed journals, *Adult Education Quarterly, Adult Learning,* and *Community Education Research Digest.* He is also editor in chief of the national book series *Professional Practices in Adult Education and Human Resource Development.* He has received numerous national, regional, and state awards for his leadership in the field of adult and continuing education from various professional associations.

THOMAS W. GRACE has served in a variety of administrative positions in student affairs, including director of residence life, dean for student services, ombudsman, and judicial affairs officer. He has also held appointments as an adjunct faculty member at two institutions and is currently adjunct associate professor in the School of Education at New York University. Grace has presented many programs at national, regional, and state conferences of the American College Personnel Association and the National Association of Student Personnel Administrators on the development of collaborative strategies to respond to issues associated with students with psychological disorders, students who are HIV positive, and initiatives to enhance the role and involvement of adjunct faculty members. He also has conducted workshops for the Rotary Club International, the In-Roads Corporate Internship Program for students of color, and other private and civic organizations on topics such as stress management, multiculturalism in the corporate environment, and the dynamics of power and leadership. He is the coauthor of the ASHE-ERIC publication *New Perspectives for Student Affairs Professionals: Evolving Realities, Roles, and Responsibilities.* Grace received a bachelor of arts degree in American history (1974) and a master of science degree in counseling and college student personnel services (1977) from the State University of New York and a doctor of education degree in educational, career, and counseling psychology from Pennsylvania State University (1983).

PATRICIA MASLIN-OSTROWSKI is associate professor of educational leadership at Florida Atlantic University in Boca Raton, where she is director of research and teaches graduate courses in organizational behavior and change and in middle school administration. Maslin-Ostrowski received a bachelor of arts degree in psychology from Syracuse University (1972) and earned a master's degree (1986) and a doctor of education degree (1994) from Harvard University, where her thesis won a policy research competition sponsored by the Goldie-Anna Charitable Trust and the University of Pennsylvania. She also holds a master of arts degree (1974) and a master of education degree (1975) from Columbia University, and has worked in a variety of educational settings over the past twenty years, including a New York middle school, the Rhode Island Department of Education, the University of Rhode Island, and Rhode Island College. While at the University of Rhode Island, she instituted a mentoring program, Career Advocates for the University of Rhode Island where undergraduates are paired with alumni. She presently works with mentors for disadvantaged youth. Maslin-Ostrowski's research has focused on students at risk of school failure, grouping policies, the development of case stories for teaching educational leadership, and case story as a collaborative inquiry approach to professional development. Currently, she is principal investigator for the South Florida Consortium of Schools and serves on the Middle School Council for Broward County. She writes and lectures regularly about educational matters.

ALENOUSH SAROYAN is associate professor of educational psychology and member of the Centre for University Teaching and Learning at McGill University. She earned her master of arts degree in education from Loyola University of Chicago (1978) and her doctorate from McGill University (1989) in educational psychology. Saroyan's main research activities have focused on the development and assessment of the pedagogical expertise of university professors.

She has published several articles on these topics, including "Incorporating Theories of Teacher Growth and Adult Education in a Faculty Development Program," "Changing Methods and Metaphors: A Case Study of Growth in University Teaching," and "Variations in Lecturing Styles." This research informs her practice as a faculty developer and as a consultant to local colleges and international organizations such as the World Bank. She is currently a member of the Executive of the Canadian Society for the Study of Higher Education and chairs the publications committee of this organization.

BRUCE W. SPECK is associate vice chancellor for academic affairs and professor at the University of North Carolina at Pembroke. He earned his bachelor of arts degree (1975) magna cum laude in English from the University of Northern Colorado, his master of arts in education degree (1980) in English from Wayne State College in Nebraska, and his doctorate (1984) in rhetoric and composition from the University of Nebraska-Lincoln. He has been a technical writer in industry; an assistant professor in English at Indiana-Purdue University at Fort Wayne; and the acting director of the Center for Academic Excellence, Coordinator of the Writing-Across-the-Curriculum Program, and professor of English at the University of Memphis. For the past six years, he has been the coordinator of the Writing-Across-the-Curriculum Program at the University of Memphis. Speck's research interests include both writing and faculty development. He has published articles on writing in relation to ethics, editing, and pedagogical theory and is the coeditor of two Jossey-Bass volumes in the *New Directions for Teaching and Learning* series. In addition, he is the author of four volumes of annotated bibliographies published by Greenwood Press, including *The Grading of Writing*. His *Assessing Students' Classroom Writing: Issues and Strategies* is forthcoming with ASHE-ERIC Higher Education Reports, and he has produced several articles and book chapters on grading students' performance. Speck was appointed acting director of the Center for Academic Excellence (CAE), the faculty development unit at the University of Memphis, to develop the newly instituted CAE. He has initiated a variety of programs, including a teaching certificate for graduate students, a program for international teaching assistants, and numerous faculty development workshops, and has published a semiannual newsletter, *The Mentor*, as a forum for discussing faculty development issues. In his current position at the University of North Carolina at Pembroke, his responsibilities include administering a wide range of faculty evaluations, including tenure and promotion, and post-tenure reviews.

RICHARD G. TIBERIUS earned his bachelor of science degree (1964) in general science, his master of arts degree (1966) in psychology, and his doctorate (1975) in applied psychology, all at the University of Toronto. He holds the position of professor in the Department of Psychiatry and the Centre for Research in Education, where he collaborates with medical faculty in designing and conducting educational research and faculty development efforts. His scholarly work and consulting practice have focused on the improvement of the teaching and learning process. His current research interest is the role of the teacher-student relationship in learning. He has conducted workshops and lectured throughout North America and Europe. His written works include a book entitled *Small Group Teaching: A Trouble-Shooting Guide*, several chapters in *Practically Speaking: A Sourcebook for Instructional Consultants in Higher Education* by K. T. Brinko and R. J. Menges, and journal articles on various topics, including "Implications of the Nature of 'Expertise' for Teaching and Faculty Development" in *To Improve the Academy*, "Metaphors Underlying the Improvement of Teaching and Learning" in *The British Journal of Educational Technology*, and "Alliances for Change: A Procedure for Improving Teaching Through Conversations with Learners and Partnerships with Colleagues" in *Journal of Staff, Program and Organization Development*.

JANE TIPPING is an educational consultant with the Office of Continuing Education, Faculty of Medicine, University of Toronto. Her career in faculty development began in Montreal in 1976. Since then, she has acquired an extensive theoretical and practical background in both adult education and faculty development. In recent years, she has focused on these fields as they apply specifically to continuing professional and medical education. She has presented many workshops across Canada and the United States. Currently, she holds a master of arts degree in adult education from St. Francis Xavier University and is pursuing a doctor of education degree at the University of Toronto. She is a member of the editorial board for the Journal of Continuing Medical Education and is a director on the board for the Alliance of Continuing Medical Education. Her publications include articles on small group teaching and focus on methodology as it applies to education.

Teaching Alone, Teaching Together

Chapter One

Tasks, Talents, and Temperaments in Teaching

The Challenge of Compatibility

James L. Bess

The question of the effectiveness of colleges and universities has assumed a new salience in America. A fresh set of demands on institutions and their faculty for increased productivity has set in motion a variety of efforts by faculty and administrators to examine the processes by which higher education is carried out. Both administrators and faculty have been besieged by angry parents severely disappointed with the results of their children's education for which they, the parents, conscientiously saved, then spent, considerable sums of money. Their hope, as well as their expectation, was that the respected and exalted institutions of higher learning would elevate their students to greater sophistication in matters of culture and general education, as well as in practical skills of value to their lives immediately upon graduation. The unhappiness of parents has been vociferously expressed directly to the colleges and universities, whose teaching staffs have usually been at a loss as to how to respond, except defensively. In addition, as the undercurrent of parental dissatisfaction has made its way to the legislators who vote on educational policy and budgets, the states and federal government—who provide external funds in the form of direct institutional support or financial aid to students—have been demanding that institutions of higher learning take more responsibility for the outcomes of their teaching efforts (Massey & Wilger, 1992).

On some campuses, these pressures have produced a modicum of useful change, especially in the domain of curricular configurations. An increased recognition of the need for more integrated learning experiences for students has provoked some campuses into planning and instituting new formats for linking related (and sometimes unrelated) subject matters—for example, in "federated" systems of courses (Hill, 1984). As with most important innovations, however, those of today are adopted by a relative few and are sustained only as long as the innovators themselves remain committed.

The frustrations of administrators and faculty leaders, moreover, have frequently induced a recourse to practices such as downsizing, replacing tenure with contracts, increasing the use of part-time faculty, disenfranchising faculty from critical decision making, and making demands for evaluation of teaching under threat of punitive action, all of which create an anxiety-ridden ambience that is more likely to make teaching an odious chore than a source of reward and commitment.

What is missing from these efforts is the recognition that what teaching in higher education needs is a *fundamental* change in its organization that yields rewards for faculty that are readily perceived, are significant, meaningful, and sustained, and extend to the entire faculty, rather than to an experimental group. These rewards, which need to be both intrinsic and extrinsic, would result in a new legitimacy for full engagement in *teaching* by faculty, leading ultimately to parity with the rewards of research and publication.

At present, the intellectual and physical isolation of the faculty member as teacher results in a paucity of opportunities for significant reward, save through the professional and personal satisfaction of faculty from seeing students learn and grow under their tutelage. Although this is by no means insignificant, as will be discussed later, many if not most faculty are recruited from the ranks of applicants who show promise for research, not teaching, and hence are unprepared to seek and find the kinds of satisfactions available through teaching. The absence of a structure for the work of teaching that *requires* faculty interaction inhibits the development of peer norms that would support excellence in teaching.

The recognition of the necessity and possibility of disaggregating the basic components of the teaching process raises new and interesting organizational questions about the nature of "specialization" in higher education. In other kinds of professional organizations (for example, hospitals and large law firms) with multifunctioned professionals, there has been a recognition of the limitations on effectiveness of asking professionals to assume roles that are so broad as to diminish their ability to focus on and carry out the separate functions (Charns, Lawrence, & Weisbord, 1977; Charns & Smith, 1993). For faculty in American higher education, on the other hand, subspecialization beyond the broad, general roles of teaching, research, and service has rarely taken place, if it has occurred at all. Most faculty play all of the roles, though with different allocations of time depending on type of institution. Indeed, role overload has come to be the standard lament of faculty throughout higher education (Sorcinelli & Gregory, 1987). There are fewer roles in institutions whose mission is primarily teaching, but even in these, faculty complain of having to wear too many hats and many that are ill fitting.

Recently, however, in higher education, a modicum of de facto specialization has begun. As one example only, some institutions are beginning to hire professional actors to present taped materials that have been prepared by scriptwriters for use in distance or on-line education (Arenson, 1998). To continue to expect faculty competently to perform an ever more sophisticated set of subroles (each of which, not incidentally, requires extensive preparation to develop) may be to risk a further deterioration in teaching effectiveness. Indeed, what this book will attempt to show is that the current clustering of faculty roles in general, and teaching roles in particular, results in neither effectiveness for the institution nor satisfaction for the faculty.

Organizational Forms

The issues of the appropriate organization for effective teaching raised by budget problems and the introduction of new technologies serve as prompts for rethinking the essential bases of specialization in organizations like colleges and universities. The departmental form of organization originated in the knowledge structure of the trivium (the group of studies considered in Greek times the lower division of the liberal arts, consisting of grammar, rhetoric, and logic) and the quadrivium (the group of studies considered the upper division of the liberal arts, consisting of arithmetic, music, geometry, and astronomy) from the Middle Ages. That curriculum and its associated organizational staffing structure were reinforced with the rise of research and its knowledge boundaries in the late nineteenth century. It has ill served liberal education for late twentieth-century undergraduates, however, who suffer from exposure to course-circumscribed fragmented knowledge, unintegrated by purposeful, planned professional faculty cross-course and cross-disciplinary efforts. As a result of this approach, students themselves are asked to make conceptual and philosophical bridges across their disparate courses and to relate that variegated spectrum of knowledge to their developing self-concepts and affective dispositions.

Attempts to breach the disciplinary insularity of academic departments in higher education have bred a small number of successful cross-departmental, team-taught courses. These are usually initiated, however, by individual faculty stimulated by a happenstance discovery of interests in common with other faculty. Only occasionally are these ventures institutionalized as formal curricular programs. They die as originating faculty lose interest (Hill, 1984). Team teaching within disciplines also is not uncommon, but the rationale for the collaboration of faculty again lies in the perceived linkages across course subject matters. That is, the specialized knowledge in the courses that are joined for team teaching are founded in the similarities of the subject matters being taught or their connections to some field of practice.

It is useful at this point to step back and ground the common curricular models in colleges and universities in organizational theories that can help explain the unique "division of labor" for teaching. The organizational structure of colleges and universities can be said to be organized by *product*. In this case, the product is conceived as packages or "bundles" (Parsons, 1974) of knowledge. As Hellriegel, Slocum, and Woodman (1998) note: "Product design involves the establishment of self-contained units, each capable of developing, producing, and marketing its own goods or services" (p. 522). Thus, academic departments essentially establish their knowledge "products" and offer them to the market of current and prospective students at an institution.

An alternative organizational configuration is design by *function*, which focuses on the common required tasks of workers.

Again, from Hellriegel et al., "Functional organizational design involves the creation of positions and units on the basis of specialized activities. Functional grouping of employees is the most widely used and accepted form of departmentalization. Although the functions vary widely depending on the organization . . . grouping tasks and employees by function can be both efficient and economical" (p. 520).

Functions of faculty in colleges and universities are typically described in terms of the tasks of teaching, research, and service. The organizational "units" to which these functions are assigned, however, are individual, multidimensional faculty, who perform all three functions in product-type, discipline-dominated departments. Within the teaching function, moreover, there are many subfunctions—for example, planning pedagogy, gathering information for teaching, lecturing, holding discussion classes, evaluating, mentoring, and working with other institutional personnel—the topics of subsequent chapters. And even within these subfunctions, there are smaller subdivisions. As with the overall three functions faculty perform (teaching, research, and service), so also within the teaching function, traditionally, all of the functions and subfunctions are assigned to individual faculty members, each of whom is responsible for integrating the lot into the preparation and delivery of teaching services.

The idea for this book stemmed from an awareness of a fairly common lament among faculty that there simply is not enough time to perform effectively even in each of the required *major* functions—teaching, research, and service work—that are required of them, nor time to devote to desired work that is elective (Seldin, 1987). Many faculty experience a role overload that reduces the quality of their work and hence the effectiveness of their contribution to their institution. They suffer also from personal anguish when they see that the often considerable time required to be spent on work in which they have little interest or little talent does not either advance them toward their professional goals or result in personal satisfaction. Such phenomena point to the need for a reorganization of faculty into narrower and smaller functional subspecializations.

As noted in the Preface, however, many argue that narrowing the role set represents a cure that may be worse than the disease. They suggest that it is the very diversity of the array of faculty roles that makes the performance of each subrole more effective—the roles allegedly being intimately connected and rewarding—as well as less repetitive and hence less boring and enervating. This argument reaches to the heart of fundamental questions about work design in organizations—in particular, to the optimal balancing of the repetition of tasks performed with acquired expertise and the introduction of new tasks that may challenge existing skill repertories, require new knowledge, and test new skills. Both the exercise of expertise and the challenge of new tasks are critical features in the sustaining of worker motivation. What diminishes motivation, on the other hand, is the repetition of tasks that do not appear difficult and for which skills and interests do not exist.

In this book, we suggest that both the desirable and undesirable aspects of role variety can be organizationally structured in ways that do not demand excessive faculty attention to undesired and unrewarding tasks and yet provide fresh and challenging opportunities for knowledge and skill demonstration. To the argument that the omnibus role for each individual faculty member is necessary because the subroles are intimately related and mutually reinforcing (research feeds teaching and the reverse), we suggest that this interconnectedness can be accomplished more effectively through structured *inter*personal (that is, team-based) rather than the traditional *intra*personal (that is, single-person) integration of tasks. Rather than one faculty member being responsible for all roles, different faculty members can take on different roles and interact to enhance all performances. This notion of interpersonal linkages is central to the idea of team teaching and to the themes developed in the chapters that follow. (Because of space limitations, we omit from the discussion critical and related issues pertaining to the organization of national systems of education. See, for example, Clark, 1997.)

Not all faculty actually want to do research, though this seems to be the near-universal bureaucratic, if not normative, expectation throughout the higher education system (with the possible exception of the two-year colleges). And relatively few faculty are successful at research, at least as measured by publications; nor in fact, do all faculty want to teach, many preferring other faculty roles, like research. Again, effectiveness varies. Such preferences and limited skills are not without precedent in the history of higher education. Recall that the tutors of early American colleges were ill suited to manage the *in loco parentis* responsibilities that accompanied their more intellectual tasks.

Thus, it is not at all clear that either teaching or research in institutions of higher education is carried out with a high level of effectiveness, though to be sure, there are many examples to the contrary; and historically the long-term survival of the higher education system as a whole is some validation of its success. The recent, quite evident dissatisfaction of the general public, however, with the outputs of higher education—that is, largely with the qualities and qualifications of recent bachelor of arts recipients—speaks to the general failure of the system to figure out how best to carry out its teaching mission. It may be that as postsecondary education has continued to expand its access to greater and greater percentages of many different cohort groups (Gumport, Iannozzi, Shaman, & Zemsky, 1997), the public has been "getting wise" to the deficiencies in a large number of existing colleges and universities. The admission of many more students with lower—or at least different—levels and kinds of intellectual ability and intelligences (Gardner, 1993) has created challenges to faculty that they have not had to meet before because the majority have had almost universally bright students in their classes. Those challenges continue unmet or, in many cases, even unrecognized in much of higher education, particularly those institutions employing a traditional instruction paradigm (Barr & Tagg, 1995).

So, at least four constituencies are unhappy with the present state of teaching—the paying public, the receiving or employing public, the student recipients, and the practitioners (the faculty). Doubtless, administrators are also unhappy—in their own ways—to paraphrase Tolstoy. Yet, the *status quo* or even the *status quo ante* organizational structures and methods of teaching persist. There are pockets of experimental teaching with new methods, and the faculty professional development field is active; but for most faculty, teaching remains premised on the technology of the log-linear model—an inspired Mark Hopkins–type teacher and the sequential learning that is carried out in periodic contacts with students.

To reiterate the premise of this book: instructional subfunctions or roles are so diverse and require such different mixes of tasks, talents, and temperaments that the smaller parts must be played by more than one person. Yet, competency in any one of these is a necessary but not sufficient condition. In all work organizations, for successful outcomes to emerge, in addition to proficient workers performing the required tasks, there must be a compatibility among the three elements—the tasks to be performed, the talents needed for the tasks, and the temperaments that are likely to result in satisfaction and motivation (see Cannon-Bowers, Tannenbaum, Salas, & Volpe, 1995). Further, there must be a recognition of the role relationships and associated social relationships among the workers. This means that differentiated functions must be successfully integrated across interdependent workers, or there will be a breakdown in the performance of the overall function (Lawrence & Lorsch, 1967).

The belief of the authors in this book is that in most colleges and universities, the matching of tasks, talents, and temperaments has not been properly addressed in the last fifty years, as the complexities of the delivery of higher education services have become more profound. The structural division of faculty labor for teaching and research and within teaching in most colleges and universities does not attend to this "matching" prerequisite, thus a large majority of faculty are less effective than they might be and are less personally satisfied.

In addition, the usual approach of recruiting allegedly "multi-talented" faculty to perform the vast variety of different roles they play (as many as 325—see Bess, 1982) is now largely inappropriate. The subject of the connections among faculty roles is not new, of course, especially in the light of the extensive literature exploring the relationship between teaching and research (Faia, 1980; Finkelstein, 1984; Clark, 1987; Hammond, Meyer, & Miller, 1969; Cohen & Brawer, 1996; Bess, 1997). The argument suggested here is that the manifold functions and tasks required of faculty are now so extensive that effective professional education and training for each of them are not possible in the time frame of the typical doctoral degree period of study. Moreover, and equally important, it is highly unlikely that the psychological dispositions that are needed for faculty to find enjoyment and satisfaction in all or even most of the tasks will be present in single individuals. Indeed, the opposite is more probable. The composite of different tasks in the current faculty role and the teaching subrole require not only different skills and talents but also varied personality dispositions, some of which may be "intrapsychically incompatible." This means that if a person is psychologically inclined to engage in one, it is quite possible that he or she will not wish to do the other.[1] In sum, the complex mix of tasks, talents, and temperaments required for performing the faculty role demands a fresh look at how the entire enterprise is "packaged" and who should carry out the tasks. This enormously complicated subject is limited in this book to the role of teaching in higher education, the work of which is itself extremely complicated and multifaceted.

Before discussing the tasks of teaching, however, it is important conceptually to lay out the framework for understanding tasks in general and their place in an organizational system with intentional outcomes (Tschan & von Cranach, 1986). It will then be possible to apply this conceptual model to the analysis of teaching tasks. Typically, a task in an organization refers to a concrete segment of work that is performed by a single organizational member. It can be characterized by its relative complexity, divisibility, novelty, interdependence, and capacity for standardization (a function in part of its conceptual nature), different tasks varying in these dimensions (Tschan & von Cranach, 1986). Tasks are set in a bureaucratic structure that is partially constrained by the technologies needed to accomplish them (and often by philosophical or value assumptions about the technologies). For example, some organizations can employ simple technologies that allow workers to follow published manuals or guidebooks, whereas other types of organizations face uncertain environments or variable raw material quality that require their workers continually to invent solutions to unique problems (Perrow, 1970). Still other organizations require processing of raw material involving sequential, reciprocal, or pooled interdependence of tasks that at least partially dictates the organizational structures (Thompson, 1967). Structures are also bound by accepted or intentional cultures and by the

---

1. Dawis and Lofquist, 1984, include skills and abilities in their definition of personality "structure," which is differentiated from personality "style." In this chapter, both are included in the definition of temperament. Data from the Center for Applications of Psychological Type, for example, reveal a wide distribution in faculty personality dispositions (Macdaid, McCaulley, & Kinz, 1986).

uniqueness of the people who are employed. As will be seen later, it is reasonable to question the bases for the conceptualization of teaching tasks and the associated constraints on organizational arrangements for the accomplishment of organizational purposes.

Task complexity, divisibility, novelty, standardization potential, and interdependence are the ingredients of the field of *job design* in the organizational theory literature, particularly that part of it that is concerned with *reengineering* (Hammer & Stanton, 1994). The latter involves the replacement of the dated conceptions of the ways tasks have been performed previously and of the static, unexamined current task relationships. This is followed by attempts to connect more intimately the work that needs to be done with the needs of clients to be served.

As the basic ingredient of job design and reengineering is the "task," attempts have been made to develop exhaustive lists of categories describing task dimensions. In Exhibit 1.1, for example, are some categories from the Position Analysis Questionnaire developed at Purdue University, with some refinements offered by Richard Tiberius that suggest one way of meaningfully differentiating among tasks (see Homans, 1950; Freidson, 1973; Abbott, 1988). These distinctions can usefully be applied to the domain of teaching.

Tasks of Teaching

As the authors of this book reviewed the tasks of teaching in the light of these and other categorization schemes, it became clear that teaching policies and practices depend very much on conceptualizations of, or at least assumptions about, the goals of postsecondary education. As these vary by and within institution, discipline, and constituency (faculty, students, administrators, and external stakeholders), the conception of which tasks are considered within the realm of teaching differs markedly, partly because of the goals of each constituency (Hativa & Marincovich, 1995).

For example, across the range of Carnegie-type institutions and others outside (such as the military and the corporate sector), what constitutes teaching differs in important ways. A related set of differences occurs with respect to the structure of knowledge across disciplines (Donald, 1983). The work of the teacher is specialized

Exhibit 1.1. Sample Categories of Analytical Task Dimensions.

Knowledge

How much "formal" knowledge about the field is required? How much "informal" knowledge in the form of "common sense" and background knowledge is required?

Information Input

Where and how does the worker get the information used in performing the job?

Mental Processes

What reasoning, decision-making, planning, and information-processing activities are required to perform the job?

Attitudes and Sentiments

For expert performance on the job, what kinds and strengths of beliefs and what attitudes (for example, toward students, toward education in general, toward the institution and its values) are necessary?

Formal Skills

What explicit self-regulatory strategies are necessary for dealing with people, data, and things in the work? That is, to what degree must the job incumbent be consciously in control of the attitudes and behavior that are involved in his or her duties?

Implicit Skills

What latent or tacit self-regulatory skills are utilized in the performance of the job?

Job Context

In what physical and social contexts is the work performed? For example, what structure of the work organization, "climate" for tolerance and human development, and degree of autonomy are required for the work to be done well?

Relationships and Interactions

How much and what kind of interpersonal contact is involved in the work?

Mechanical Support

What machines, tools, and equipment are needed?

Other Job Characteristics

What activities, conditions, or characteristics other than those described above are relevant to the job?

Note: Items in bold are taken from Bemis, Belenky, and Soder, 1983, pp. 30–31.

depending on the structure of knowledge in the course or seminar being taught. Thus, not only is English different from physics, but the philosophical assumptions and sociological characteristics of each discipline and even departments within them vary (Adkinson, 1979). One department may see truth as "personal meaning," another as "empirically verifiable facts," and so forth. What is taught and how it is taught and what kinds of teachers are necessary to teach it are also different. As noted earlier, in higher education, these epistemological differences among the faculty in the various disciplines (see Mannheim, 1952; Bell, 1966; King, 1966) represent a somewhat arbitrary acceptance of the structure of knowledge as it has evolved as legitimate grounds for the division of labor, not only for research but also for the proper organization of teaching.

In addition to the qualitative or philosophical differences by disciplines, the constituencies that use the products of teaching also have different conceptions of their nature. The corporate sector, for example, may expect skilled novices to be produced at colleges and universities. Hence, to meet their expectations, "training" would constitute the prime appropriate method of teaching. The external public at large, on the other hand, may expect to receive as college graduates "civilized" men and women, who can and will participate meaningfully in civic and cultural affairs. Education in values and values sensitivity may thus be required, and educational processes such as multicultural awareness workshops and peer-led philosophy discussions would be legitimate. The science community may wish to have sophisticated problem solvers, who are knowledgeable about pressing contemporary technological issues and problems, thus requiring much laboratory experience and mentoring. As a final example, students themselves may be seeking personal, vocational, and even racial "identity." Such objectives may involve still other pedagogical approaches. Thus, not only does the subject matter for teaching differ according to goals, but the methods to be employed vary as well according to the expectations of the final student product.

In point of fact, each of these examples of expectations of goals and methods of teaching may demand an entirely different set of skills of the teacher. For the purposes of explaining the themes of this book, however, the authors have made some fairly traditional assumptions about the goals of instruction in undergraduate education. Among these are that the instruction is primarily intended to introduce new ideas; expand interests; develop critical thinking skills and habits; encourage divergent thinking; engender exploration of alternative ranges and manifestations of personality; foster relativistic thinking, especially about values; and generate tentative commitment to some of these values. (Training in vocational skills, especially at community colleges, might be added.) No mean feat! This is obviously a simplification, but it permits a unifying approach for the authors of the chapters. Doubtless, others with different conceptions of teaching will see alternative configurations for designing the system.

Even this restricted definition of the goals of instruction in colleges and universities, however, evokes a wide variety of processes that must be mastered in order to achieve the ends of teaching. Note that the word *processes* is the focus of the design. This is not to suggest that subject matter should be abandoned as a basis for organizing teaching in higher education, though as noted above, there is some reason to believe that the current disciplinary boundaries that now define the tasks are more responsive to the epistemological and ontological assumptions of researchers in the fields than to the needs of learners. Reconceptualizations of the curriculum across disciplines, however needed, are beyond the scope of this volume.

The tasks of teaching that the chapter authors take up constitute subfunctions or roles traditionally performed by faculty as teachers in higher education. The core of essential tasks that are associated with each are described, and their relations to other subfunctions are indicated.

Talents (Skills) of Teaching

The argument put forth here is that the processes of transferring knowledge, of engendering value awareness, of developing critical thinking, or of facilitating growth and development require not only mastery by the faculty member qua expert of a body of knowledge but also high-level competencies in multiple teaching methods and technologies—each of which, in turn, involves a diverse set of skills, as the chapters that follow illustrate. The enormous variety of teaching tasks demanded of faculty gives rise to the question of whether they can do all of them equally well. It is likely that few individual faculty members have the skills to perform with equal competence all or most of the major roles in their academic assignments or even the main teaching tasks that are required of them.

Teachers, therefore, must become specialized "experts." Hence, the relationship of skills and talents to the concept of expertise is important to clarify. In our view, teaching expertise is not a generalized capability. It is quite specific and is acquired through the course of long study and experience. The exercise of expertise is manifested as a combination of behaviors elicited from personally organized cognitive memory banks; from informal, disorganized bits of knowledge; and from intuition informed by experience. The focus of faculty in seeking to enhance their expertise is circumscribed. As Johnson (1988) notes, experts (in contrast to amateurs) "appear to use their knowledge to examine only information that they consider diagnostic, limiting their search to a smaller subset of the available information" (p. 217). Walton (1997) has much to say on this subject, and it is worth citing a long section of his work. He notes that:

[S]omeone is an expert not only because she knows a lot of facts, but because she can carry out certain actions in a skilled, smooth, and practiced manner, applying their knowledge in a clever way to specific tasks and problems. Emphasizing this practical nature of expertise, Dreyfus and Dreyfus stress that expert actions are carried out smoothly and automatically, and that an expert action is not characteristically carried out by detached or conscious decision-making or problem solving. Dreyfus and Dreyfus distinguish five stages in the skill acquisition process of an expert: (1) novice, (2) advanced beginner, (3) competence, (4) proficiency, and (5) expertise. In the evolution through these stages to expertise, Dreyfus and Dreyfus see a refinement of intuitive skills that become so ingrained in the expert that she is hardly aware of them. 'An expert's skill has become so much a part of her that she need be no more aware of it than she is of her own body' (1986, p. 31). According to their account, expertise is a kind of holistic, situational understanding that cannot be expressed as a calculative or conscious sequence of reasoning that proceeds by applying rules to facts. Although decisions are made in a more analytical way at the four lower stages of skill acquisition, the fifth stage of expertise is more intuitive [p. 111].

This is a somewhat surprising notion of an expert since an expert is usually conceived as a "source of information." However, as Walton notes, expertise involves more than cognitive skills—or, in the case of teaching, more than subject matter knowledge. It embodies the skills and talents of "knowing how"—the practical reasoning and tacit or intuitive knowledge that the *craft* of teaching requires. Further, as Johnson notes, in many ways, *expertise* is paradoxical. He notes, "As individuals master more and more knowledge in order to do a task efficiently as well as accurately, they also lose awareness of what they know" (1983, p. 79). The question of expertise has relevance for the reorganization of teaching as it is put forth in this book since it asks whether the knowledge of subject matter and the knowledge of how to engage in the tasks of teaching can be incorporated in single individuals. If it is true that experts as qua possessors of knowledge lose the ability to discern how the complexities and nuances of the subject matter can be conveyed to novices, then it may be more sensible to assign the tasks of knowing (and finding out) to specialists with talents and skills in that area and the tasks of utilizing that knowledge to other specialists with other talents and skills. As Walton (1997) also notes: "On account of the inaccessibility problem and the paradox of expertise, the interface between the expert source and the layperson user needs to be a complex layer of judgments, explanations, questions, and so forth. When dealing with encounters of the kinds of high-level human experts encountered in typical cases where the *argumentum ad verecundiam* might be a fallacy, there is a gap between possessing knowledge and transmitting it to a nonexpert" (p. 114).

An additional argument for separating the teaching subroles involves the sensitivity of teachers to their students. Bereiter & Scardamalia (1993), for example, citing Robert Welker's work, note that "teachers must be caring, sensitive people and . . . teaching is a complex human enterprise that cannot be reduced to technique. Teachers ought not to seal themselves off as an elite community of experts, but ought to be involved with and responsive to the communities in which they serve" (p. 8).

The point is not that teachers do not have to be experts but that different kinds of expertise are required for competent teaching, and not all faculty possess them all. Certainly, not all faculty can be characterized as "sensitive" experts in teaching in the sense cited above, but most assuredly, some faculty can be so described. Their special talents and expertise, then, might better be attached to a team effort in which it will complement other kinds of expertise needed for teaching and held by other team members.

Temperaments of Teachers

Temperaments refer to the variety of psychological characteristics that individuals possess that are primarily derived from genetic dispositions and that are sustained throughout the life cycle. As Roe (1984) suggests, in attempting to conceptualize individual characteristics, it is important to identify "basic" features that cannot further be reduced to other, more fundamental constructs and that are not subject to change owing to temporal vicissitudes. He suggests that it is possible to create an exhaustive vocabulary for individual characteristics that includes three dimensions—*dispositional characteristics* or personality traits; *habitual characteristics* or knowledge, aptitudes, skills, attitudes, expectations, and habits, which are acquired through learning and then form a stable resource set guiding action; and *motivational characteristics* or relatively enduring mental states, which direct behavior that is evoked repeatedly when exposed to the same or similar stimuli over a period of time. Of these, personality has appeared through research to be the most powerful predictor of behavior, though Roe identifies other individual characteristics that are important differentiators—intellectual abilities, character traits, interests and values, motor abilities, sensory abilities, knowledge and skills, and biographical characteristics. Certainly, the works of Howard Gardner (1983, 1993) and Daniel Goleman (1995) have introduced the notion that there are wide ranges of personal characteristics that differentiate people. In higher education, Blackburn and Lawrence (1995) found that preferences for teaching versus research varied by personality type.

With more specific reference to the teaching function, when William McKeachie (1997) asks the question, "How do teachers differ from one another?" (p. 396) his purpose is to revisit the question of whether certain personality characteristics are related to effectiveness in teaching (as rated by students). McKeachie believes that the now well-researched personality dimensions in the Big Five (Hogan, 1991) constitute a reasonably exhaustive set. These are *extroversion-introversion, agreeableness, conscientiousness, emotional stability-neuroticism,* and *culture* (openness to experience). (This five-factor model is intended to be illustrative only. Some recent research suggests, for example, that it does not appear to measure interest and activity patterns that are covered in other personality measures. See Schinka, Dye, & Curtiss, 1997.)

Hypothetically, these same five dimensions can be related to the preferences of faculty for the widely varied multiple tasks of instruction and the skills needed to accomplish them. Moreover, given equal levels of competence, individuals whose temperaments are matched to their assigned tasks will perform more effectively (on the assumption that higher motivation and commitment are generated). For example, it is entirely possible that "introverts" prefer certain kinds of teaching tasks that do not require overt expressiveness and that they are more effective when they are called on to act out these less emotionally revealing roles. "Extroverts," on the other hand, prefer another set of tasks and would not be happy, say, closeted in a library doing research for teaching all day.

What is important for the theme of this book is to note the probability that for each of the different subroles identified above and described in later chapters, different kinds of personality are more suitable. Presumably, a "profile" of scores on each of the Big Five would characterize each of the major teaching roles in higher education, and the profiles would be significantly different from one another. Thus (to present one hypothetical characterization), a teacher qua researcher might be found to be introverted, disagreeable, conscientious, emotionally stable, and closed to experience; whereas a teacher qua lecturer in the performance part of that role might have a personality that is extroverted, agreeable, not too conscientious, slightly neurotic, and open to experience. (Readers who find these caricatures to be stereotypes are invited to reverse the attributions, which were created only to illustrate a point and are not based on any empirical research whatsoever nor intended to reflect any judgment on the tasks or the faculty who perform them.)

There is a considerable record of research in the area of matching personality and vocational choice, especially in the work associated with the production of the *Dictionary of Occupational Titles* (U.S. Department of Labor, 1986) and with career counseling in general, especially Holland's (1992) work. As contemporary organizational psychologists now report, the efficient utilization of human resources in organizations is advanced when there is a "fit" between individuals and their jobs.

Job analysis in general involves a scientific study of jobs and the preparation of descriptions of the extant tasks and mental states. Here, for teaching, we have disaggregated the usual "job" of teaching into component parts and are suggesting, sometimes speculatively, what knowledge, skills, and attitudes are required. Further, this book, in contrast to past literature on teaching, introduces the idea of "person-environment fit" (Ostroff, 1993; Pervin, 1989; Tranberg, Slane, & Ekeberg, 1993; Livingston, Nelson, & Barr, 1997). Commonly in the past, task analysis meant the examination of jobs from the perspective of the employer only—seeking to describe jobs in terms that would maximize the output of an incumbent job-holder. In the case of this book, we add a motivational component: we argue that it is not only necessary to identify job characteristics that will maximize output, but it is also important to place only those workers whose personal characteristics match the requisite job requirements, because such a match will ensure a continuity of satisfactions and motivation (Dawis & Lofquist, 1984). For example, whereas from the perspective of the organization, a job may not require the job characteristic "autonomy," from a motivational point of view, autonomy, especially for most professionals, will contribute to sustained satisfaction.

To illustrate, in a meta-analysis of the congruence between interests and occupational satisfaction for adults who were no longer students, Tranberg et al. (1993) found an average correlation of .317 (see also Edwards, 1991; Kilmann & McKelvey, 1975; Mitroff, 1983; Chatman, 1989; Ostroff, 1993). Translated to organizations like colleges and universities, this finding suggests that faculty who are "fitted" psychologically to the tasks will find greater satisfaction in their work and presumably will be motivated to work hard (though, see Blackburn and Lawrence, 1995, p. 98).

Faculty not only must have the dispositions that match the knowledge-based disciplines in which they have been trained and which they now teach but also must be matched psychologically to the processes in which they engage to connect the material of their disciplines to the constituents they are serving. The fit, in other words, is both to the character and structure of the knowledge in their field and to the procedures they follow to extract that knowledge, transform it, and communicate it. Note that the "processes" themselves are embedded in specialized bodies of knowledge that must be mastered by the role players. Thus, the teacher as actor must have profound knowledge of the "methods" of acting *("knowing that"* in addition to *"knowing how")*. The proper fit of temperament to both subject matter discipline and methods involved in the task will enhance motivation, commitment, and ultimately, personal and organizational effectiveness.

Sociotechnical Organizational Design

Research has demonstrated that the most effective organizations have found ways to integrate the three realms discussed above—tasks, talents, and temperaments. *Sociotechnical design* suggests that when it is necessary for workers in organizations to be engaged in tasks that are interdependent—that is, when there is a logical and practical connection among them—workers must also be connected psychically. Sociotechnical systems design focuses on both the technological and the social conditions of tasks, so that they account for both the technical and social relationships among workers (Klimoski & Jones, 1995). It also involves the creation of self-managed teams of workers who have confidence in one another and whose work is complementary. More will be said on the subject of teams in Chapter Nine.

Compare, for example, the idea of groups of faculty members working together in teams with the finding of Trist and Bamforth (1951; see also Herbst, 1974; Cherns, 1987; Trist & Murray, 1993), early researchers on sociotechnical systems, regarding the wisdom of self-managed teams in underground coal mining.

In the underground situation external dangers must be faced in darkness. Darkness also awakens internal dangers. The need to share with others anxieties aroused by this double threat may be taken as self-evident. In view of the restricted range of effective communication, these others have to be immediately present. Their number there is limited [p. 7].

Under these conditions, as Miles (1980) notes, the difficulty of seeing in the dark and the autonomy of the work groups in the underground tunnels prevented continuous close supervision. Citing Trist and Bamforth, he notes,

The small group, capable of responsible autonomy, and able to vary its work pace in correspondence with changing conditions, would appear to be the type of social structure ideally adapted to the underground situation. It is instructive that the traditional work systems, evolved from the experience of successive generations, should have been founded on a group with these attributes" [Trist & Bamforth, 1951, p. 7].

Instead, then, of autonomous individual faculty, isolated in their classrooms, who rarely discuss their instructional challenges or problems, rarely confess their teaching failures and perceived inadequacies, and seldom even laud their successes, the potential "social dimension" of the work of teaching suggests an alternative, more collaborative mode. Such an organizational arrangement would permit complementary talents and temperaments to be joined in a social setting that encourages high sustained motivation and results in both individual and group satisfaction. It would also facilitate the smooth communications required for interdependent tasks.

The policy implication of these theses, if true, suggests that the teaching role as comprising many subroles must be "repackaged" in personally and organizationally desired ways and that the new task clusters must be performed by more narrowly specialized (and hence more competent and motivated) faculty in "teams." Thus, a reconstituted teaching role in higher education would call for more role specialization and the assignment of faculty with dispositions appropriate to these more technological processes, rather than (or in addition to) the more traditional subject matter departments. Further, a new form of "team teaching" that integrates the technological and pedagogical specializations would be required. This team teaching is quite different from usual notions of team teaching that aggregate faculty from different subject matter disciplines (though such mergings of subject matter interests would still be quite appropriate). Rather, it brings together specialists from the *same* subject matter area who possess different job skills and who perform significantly different tasks (see Orsburn, Moran, Musselwhite, & Zenger, 1990).

Differences Among the Subroles

As noted in the Preface, there are seven central subroles that constitute teaching—pedagogy, research, lecturing, leading discussions, mentoring, curricular-cocurricular integration, and assessment. It should be plain from this mode of disaggregation of the usual composite teaching role that each of the subroles is quite different, requiring among faculty dramatically different skills, interests, and personalities. A summary of these differences is presented in Exhibit 1.2. It is suggested here that very few, if any, faculty members are so broadly talented or psychologically disposed as to engage in all of the roles. This conclusion directs us to a reconceptualization of this portion of the teaching role (also, incidentally, of other portions). What is needed is a formal organizational reclassification of the different kinds of college teaching subroles, with faculty recruited as specialists for those positions. Concomitantly, universities would have to change their graduate education modes radically in order properly to train new faculty in the subroles. Needless to say, they should already be providing such instruction, but as is quite clear to most observers, the typical faculty career track prepares would-be faculty only for the first of the disaggregated roles—researcher for publication.

Implementation

In these days of severe budget stringency, some may wonder how these subroles can be filled without the addition of new faculty with the required specialized skills. In point of fact, more faculty may not be needed. What is proposed is not additional teaching tasks, but the assignment to interested specialists already on staff of tasks currently being carried out by other faculty as generalists (and the reassignment of unwanted tasks of the recipients of the new roles to others who view them as desirable). Thus, "researcher types"

**Exhibit 1.2. Samples of Contrasting Tasks,
Talents, and Temperaments Associated
with Different Teacher Subroles.**

Teaching Subrole	Pedagogical Technology or Setting	Personality and Sources of Teacher Satisfaction
Researcher	Library and laboratory	Rationality; knowledge acquisition, integration, theory analysis
Pedagogue	Classroom observation, media, textbooks	Intuition; knowledge and person synthesis, integration of disparate fields
Lecturer	Oratory	Extroversion; self-expression; immediately manifested student enlightenment
Discussion Leader	Group setting	Personal self-awareness; interpersonal honesty; successful group dynamics; student growth and development
Integrator	Residence hall	Immediacy of experience; successful merging of current events and learning objectives
Assessor	Classroom or office	Reflective judgment; comparative analysis; interpersonal sensitivity; interpretive applications of data
Mentor	Office or home	Sensitivity; idiosyncratic psychological insights; role modeling

Source: From Sedeleck.

might expand their knowledge vistas, while others, freed from research responsibilities, might concentrate on pedagogy, lecturing, conducting discussions, mentoring, working with out-of-class constituencies, or evaluation.

The adoption of this plan could make colleges and universities more efficient through the usual savings derived from specialization of labor in any field—that is, having more highly skilled, motivated, and trained people performing tasks that they find intrinsically satisfying. With this redistribution of labor, faculty who like to do research will simply do more of it; those preferring to do different types of teaching will do more of that (Bess, 1982). An additional expense may be occasioned by the minor bureaucratic cost of coordination of team members performing the subroles. Recall that such coordination has historically been hidden in the intrapersonal linking of the teaching and research roles—that is, by each faculty member, rather than across different faculty members. Theorists of organizational decision making suggest that individual decision making is more efficient when tasks are simple and skills of workers are homogeneously distributed. When tasks are complex (requiring a variety of skills and knowledge) and when those attributes are distributed across many workers, then group decision making becomes more efficient. (See the classic literature on this subject beginning with Kelly & Thibaut, 1969.)

The new costs of interpersonal coordination of team members, however, may be quite small, as self-managed teams of professional role specialists learn to link their differing responsibilities (Orsburn et al., 1990; Wellins, Byham, & Wilson, 1991; Manz & Angle, 1986). Such a restructuring, then, does not deny the position of Boyer (1990), who asserts that the four categories of scholarship—discovery, integration, application, and teaching—"are tied inseparably to each other" (p. 25), nor of Clark (1987), who says that academic work requires a seamless blend of activities. The case for this new restructuring alleges instead that interpersonal rather than intrapersonal linkages across these functions must be structured into the occupation of teaching. Indeed, it is likely that the interactions among faculty surrounding teaching tasks—an infrequent occurrence in today's academic environment—might generate new norms of commitment and excellence to teaching.

Not Scientific Management

Some might object to this proposal on the grounds that its emphasis on specialization makes it vulnerable to criticisms similar to those rendered against Taylor's scientific management philosophies in the early part of the twentieth century. As Taylor (1978) noted:

> It becomes the duty of those on the management's side to deliberately study the character, the nature, and the performance of each workman with a view to finding out his limitations on the one hand, but even more important, his possibilities for development on the other hand; and then, as deliberately and as systematically to train and help and teach this workman, giving him, wherever it is possible, those opportunities for advancement which enable him to do the highest and most interesting and most profitable class of work for which his natural abilities fit him, and which are open to him in the particular company in which he is employed [p. 18].

Faculty are not, clearly, replaceable parts of a machine. They are autonomous professionals, now moving into a technological age that requires interdependent relations with other professionals (Adler, 1997). To avoid both "deprofessionalization" and "deskilling" (and their associated dehumanization and demoralizing consequences), faculty would need to have opportunities with reasonable frequency to rotate through the various teaching subroles, as developing interests and needs dictate (their "permanent" temperaments to the contrary, notwithstanding). Indeed, all faculty in their successive role incumbencies will benefit from the comprehensive education they will gain in the diverse phases of teaching that they will experience. They will thus be better able to understand and deal with others performing specializations different from their own. This redefinition of the faculty role may enlarge the discussion of graduate education to include a fresh look at preparation for teaching. It is beyond the scope of this chapter to speculate on the nature of professional specialization and external associations that might support these activities, though in truth, both now exist in inchoate form. Most workers in Japanese organizations are shifted through many roles in order partly to give them a broader set of skills and partly to enhance cooperativeness in interdepartmental decision making. So also in higher education, faculty must want to collaborate and be able to do so with skill.[2]

Summary

It is important to end the myth of the necessary integrity and effectiveness of a single multifunctioned professional faculty member (Charns et al., 1977). Few persons can competently perform all of the parts of this highly complex role, nor even of the instruction segment illustrated here. Few persons are likely to be interested in and to derive satisfaction from performance of each of the diverse aspects of the role, which demand quite different skills and provide very different kinds of rewards. It is necessary, therefore, to recognize the need for more role specialization that will use skills more efficiently and will provide more satisfactions to those performing the tasks. The omnibus role of teaching in higher education might well be formally disaggregated and candidates found to fill the different parts. Teaching by means of teams of experts in the tasks, rather than (or in addition to) the subject matters, must be considered as the organizational paradigm of the future.

Such organizational designs are not new in the corporate world and have been found to be both organizationally efficient and personally rewarding.[3] Moreover, the development of organizational structures in colleges that "require" the formal interaction of faculty role players will have the additional benefit of enhancing the sense of community on college campuses. The current practice of leaving self-serving faculty to their own parochial interests has long been lamented for its resulting isolation and insularity. Although the essence of professionalism demands individual autonomy, to improve teaching effectiveness

---

2. Whether such faculty are currently attracted to the profession or are socialized into these dispositions in graduate school is a subject for research.

3. It is conceivable that a further elaboration of the idea of team teaching would result in "matrix" organizational forms, which are often found in the corporate world. It is more likely, however, that small, subject-circumscribed "permanent" teams would work in conjunction with the ancillary experts noted earlier. These latter, however, might well be employed in a matrix format that provides service to the teaching teams. One matrix format is discussed in Chapter Nine.

amid the complexity of new technologies, that autonomy must be set in the context of group efforts.[4]

Planning for these emerging events will be difficult because significant changes in roles and role players are involved. In most cases, a full complement of faculty personnel willing and able to fill new roles may not presently be available on campuses, especially smaller ones. A first step in the planning process, then, requires an assessment of the requisite organizational positions and following that of the faculty preferences for those positions (see Kilmann, 1977; Kilmann & McKelvey, 1975). Clearly, the open and complete involvement of faculty in the planning stages is an absolute necessity. Implementation of the plan will take a long period of time, since recruitment of new faculty will be needed to fill missing slots. Furthermore, as with any change, there will be resistance, as faculty career tracks typically are well established, both internally and externally. The system does not presently reward the kinds of specialization prescribed above. In many ways, however, the gradual implementation of the program can be expected to result in the generation of external rewards—within and across campuses that support it. (There is already some movement in this direction. See, for example, the "excellence-in-mentoring" awards for faculty at Harvard [John Harvard's Journal, 1999].) The reason is that the plan is based on the assumption that the organization's new role system will make more readily available the satisfaction of intrinsic faculty needs. The manifestation of these satisfactions among faculty will cause them to move toward the implementation of an external reward system that supports the continuing satisfaction of those intrinsic needs. Such is the case for the current reward system that supports intrinsic faculty satisfactions from research successes.

College and university organizations are creaking with old age. They have not responded to the new waves of technology, nor even to the basic requirements for effective teaching. The time is upon

---

4. This is not to suggest that individual discretionary behavior will not be appropriate in this system. This chapter has not considered the nature of nonteaching roles; for example, researching for publication, which more frequently than not is a single-person activity (although there are variations by field). Designing an organization for faculty that involves these other roles is a still more formidable venture.

us for a fresh look at the organizational requirements for high-quality teaching in the twenty-first century. If we do not take this fresh look, the critics alluded to in the Preface will become even more vociferous—and rightly so.

References

Abbott, A. (1988). *The system of professions: An essay on the division of expert labor.* Chicago: University of Chicago Press.

Adkinson, J. (1979). The structure of knowledge and departmental social organization. *Higher Education, 8,* 41–53.

Adler, P. S. (1997). From Taylorism to teamwork. *Perspectives on Work, 1*(1), 61–65.

Arenson, K. W. (1998, November 2). More colleges plunging into uncharted waters of on-line courses. *New York Times,* p. A16.

Barr, R. B., & Tagg, J. (1995). From teaching to learning: A new paradigm for undergraduate education. *Change, 27*(6), 13–25.

Bell, D. (1966). *The reforming of general education: The Columbia College experience in its national setting.* New York: Columbia University Press.

Bemis, S. E., Belenky, A. H., & Soder, D. A. (1983). *Job analysis: An effective management tool.* Washington, DC: Bureau of National Affairs.

Bereiter, C., & Scardamalia, M. (1993). *Surpassing ourselves: An inquiry into the nature and implications of expertise.* Chicago: Open Court.

Bess, J. L. (1982). *University organization: A matrix analysis of the academic professions.* New York: Human Sciences Press.

Bess, J. L. (Ed.). (1997). *Teaching well and liking it: Motivating faculty to teach effectively.* Baltimore: Johns Hopkins University Press.

Blackburn, R. T., & Lawrence, J. H. (1995). *Faculty at work: Motivation, expectation, satisfaction.* Baltimore: Johns Hopkins University Press.

Boyer, E. L. (1990). *Scholarship reconsidered: Priorities of the professoriate.* Princeton, NJ: Carnegie Foundation for the Advancement of Teaching.

Cannon-Bowers, J. A., Tannenbaum, S. I., Salas, E., & Volpe, C. E. (1995). Defining competencies and establishing team training requirements. In R. A. Guzzo, E. Salas, & Associates, *Team effectiveness and decision making in organizations* (pp. 333–380). San Francisco: Jossey-Bass.

Charns, M. P., Lawrence, P. R., & Weisbord, M. R. (1977). Organizing multiple-function professionals in academic medical centers. *Studies in the Management Sciences, 5,* 71–88.

Charns, M. P., & Smith, L. J. (1993). *Collaborative management in health care: Implementing the integrative organization.* San Francisco: Jossey-Bass.

Chatman, J. A. (1989). Improving interactional organizational research: A model of person-organization fit. *Academy of Management Review, 14*(3), 333–349.

Cherns, A. (1987). Principles of sociotechnical design revisited. *Human Relations, 40,* 153–162.

Clark, B. R. (1987). *The academic life: Small worlds, different worlds.* Princeton, NJ: Carnegie Foundation for the Advancement of Teaching.

Clark, B. R. (1997). The modern integration of research activities with teaching and learning. *Journal of Higher Education, 68*(3), 241–255.

Cohen, A. M., & Brawer, F. B. (1996). *The American community college.* (3rd ed.) San Francisco: Jossey-Bass.

Dawis, R. V., & Lofquist, L. H. (1984). *A psychological theory of work adjustment: An individual-differences model and its applications.* Minneapolis: University of Minnesota Press.

Donald, J. G. (1983). Knowledge structures: Methods for exploring course content. *Journal of Higher Education, 54*(1), 31–41.

Dreyfus, F., & Dreyfus, S. (1986). Why expert systems do not exhibit expertise. IEEE Expert, *1*(2), 86–90.

Edwards, J. R. (1991). Person-job fit: A conceptual integration, literature review, and methodological critique. In C. L. Cooper & I. T. Robertson (Eds.), *International review of industrial and organizational psychology* (pp. 283–357). New York: Wiley.

Faia, M. A. (1980). Teaching, research, and role theory. In P. G. Altbach & S. Slaughter (Eds.), *The academic profession: The annals* (Vol. 448, pp. 36–45).

Finkelstein, M. J. (1984). *The American academic profession.* Columbus: Ohio State University Press.

Freidson, E. (1973). The professions and their prospects. Beverly Hills, CA: Sage.

Gardner, H. (1983). *Frames of mind: The theory of multiple intelligences.* New York: Basic Books.

Gardner, H. (1993). *Multiple intelligences: The theory in practice.* New York: Basic Books.

Goleman, D. (1995). *Emotional intelligence: Why it can matter more than IQ.* New York: Bantam Books.

Gumport, Patricia J., Iannozzi, M., Shaman, S., & Zemsky, R. (1997). Trends in United States higher education from massification to post-massification. In A. Arimoto (ed.), *Academic reforms in the world.* RIHE International Seminar Reports No. 10, pp. 57–94. Hiroshima: Research Institute for Higher Education, Hiroshima University.

Hammer, M., & Stanton, S. (1994). *The reengineering revolution.* New York: HarperBusiness.

Hammond, P. E., Meyer, J. W., & Miller, D. (1969). Teaching versus research: Sources of misperceptions, *Journal of Higher Education, 40,* 682–690.

Hativa, N., & Marincovich, M. (Eds.). (1995). *Disciplinary differences in teaching and learning: Implications for practice*. New Directions for Teaching and Learning, no. 64. San Francisco: Jossey-Bass.

Hellriegel, D., Slocum, R., & Woodman, R. W. (1998). *Organizational behavior* (8th ed.). Cincinnati: South-Western College Publishing.

Herbst, P. G. (1974). *Socio-technical design: Strategies in multidisciplinary research*. London: Tavistock.

Hill, P. (1984). Creating a lively academic community. In Z. F. Gamson & Associates (Eds.), *Liberating education* (pp. 83–94). San Francisco: Jossey-Bass.

Hogan, R. T. (1991). Personality and personality measurement. In M. D. Dunnette & L. M. Hough (Eds.), *Handbook of industrial and organizational psychology* (2nd ed.). (Vol. 2, pp. 878–879). Palo Alto, CA: Consulting Psychologists Press.

Holland, J. L. (1992) *Making vocational choices*. Odessa, FL: Psychological Assessment Resources.

Homans, G. C. (1950). *The human group*. Orlando: Harcourt Brace.

John Harvard's Journal. (1999). *Harvard Magazine, 101*(6), 58–88.

Johnson, E. J. (1988). Expertise and decisions under uncertainty: Performance and process. M. T. H. Chi, R. Glaser, & M. J. Farr (Eds.), *The nature of expertise* (pp. 209–228). Hillsdale, NJ: Erlbaum.

Johnson, P. E. (1983). What kind of expert should a system be? *Journal of Medicine and Philosophy, 8,* 77–97.

Kelly, H., & Thibaut, J. (1969). Group problem solving. In G. Lindsey & E. Aronson (Eds.), *The handbook of social psychology* (2nd ed.). Reading, MA: Addison-Wesley.

Kilmann, Ralph H. (1977). *Social systems design, normative theory and the MAPS design technology*. New York: North-Holland.

Kilmann, R. H., & McKelvey, B. (1975). The MAPS route to better organizational design. *California Management Review, 17*(3), 23–31.

King, A. (1966). *The curriculum and the disciplines of knowledge*. New York: Wiley.

Klimoski, R., & Jones, R. G. (1995). Staffing for effective group decision making: Key issues in matching people and teams. In R. A. Guzzo, E. Salas, & Associates (Eds.), *Team effectiveness and decision making in organizations* (pp. 291–332). San Francisco: Jossey-Bass.

Lawrence, P. R., & Lorsch, J. W. (1967). *Organization and environment: Managing differentiation and integration*. Boston: Division of Research, Graduate School of Business, Harvard University.

Livingston, L., Nelson, D., & Barr, S. (1997). Person-environment fit and creativity: An examination of supply-value and demand-ability versions of fit. *Journal of Management, 23*(2), 119–146.

Macdaid, G. P., McCaulley, M. H., & Kinz, R. I. (1986). *Atlas of type tables.* Gainesville, FL: Center for Applications of Psychological Type.

Mannheim, K. (1952). *Essays on the sociology of knowledge.* (P. Kecskemeti, Ed.). New York: Routledge.

Manz, C. C., & Angle, H. (1986). Can group self-management means a loss of personal control: Triangulating a paradox. *Group and Organization Studies, 11,* 309–334.

Massey, W. F., & Wilger, A. K. (1992). Productivity in postsecondary education: A new approach. *Educational Evaluation and Policy Analysis, 14*(4), 361–376.

McKeachie, W. J. (1997). Good teaching makes a difference—and we know what it is. In R. P. Perry & J. C. Smart (Eds.), *Effective teaching in higher education: Research and practice* (pp. 396–408). New York: Agathon Press.

Miles, R. H. (1980). *Macro organizational behavior.* Santa Monica, CA: Goodyear.

Mitroff, I. (1983). *Stakeholders of the organizational mind: Toward a view of organizational policy-making.* San Francisco: Jossey-Bass.

Orsburn, J. D., Moran, L., Musselwhite, E., & Zenger, J. H. (1990). *Self-directed work teams: The new American challenge.* Homewood, IL: Irwin.

Ostroff, C. (1993). Relationships between person/environment congruence and organizational effectiveness. *Group and Organizational Management, 18*(1), 103–122.

Parsons, T. (1974). Epilogue: The university "bundle": A study of the balance between differentiation and integration. In N. J. Smelser & G. Almond (Eds.), *Public higher education in California* (pp. 275–299). Berkeley: University of California Press, 1974.

Perrow, C. (1970). *Organizational analysis: A sociological view.* Belmont, CA: Wadsworth.

Pervin, L. A. (1989). Persons, situations, interactions: A history of a controversy and a discussion of theoretical models. *Academy of Management Review, 14*(3), 350–360.

Roe, R. A. (1984). Individual characteristics. In P. J. Drenth, H. Thierry, P. J. Willems, & C. J. de Wolff (Eds.), *Handbook of work and organizational psychology* (pp. 103–127). New York: Wiley.

Schinka, J. A., Dye, D. A., & Curtiss, G. (1997). Correspondence between five-factor and RIASEC models of personality. *Journal of Personality Assessment, 68*(2), 355–368.

Seldin, P. (Ed.). (1987). *Coping with teacher stress.* San Francisco: Jossey-Bass.

Sorcinelli, M. D., & Gregory, M. W. (1987). Teacher stress: The tension between career demands and "having it all." In P. Seldin (Ed.), *Coping with teacher stress.* San Francisco: Jossey-Bass.

Taylor, F. W. (1978). Scientific management: Testimony before the U.S. House of Representatives, January 25, 1912. Cited in J. M. Shafritz & A. C. Hyde, *Classics of public administration.* Oak Park, IL: Moore.

Thompson, J. D. (1967). *Organizations in action.* New York: McGraw-Hill.

Tranberg, M., Slane, S., & Ekeberg, S. E. (1993). The relation between interest congruence and satisfaction: A meta-analysis. *Journal of Vocational Behavior, 42,* 253–264.

Trist, E., & Bamforth, K. W. (1951). Some social and psychological consequences of the longwall method of coal getting. *Human Relations, 4,* 3–38.

Trist, E., & Murray, E. (Eds.). (1993). *The social engagement of social science: An anthology, vol. II: The sociotechnical perspective.* Philadelphia: University of Pennsylvania Press.

Tschan, F., & von Cranach, M. (1986). Group task structure, processes and outcome. In M. A. West (Ed.), *Handbook of work group psychology* (pp. 95–121). New York: Wiley.

U.S. Department of Labor. (1986). *Dictionary of occupational titles.* Washington, DC: U.S. Department of Labor.

Walton, D. (1997). *Appeal to expert opinion: Arguments from authority.* University Park: Pennsylvania State University Press.

Wellins, R. S., Byham, W. C., & Wilson, J. M. (1991). *Empowered teams: Creating self-directed work groups that improve quality, productivity, and participation.* San Francisco: Jossey-Bass.

Part One

Preparatory Roles

Chapter Two

The Pedagogue
Creating Designs for Teaching
Janet G. Donald

Until relatively recently, pedagogy has been a tacit role of the university professor. Tacit roles are assumed but not examined; the pedagogical role of organizing knowledge to ensure learning is therefore less well understood than the research role of producing knowledge or the manifest instructional role of lecturing. In the evaluation of university teaching over the past thirty years, the focus has been almost exclusively on professors' presentation skills. Course planning, the organization of knowledge into dynamic learning sequences that take into account students' prior knowledge and the evolution of their knowledge and skills, is still a hidden, and some might say mystic, art. With the sophisticated delivery systems that the Internet and other forms of technology are now able to supply, the need to understand and develop a working vocabulary of postsecondary pedagogy becomes essential. What kind of vocabulary is needed? Major entries would include the tasks of syllabus review, program alignment, and organization of instruction and its assessment. In this chapter, I explore the role of the faculty member as an expert pedagogue and lay out the diverse tasks that constitute this demanding role, from listener to leader. Compared with lecturer or discussion leader, pedagogy is

Note: This chapter is based on research funded by the Québec Fonds pour la Formation de Chercheurs et l'Aide à la Recherche (FCAR) and the Social Science and Humanities Research Council of Canada.

a new role, one that has been fulfilled largely by educational psychologists in instructional development centers on those campuses that have them.

As an initial strategy in understanding the role of university pedagogy, we can call on the general educational research literature, which explores the functions of the expert pedagogue. The notion of expertise is central to this discussion because it provides the merit-based authority that is foundational to a professor's influence in the instructional context. Because the research on expertise in education has been situated primarily at the elementary and secondary school level, which differs in several important ways from the teaching and learning context in postsecondary education, a second step will be a situated interpretation of expert pedagogy in postsecondary education. Three major contextual factors—the breadth of the postsecondary educational environment, the skills that students bring to the learning milieu, and the effects of a policy of mass higher education translated on campus primarily into large classes—must be taken into account. An analysis of the pedagogical goals, tasks, and the skills needed to execute these tasks across domains is the third step in understanding this complex role.

The Expert Pedagogue in the Educational Research Literature

In two groundbreaking articles on knowledge and teaching, one entitled *Those Who Understand: Knowledge Growth in Teaching*, published in 1986 in the *Educational Researcher*, and the other, entitled *Knowledge and Teaching: Foundations of the New Reform*, published in 1987 in the *Harvard Educational Review*, Lee Shulman portrayed the knowledge base and the processes of pedagogical reasoning and action needed for expertise in teaching. He distinguished seven categories of teacher knowledge—subject matter content knowledge, general pedagogical knowledge, curriculum knowledge, pedagogical content knowledge, knowledge of learners and their characteristics, knowledge of educational contexts, and knowledge of educational ends. These categories of teacher knowledge suggest the breadth and complexity of the pedagogical role. They are defined in the following manner.

Subject matter content knowledge refers to the way in which the concepts and principles of a domain are organized and the methods used to validate this knowledge (Shulman, 1986). *General pedagogical knowledge* concerns those broad principles and strategies of classroom management and organization that transcend subject matter (Shulman, 1987). *Curriculum knowledge* refers to the range of programs and materials available to teach a particular content area, lateral knowledge of topics being taught at the same time in other courses, and vertical knowledge of topics and issues that were taught earlier or will be taught later in the program (Shulman, 1986). *Pedagogical content knowledge* refers to useful alternative forms of representing and formulating concepts and principles that make them comprehensible to others, to the conceptions and misconceptions that students bring with them, and to the strategies for reorganizing students' conceptions (Shulman, 1986). *Knowledge of learners* includes both their physical and psychological characteristics (Shulman, 1987). *Knowledge of educational contexts* encompasses the workings of the group or classroom, governance and financing, and the character of the community and culture (Shulman, 1987). *Knowledge of educational ends* includes purposes and values and their philosophical and historical grounds.

Of these categories of teacher knowledge, some cross disciplinary boundaries—general pedagogical knowledge, knowledge of educational contexts, and knowledge of educational ends. Others are discipline specific—subject matter content knowledge, curriculum knowledge, and pedagogical content knowledge—and would be expected to be closely tied to scholarship in the academic discipline or program. Knowledge of learners and their characteristics would be general in some respects, such as age cohort and general knowledge of students, but particular in the program elected by the students and their reasons for so doing. The categories of knowledge therefore require different although overlapping strategies to elucidate. This means that the domain of pedagogical expertise is enormous and requires continual professional study.

The processes of pedagogical reasoning and action evolve in a series of steps from the comprehension of purposes and ideas through transformation, instruction, evaluation, reflection, and new comprehensions that consolidate learning (Shulman, 1987).

A critical capacity is the transformation of content knowledge into forms that are pedagogically powerful and yet adaptive to the variations in ability and background presented by students. According to Shulman, transformation involves critical interpretation of text, representation of the ideas in the form of new analogies or metaphors, selection of teaching methods, adapting them to the students to be taught, and tailoring adaptations to specific students in the class. We see here the first major problem in applying general pedagogical wisdom to postsecondary learning situations, in which classes of three hundred preclude adaptation and tailoring to the needs of individual students. Evaluation of student understanding is another process that is complicated by large numbers, as the evaluation of understanding requires far greater time to analyze and provide feedback than establishing the acquisition of facts. This situation then renders the next steps—reflection of the process of teaching and its effects on students' learning, and new comprehension of instruction and consolidation—more difficult. These are challenges for the team as a whole, however.

Most demanding in this conception of pedagogical reasoning is the emphasis on the intellectual basis of teaching performance. Shulman points out that the increased importance of the role of pedagogical content knowledge implies greater attention to the ability to reason within a content area, and a concomitant focus on the particular learners being served. Our research has shown that professors and students prefer educational experiences that incorporate higher-order learning. This requires a shift from the representation of learning as occurring in bits and bytes to one in which thought processes are central. It also requires an immediate understanding of students' background in terms of their capacity and experience in thinking, rarely within the investigative capacity of the traditional professor.

Research on the forms of instructional expertise needed show that expert teachers represent an instructional situation very differently from novices (Berliner, 1986). Experts make higher-level inferences about instructional situations. They use higher-order systems of categorization to analyze problems, recognize patterns, and think through problems differently. They are sensitive to particular situations and the social structure, and plan and use time efficiently. Efficiency features of the expert pedagogue consist of automatization of tasks, executive control in planning, monitoring and evaluating, and the reinvestment of cognitive resources as in the use of classroom feedback (Sternberg & Horvath, 1995). Because expertise is highly contextualized, and therefore domain dependent (Berliner, 1991), academic disciplines or programs must take major responsibility for pedagogical expertise. What does this mean for the pedagogical expert on the faculty team?

Comparative studies across disciplines have confirmed differences in teaching goals and matching student progress (Cashin & Downey, 1995; Donald & Denison, 1997). Most notable are the disciplinary variations in professors' and students' recognition of such higher-order goals as learning to apply course material to improve rational thinking, problem solving, and decision making. Even more striking differences occur across levels of education and between large and small universities (Donald, 1991). To what extent would these situational differences affect the conceptualization of pedagogical expertise?

Postsecondary Learning Environment

Three major factors distinguish the postsecondary learning situation from that of education in elementary and secondary schools. First, even in a classic postsecondary institution based on a single campus, the educational environment is both more diffuse and more complex than at earlier stages, with more options from which students may select. Second, the knowledge base and skills that students bring to the learning milieu, as well as their stage of development and the transition many are making from family life to independent living, mean that students have a larger and less stable personal environment than before. Third, a policy of mass higher education over the past thirty years has led in many postsecondary institutions to large classes and limited attention to individual learners. Institutional size has clear negative effects on student affective development, satisfaction, and the perception that faculty care about them (Astin, 1993). These factors contribute to a set of issues concerning pedagogical locus of control or influence: the influence that professors have differs radically from that of the elementary or high school teacher in the following ways.

To begin with, the learning environment in postsecondary learning situations is not the classroom but the entire campus, and increasingly, it extends beyond the campus (see Exhibit 2.1). On campus, students may spend as little as fifteen hours per week in classes, and the class setting may vary radically, from large lecture hall to seminar room, leading to further ecological instability. Other venues, such as the library, laboratory, cafeteria, work or field placements, or the student's own room, assume greater importance as learning settings. With the broader array of learning milieus, influence over learning per se is dispersed. More to the point, undergraduate students report that their learning takes place when they do their assignments, and not in the classroom (Donald & Denison, 1997). The overall attitude toward learning on campus then increases in importance, and support for a learning community becomes requisite for the following reasons.

The primary reason for a learning community is that it promotes relationships and provides a psychologically manageable environment (Davis & Murrell, 1993). In a psychologically manageable environment, students have the perception that they are in a place

Exhibit 2.1. Issues of Locus of Control in Postsecondary Learning Environments Compared with Previous Educational Levels.

Issue	Elementary Education	Secondary Education	Postsecondary Education
Learning environment/ context	Classroom	Classroom	Entire campus +
Students	Dependent	Increasingly independent	Independent
Instructors' relationship to learning	High control/ high responsibility	High control/ responsibility	Minimal control/ minimal responsibility
Administrators	High control	High control	Minimal control
Curriculum/ domain control	General/ external (government)	Specific/ external (government)	Specific/ internal (instructor)

that supports learning in general and their own development in particular. Learning communities thus increase commitment to learning. Recognition of the influence of the campus zeitgeist on learning has led some universities to develop policy statements of a commitment to learning to guide campus practice (Donald, 1997). For example, one university, which describes itself as a student-centered research university, has pledged to support scholarly learning as the central mission of the university. Instilling a sense of the importance of a learning community is a challenge for the entire campus, but the onus frequently falls on the individual instructors to contend with nonscholarly campus influences. Student attention spans in class are as low as twenty minutes; students spend half their class time in nonscholarly activities—watching other students, looking at the time, and fantasizing—rather than attending to the lecturer or taking notes (Gardiner, 1994).

Another reason to promote a learning community is that university and college students are most frequently newly independent and are known to test their newfound independence from family and hometown constraints. However, students frequently arrive at university lacking the strategies needed for independent learning, so their own desired independence may work against success in learning. Although this independence is consistent with their stage of development and the amount of knowledge they have acquired, it also means that they are less likely to respect authority, on which instructors at earlier levels have been able to rely.

At the same time, students in postsecondary institutions are asked to provide indices of their satisfaction with their learning situation in course evaluations, even though they may have limited insight into their own responsibility for learning. This problem requires a set of strategies on the part of instructors to enlighten students on their new role as independent learners. The largest contributor to student learning gains at the postsecondary level is the quality of effort students put into their work (Pace, 1982). To date, however, institutions have not been highly successful in getting across this message.

Given these limitations, instructors at the postsecondary level are placed in a dilemma of major proportions: their authority rests on the extent of student respect for instructor knowledge base and intellectual skills, but those same undergraduates may lack a clear understanding of what the knowledge base and skills are and what their own responsibilities as learners are. Professors meet with their students for a very limited period of time. This makes it difficult to establish personal contact; and larger classes, which increasingly constitute the majority of courses, inhibit recognizing students, let alone establishing personal contact. Administrators see less of students, and their multiple and diverse tasks preclude continued interaction; hence they tend to have little influence over or responsibility for students. Thus, student contact becomes an important factor to be considered.

The final issue of locus of control is the curriculum, and here traditionally the pendulum has shifted to the professor. Setting the syllabus, defining how the subject matter will be taught, and evaluating the results of students' attempts to learn are professorial responsibilities protected by the principle of academic freedom. Program review, the publication of course outlines on the Web, and thirty years of course evaluations act as constraints to this freedom; but in the current situation, the individual professor has major responsibility for the content and delivery of a course. Over the years in many disciplines, course content has become more specialized and may not necessarily cohere with that in other courses. Although educators have called for increased coherence and the provision of an overview of the discipline on the part of pedagogues (Holmes Group, 1986), the means for accomplishing this are not readily available.

Given the differences between the postsecondary learning environment and the learning milieu at earlier stages for which the concept of the expert pedagogue has been developed, what are the tasks of the expert pedagogue on the faculty team? What are the responsibilities and constraints surrounding this role? Analysis of the postsecondary learning environment suggests that although some tasks may be consistent with those at earlier levels of education, different and as yet unexplored tasks are important to aid student learning and will require the team's consideration.

Tasks of the Expert Pedagogue in Higher Education

The tasks of the pedagogical expert proceed from the central goal of assisting students to develop intellectually. As postsecondary students are expected to learn in a much larger and more diffused context, a subset of tasks arises from consideration of what is needed to make the learning context manageable and supportive. The comparative analysis of the postsecondary learning environment has indicated that provision of an intellectual context includes the tasks of instilling the sense of importance of scholarly learning within the learning community, providing increased coherence in the curriculum and an overview of the guiding discipline, establishing personal contact, and transmitting the message to students that they have a new responsibility as independent learners (See Exhibit 2.2). As these pedagogical tasks provide the intellectual context that will enable students to learn, and set the stage for it, they are discussed first. A second subset of tasks deals directly with instructional planning and evaluation and reflects the features of the expert pedagogue as discussed by Berliner (1986), Shulman (1986), and Sternberg and Horvath (1995), and the pedagogical reasoning processes advocated by Shulman (1987). Although some of these tasks may be performed by instructors, the pedagogical expert must align and integrate the learning context and the instructional plan.

Provision of Intellectual Context

Mission statements, compacts, and student orientations may provide students with a sense of the goals of the higher education institution generally, but it falls to the expert pedagogue on the faculty team to interpret and operationalize institutional goals. The process of interpreting the intellectual context has multiple facets, beginning with understanding and being able to explain higher educational goals.

Explaining Educational Goals

In order for students to actively control and organize their learning, they need to see the relationship between understanding their field and gaining credentials in it (Donald, 1997). Obvious as this might sound, it runs counter to the dominant perspective of today's students. Students give greater weight to career preparation and are less interested in broader intellectual issues (Donald, 1998; Williams & Schiralli, 1991). Financial well-being is a more

Exhibit 2.2. Tasks of the Expert Pedagogue in Higher Education.

Provision of Intellectual Context

Explaining educational goals	Explain educational goals, purposes and values, and their epistemological grounds.
Understanding the institutional context	Clarify institutional and faculty educational objectives, governance and financing, and the character of the community and culture.
Understanding students	Obtain information on students' language, culture, motivation, gender, age, ability, and interests.
Providing the disciplinary context	Provide an overview of the discipline—the way in which the subject matter is organized, and the methods used to validate this knowledge.
Providing a learning community	Instill a sense of the importance of scholarly learning, and provide personal, collaborative contact.
Establishing student responsibility for learning	Explain to students that their learning will depend primarily on the quality of effort they put into their work.

Instructional Planning and Evaluation

Designing	Interpret the knowledge base critically, and structure and segment concepts, topics, and skills to be learned, organized into learning outcomes.
Representing knowledge	Use alternative ways to represent concepts and skills in analogies, metaphors, explanations, examples, demonstrations, and assignments.

Selecting teaching strategies	Organize, manage, and arrange learning activities to achieve outcomes.
Adapting to student characteristics	Respond to student conceptions, misconceptions, aptitudes, attention, motivation, and stage of development.
Aligning instruction	Manage and present material, interact with and coach students.
Aligning through monitoring and evaluating	Test for student understanding and competence during and at the end of class, and follow with a critical analysis of instructional and student performance.

important goal for American postsecondary students than developing a meaningful philosophy of life (Astin, 1998; Astin, Green, & Korn, 1987; Stark, Shaw, & Lowther, 1989). These attitudes lead many students to skimming and rote learning rather than attempting to understand and analyze course material. As student goals mediate what instructors intend students to learn and what students actually learn, it becomes imperative that students recognize early in the course why what they are learning is important. Students need to be committed to learning in order to meet the intellectual exigencies of the course, and more broadly, to contribute to a dynamic environment for learning.

How can this be accomplished? One task of the pedagogical expert is to formulate an explanation of the process of scholarly inquiry, how it governs the lives of academics, and how postsecondary students have the opportunity to engage in this process of inquiry. There is a growing literature available to explain what the process of knowledge development consists of, the strategies essential for knowledge testing and development, and the effects of different approaches to knowledge. The work of Perry (1970, 1981) and Baxter Magolda (1992) are particularly recommended for putting the process of intellectual development into perspective for students and for encouraging students to venture into intellectual independence. We use their work as a basis for discussion in workshops with professors about how they might introduce the topic of the nature of knowledge and inquiry. The characteristics needed to undertake this task include philosophical breadth and somewhat paradoxically, goal orientation. Thus, the expert pedagogue must be able to think quietly, then act dynamically.

Understanding the Institutional Context

Related to their need for understanding something about educational ends and epistemology, but more specific to the educational institution, students need a sense of the goals of their college or university and the program they have elected. Potentially provided in orientation sessions or by word of mouth, knowledge about the institution and its programs, as well as the ways and means of getting things done, is usually tacit. Home pages are increasingly supplying information on the institution, but the view of the university on the home page and that of students as experienced in their daily lives differ in some important ways. Home pages rarely tell students where they fit in; and although some institutions have developed computerized services that, for example, remind students of their next advising appointment, in a majority of instances professors represent the university to the students in their classes.

What is the task of the pedagogical expert in clarifying the educational context to students? Advocating awareness of the campus climate on the part of all team members is the first and most basic responsibility. This means not only being up to date on campus issues and policies but also participating in the governance of the institution. Although greater responsibility rests on the shoulders of graduate advisers and supervisors to be knowledgeable about and to interpret relevant policies to students, undergraduate students need explanation about how they can actively participate in campus governance. With the knowledge that involvement and integration into the academic community has a major effect on the achievement of students (Pascarella & Terenzini, 1991), formulating and suggesting ways in which students might participate is a first step. The characteristics of the expert pedagogue needed to accomplish this task are a general interest in the campus as a whole and adeptness at the interpretive and mediational skills needed to relate campus issues and policies to the team and the program.

Understanding Students

In order to understand students' conceptions and misconceptions, it is first necessary to understand who they are and what their experiences have been. Change in the general culture has become so rapid that icons and symbols are replaced annually. Generation X, for example, faced a set of circumstances that rendered their framework of the world and their approach to learning different from any previous cohort. Change during the nineties has been as rapid and widespread as in the late sixties. More entering students report experiencing stress; over the last decade, the percentage of students overwhelmed by everything they have to do has risen from 16 percent to 29 percent (Astin, 1998). The postsecondary population has also changed and diversified (Pascarella & Terenzini, 1998). At the same time, professors are seen as impersonal and aloof, without responsibility for students (White et al., 1995).

Although the mentor on the faculty team may be able to supply an immediate understanding of student circumstances, the expert pedagogue needs an overview of the issues that are at the forefront of students' lives and the codes they use to deal with them. In spite of faculty reluctance to invest significant amounts of time in understanding students, Moore (1994) has argued that understanding students more clearly is critical to an instructor's ability to cope with and learn from the enormous social and educational changes that occur. The research on student intellectual development provides help in understanding the struggles that students face as their conception of knowledge changes from one of absolute values through relativity to a contextual approach to knowing (Baxter Magolda, 1992; Perry, 1970; 1981). Research on individual differences also provides an explanation for the varied performance levels in a class, and professors who are aware of these differences will have increased empathy for students, which is crucial to creating a positive learning environment (Moore, 1994). The task of the expert pedagogue in this instance is to ensure that the instructional team has access to students, so that their point of view is included in the planning process. The pedagogue's role is then to mediate, so that student views are heard.

Providing the Disciplinary Context

Disciplines have traditionally provided homes within the larger learning community because they determine the discourse—the domain or parameters of knowledge, the theoretical or conceptual structures, and the modes of inquiry that guide learning (Donald, 1997). Learning goals vary across disciplinary areas. For example, physical scientists emphasize facts, principles, and problem solving, whereas in the social sciences and humanities, a critical perspective and communication skills are important. The traditions of a discipline or field of studies serve as harbors for those who are learning to sail. Disciplines are prime examples of systematic scholarly inquiry, and therefore serve as scaffolding for students who are beginning to explore different bodies of knowledge.

The expert pedagogue should be able to work with the researcher on the faculty team to explain the major principles and tenets governing their field of study, to describe the major processes of establishing and validating knowledge, and to show the gaps and therefore the areas in which further research and discussion are needed. Modeling the process of inquiry used in the discipline and explaining how theory is developed and tested is foundational to students' intellectual development. The contribution of the expert pedagogue to the faculty team is then to organize this knowledge for other team members. To do this, the pedagogue requires the skills of analysis and synthesis, interpretation and organization.

Providing a Learning Community

More specific to student learning is showing students how different parts of the university or different courses in a program interact. Although the learning community is usually considered in terms of a learning environment, it may take the form of coregistration or block scheduling that enables students to take classes together (Tinto, 1998). The courses are connected by an organizing theme that gives meaning to their linkage and provides coherent interdisciplinary or cross-subject learning. Having a learning community means a sense of relatedness among learners, a more democratic rather than hierarchical approach to learning, and an openness to experience and to others (Donald, 1997). It is collaborative and consistent with the fact that the student learning environment extends beyond an individual course.

In addition to curriculum groupings, there are a number of ways the faculty team can promote a community of learning within their program. Colloquiums, in which members of a department talk about their research to other members of the department, and brown bag lunches, in which professors and students debate important issues, provide a dynamic center to learning. Advising with an open-door policy and having regular office hours, so that students know when they can approach professors, has become policy in many institutions; but ensuring that students actually have contact with instructors is a more difficult proposition. Creating research teams that allow students to collaborate on specific projects is singularly successful as a learning experience. First-year seminars provide a sense of the learning community as well as introducing students to the educational context more generally. The pedagogical expert serves as ideational instigator in the process of creating a learning community. Important characteristics are openness and a willingness to collaborate.

Establishing Student Responsibility for Learning

The majority of students enter the university from an educational setting in which the responsibility for learning has been primarily that of their teachers, who have expressed considerable concern for them and their learning (White et al., 1995). In the university, there is a shift in the balance of responsibility for learning from teacher to student; and students often find professors, especially in large introductory courses, distant and indifferent rather than concerned. Because postsecondary learning requires approaches or strategies that students may not yet have acquired, students need to be ready and willing to invest personally in learning, to be open to and aware of the changes that must take place in their way of thinking in order to develop intellectually. The most important factor affecting success in college, after entering grades and SAT scores, is productivity or perseverance at the task of college work (Willingham, 1985).

Methods for helping students become responsible for their learning include, first, providing choice—the freedom to choose among alternative courses of action. Control or autonomy has a positive relationship to interest and intrinsic motivation. Students who perceive their tasks to be interesting and worthwhile report more self-regulation and persistence (Pintrich & DeGroot, 1990). Challenge, in the form of moderately difficult tasks, is also motivating (Clifford, 1991). Finally, collaboration has been found to encourage further exploration; to foster the pursuit of additional models, benchmarks, or standards for one's own learning; and to promote persistence, because there is an obligation to peers in the group. Whatever method is used, the message needs to be spelled out that the quality of effort students put into their work is the greatest contributor to their learning. Study strategies couched in this validated principle, and explained in terms of essential ways of taking charge, may be the most efficient approach to helping students take the necessary responsibility. A more concrete example is the use of learning contracts—in which students elect certain pathways or options, or grading contracts—in which students opt for a specific grade based on a work plan. The pedagogical expert must then work with instructors and mentors to provide means for assisting students to become responsible learners. The added characteristic for the pedagogical expert to accomplish this task is determination.

Instructional Planning and Evaluation

The tasks of the expert pedagogue in instructional planning and evaluation are more familiar than those of providing an intellectual context, but even so, they have for the most part remained tacit rather than explicit in postsecondary educational institutions. In an environment where the individual professor is the essence of efficiency—supposedly capable of accomplishing superhuman feats in nanoseconds, the time and energy that must be devoted to pedagogical planning and evaluation appear implausible. The challenge for the pedagogical expert on a faculty team is to provide the best representation of the discipline and a particular body of knowledge and set of skills in the most efficient way. The primary measure of efficiency, however, is the extent to which students achieve the intended learning outcomes in their program. This demand illuminates a pedagogical black hole.

Although 90 percent of faculty members report that they are solely responsible for setting the goals and content of their courses (Bergquist, Gould, & Greenberg, 1981), teachers often do not know what students actually learn in a course. Professors have been shown to overestimate their students' learning in a course by approximately 15 percent (Fox & LeCount, 1991). If students are to be responsible for their learning, increased emphasis on instructional planning and evaluation is a fundamental requirement. Students' conceptions of learning are mediated by how well professors communicate their expectations to students and how they evaluate learning. The instructional dimension that has the highest correlation with student learning is teacher preparation or course organization (Feldman, 1989, 1996). The planning role of the pedagogical expert is central to the team's success. The characteristics needed for this role include breadth of insight, openness, dynamism, and determination.

Designing

The design of effective instruction begins with determining the kind of learning desired (Donald, 1997). The faculty team in a discipline or representative department has a major responsibility for determining the learning outcomes of courses and programs and the methods of evaluation employed. Higher-order learning outcomes—

that is, course goals beyond gaining factual knowledge—include learning fundamental principles, generalizations, or theories; learning to apply course material to improve rational thinking, problem solving, and decision making; developing creative capacities; gaining a broader understanding and appreciation of intellectual-cultural activity; developing skill in expressing oneself orally and in writing; and discovering the implications of course material for understanding oneself (Cashin & Downey, 1995). Shulman (1987) suggests that the expert pedagogue should be able to comprehend how the major concepts and principles relate to other ideas in the field of study and to ideas in other subjects, and to be able to aid students to make these connections.

Planning involves examining and critically interpreting the materials available; detecting weak arguments, gaps, or a lack of coherence; and determining where further research and discussion are needed. In our studies of knowledge structures in courses across disciplines, one of the most useful steps according to the participating professors was the creation of a tree structure or concept map showing the relationships between major concepts in the course (Donald, 1983; 1998). Extending the techniques of determining the knowledge structures and skills to be developed in a course to the related courses in a program would provide learning coherence for students and professors. To do this, the pedagogical expert needs a repertoire of design skills and a facility for critical interpretation, analysis, and synthesis.

Representing Knowledge

Representing concepts to students in a manner they can understand so that they can incorporate them into their own cognitive structure is a process of depiction or portrayal. Three modes of representation—enactive, iconic, and symbolic—have been described (Bruner, 1960). Enactive representation means that students can actively manipulate objects or events, as in demonstrations, laboratories, or experiential learning. Iconic representation involves graphic or image-based presentation. The most common, and most abstract, mode of representation is symbolic: language or some other symbol system is used (Donald, 1983). Experiential and image-arousing materials aid learning and retention; hence considering these modes of representation as part of the course repertoire is important. Building a bridge between the teacher's comprehension and that desired for students, according to Shulman (1987), recognizes the link between instruction and cognitive functioning.

Since the object of representation is to enable students to represent concepts for themselves, an examination of the operations that constitute the process of representation is essential to the learning process. In a study of the development of thinking processes in postsecondary education, we found four processes of representation (Donald, 1992). *Recognizing organizing principles* consisted of identifying laws, methods, rules, or basic tenets that arrange, form, or combine into a systematic whole. *Organizing elements and relations* consisted of arranging, forming, or combining units, parts, components, and connections between things into a systematic whole. *Illustrating elements and relations* was a process of making clear by examples the connections between things. *Modifying elements and relations* consisted of changing, varying, altering in some respect, or qualifying the parts or connections between things. The pedagogical expert would use these processes both to organize instructional materials and to evaluate their effect. One important added characteristic would then be expertise at visual processing and synthesis.

Selecting Teaching Strategies

Learning outcomes provide direction for the instructional strategy. If the learning outcome is gaining factual knowledge or learning fundamental principles, generalizations, or theories, lectures and reading may be efficient methods to use. If the outcomes are higher order, however, such as learning to apply course material to improve rational thinking, problem solving, and decision making, or developing skill in expressing oneself orally and in writing, other methods that require students to actively manipulate the concepts or principles are needed. Advocates of active learning techniques base their recommendations on the powerful impact these methods have on student learning (Bonwell & Eison, 1991; Silberman, 1996).

Student preferences for teaching strategies are for active and challenging learning, where they are involved, where learning is connected to real life, and where there are opportunities for mutual responsibility (Baxter Magolda, 1992). Strategies that promote active learning are comparable to lectures in promoting the mastery of course material, but are superior in promoting thinking skills and writing (McKeachie, Pintrich, Lin, & Smith, 1986). Methods of active learning range from team-building strategies and on-the-spot learning-assessment strategies to modified lectures, class discussions, peer teaching, and independent learning.

One effect of the new media is that they allow students to learn in a framework of situated cognition. The theory of situated cognition states that students learn at a higher level if they are given problems or learning goals in a particular context, so that they develop thinking abilities that can then be applied elsewhere (Brown, Collins, & Duguid, 1989). For example, engineering students are asked to solve the problem of access to campus buildings. The concretization of the learning goal enables students to develop models and frameworks that allow them to operate at higher levels of understanding, by beginning within a context and then expanding from it. Most important in terms of active student learning is the capacity of the new media for students to use a variety of information sources to explore and then build their own conceptual frameworks. The role of the faculty team then changes from providing knowledge to designing learning methods and environments. The characteristics required of the expert pedagogue include adeptness at synthesis and a willingness to experiment.

Adapting to Student Characteristics

We have discussed the importance of understanding students in order to cope with the social and educational changes that occur for each student cohort and to create a positive learning environment. In the classroom, adaptation at the most fundamental level means ensuring that examples are gender and ethnic inclusive or representative. At a more general level, flexibility of approach to the variety of learners in a class is critical in order to get students' attention and aid them to become independent learners. Adaptation requires continual monitoring and what Sternberg and Horvath (1995) describe as insight. At the postsecondary level, insight into where students are having trouble learning requires specific strategies. One-minute papers in which students say what they are most puzzled about, or would like clarification on, or what needs further discussion are used increasingly to provide this kind of feedback. Tutorials, question periods, and frequent brief tests also supply information about the extent of students' understanding and the opportunity to tailor answers to specific student needs. It is the pedagogical expert's role to alert team members to the array of strategies for adapting to student diversity. This role requires leadership and persuasion, in addition to openness and an experimental attitude.

Aligning Instruction

The instructional process will be dealt with in Chapters Four and Five and is the responsibility of other team members. Most important to actual instruction is recognition of those methods that enable students to evolve in their intellectual functioning. The methods include providing students with a guiding analogy for learning, then modeling the strategies students need to use in order to understand and assess their own thinking. Although these methods are executed primarily by the instructors, the pedagogue is responsible for organizing the framework of knowledge. The choice of specific methods should be predicated on the principle of supporting students' active learning and progress in thinking. One suggested approach is to attempt to use methods that reduce the effect of large class size, as larger classes inhibit learning (Gardiner, 1994). Individualized, problem-based, inquiry-based, experiential, and cooperative or collaborative learning all contribute to gains in student intellectual development. The pedagogical expert performs the function of aligning instruction, thus ensuring that content, learning outcomes, strategies, and evaluation are matched or consistent and hence requires the characteristics of a mediator.

Aligning Through Monitoring and Evaluating

The assessment process in courses and programs has a major effect on the way students approach learning. At its worst, it tells students what they do not have to learn, especially if evaluation methods test low-level learning outcomes. At its best, assessment is the process of evaluating student learning and development to improve learning, instruction, and program effectiveness. A process of developing and using classroom assessment techniques in projects advocated by Angelo and Cross (1993) allows instructors to enunciate their understanding of their teaching and learning goals and the ways in which they can assess how well they are achieving them. The steps for an individual classroom assessment project include focusing on an assessable teaching goal or question, designing a classroom assessment project, and assessing and analyzing learning by means of student feedback. It thus requires the skills of the entire faculty team.

Student self-assessment is a strategy for developing skills of self-reflection and helping students build active and meaningful relationships with the material they are studying (Kusniac & Finley, 1993). Student self-assessment has the effect of personalizing students' learning and allowing them to take ownership of it while creating a sense of community (Eaton & Pougiales, 1993). The concept refers to both a written product and the process that produces the writing and requires self-representation on the part of students. Kusniac and Finley describe self-assessment as consisting of an attitude of inquiry, requiring integration of learning from other courses and previous understanding or experience, which in turn creates meaning and relevance in the learning situation. It is self-directed; that is, students identify the questions that emerge for them and become conscious of themselves as learners, and they then connect more actively with the learning context. The context may include entire courses or programs, or specific exercises for planning learning or reflecting on it, as in journal keeping or one-minute papers on what was learned in class in the last hour, that in turn aid the instructional process of adaptation.

Learning from the experience of teaching, through review or reconstruction of the events and accomplishments of a teaching situation, provides the impetus to improve and to treat the learning situation as a focus of development in a team. The process of evaluation may employ team members, audio- or videotapes, or a recording student. A comparison of the intended learning outcomes with what was learned according to objective evidence from students is a major impetus for further exploration and improvement. Although this is primarily the assessor's role, the pedagogical expert needs to ensure effective incorporation of the feedback in the design of the teaching and learning process. The principal characteristic of the pedagogical expert then is adaptivity in application of the findings.

Challenges for the Expert Pedagogue

Given the complexity of the tasks of the pedagogical expert, what characteristics are most needed? The essential characteristics fall into four categories. First is awareness—philosophical breadth, insight, a general interest in the campus as a whole, and in relating campus issues and policies to the program. Second are intellectual characteristics—the abilities of analysis and synthesis, critical interpretation and organization, and a willingness to experiment and to be adaptive in the application of new strategies. Third are task characteristics, which all members of the team need—goal orientation, dynamism, and determination, but in addition, skill at visual processing and synthesis to bring things together. Finally are interpretive and mediational skills—openness and a willingness to be in contact and to listen to students, a willingness to collaborate, leadership and persuasion.

What does the expert pedagogue bring to the instructional team? First, the role of the expert pedagogue is one of the most general and extensive. The expert pedagogue is scanner of the learning environment and synthesizer of context, content, and goal-directed activity. Prime features of this team member are openness, determination, and patience. Essential attributes are the capacity to deal with different kinds of evidence and the ability to fit actions to intended goals. The expert pedagogue is both philosopher and psychologist. As philosopher, by providing an overview and context, he or she invigorates and puts meaning into the learning context. As psychologist, by linking intellectual goals to students' learning capacities, the pedagogue furnishes insight and motivation.

Within the responsibility for planning, the role includes designing, representing, strategizing, monitoring, and adapting. Although in the past these have been tacit roles of the university professor, they are increasingly becoming *necessitata* in the learning community, as we recognize the need to tailor instruction so that students can construct meaning. The characteristics of the expert pedagogue are thus in the first instance empathy and adaptability, prerequisite for enlarging the perspective of the team and for teamwork. The expert pedagogue must be persistent in order to align the many parts of a complex enterprise, using broad program and curriculum evaluation skills as well as those needed for instructional and learning evaluation in conjunction with the assessor. Risk taking needs to be tempered with reflection, so that the team can flourish. Above all, this mediator and integrator must be creative and inventive, willing to dare.

References

Angelo, T. A., & Cross, K. P. (1993). *Classroom assessment techniques: A handbook for college teachers* (2nd ed.). San Francisco: Jossey-Bass.

Astin, A. W. (1993). *What matters in college? "Four critical years" revisited.* San Francisco: Jossey-Bass.

Astin, A. W. (1998). The changing American college student: Thirty-year trends, 1966–1996. *The Review of Higher Education, 21*(2), 115–135.

Astin, A. W., Green, K. C., & Korn, W. S. (1987). *The American freshman: Twenty year trends.* Los Angeles: Cooperative Institutional Program of the American Council on Education and the University of California.

Baxter Magolda, M. (1992). *Knowing and reasoning in college: Gender-related patterns in students' intellectual development.* San Francisco: Jossey-Bass.

Berliner, D. (1986). In pursuit of the expert pedagogue. *Educational Researcher, 15*(7), 5–13.

Berliner, D. (1991). Educational psychology and pedagogical expertise: New findings and new opportunities for thinking about training. *Educational Psychologist, 26*(2), 145–155.

Bergquist, W. H., Gould, R. A., & Greenberg, E. M. (1981). *Designing undergraduate education: A systematic guide.* San Francisco: Jossey-Bass.

Bonwell, C. C., & Eison, J. A. (1991). *Active learning: Creating excitement in the classroom.* ASHE-ERIC Higher Education Report No. 1. Washington, DC: School of Education and Human Development, George Washington University.

Brown, J. S., Collins, A., & Duguid, P. (1989). Situated cognition and the culture of learning. *Educational Researcher, 18*(1), 32–42.

Bruner, J. (1960). *The process of education.* Cambridge, MA: Harvard University Press.

Cashin, W. E., & Downey, R. G. (1995). Disciplinary differences in what is taught and in students' perceptions of what they learn and how they are taught. In N. Hativa & M. Marincovich (Eds.), *Disciplinary differences in teaching and learning: Implications for practice.* New Directions for Teaching and Learning, no. 64 (pp. 81–92). San Francisco: Jossey-Bass.

Clifford, M. M. (1991). Risk taking: Theoretical, empirical and educational considerations. *Educational Psychologist, 26,* 263–297.

Davis, T. M., & Murrell, P. H. (1993). *Turning teaching into learning: The role of student responsibility in the collegiate experience.* ASHE-ERIC Higher Education Report No. 8. Washington, DC: School of Education and Human Development, George Washington University.

Donald, J. G. (1983). Knowledge structures: Methods for exploring course content. *Journal of Higher Education, 54*(1), 31–41.

Donald, J. G. (1991). The commission of inquiry on Canadian university education: The quality and evaluation of teaching. *Interamericana de Gestion y Lederazgo Universitario, 1,* 157–173.

Donald, J. G. (1992). The development of thinking processes in postsecondary education: Application of a working model. *Higher Education, 24*(4), 413–430.

Donald, J. G. (1997). *Improving the environment for learning: Academic leaders talk about what works.* San Francisco: Jossey-Bass.

Donald, J. G. (1998, Feb.). *Concepts, knowledge and learning—and the generation of meaning.* Keynote address to the collaboration for the advancement of college teaching and learning, Bloomington, Minnesota.

Donald, J. G. (1999). The link between knowledge and learning. In J. Brennan, J. Fedrowitz, M. Huber, & T. Shah, (Eds.), *What kind of university? International perspectives on knowledge, participation and governance* (pp. 36–55). Buckingham, United Kingdom: Open University Press with Society for Research into Higher Education.

Donald, J. G., & Denison, D. B. (1997, June). Postsecondary students' conceptions of learning: Exploring different facets of a complex issue. Paper presented at the annual meeting of the Canadian Society for the Study of Higher Education, St. John's, Newfoundland.

Eaton, M., & Pougiales, R. (1993). Work, reflection and community: Conditions that support self-evaluations. In J. MacGregor, (Ed.), *Student self-evaluation: Fostering reflective learning.* New Directions for Teaching and Learning, no. 56 (pp. 5–14). San Francisco: Jossey-Bass.

Feldman, K. A. (1989). Instructional effectiveness of college teachers judged by teachers themselves, current and former students, colleagues, administrators, and external (neutral) observers. *Research in Higher Education, 30*(2), 137–194.

Feldman, K. A. (1996). Identifying exemplary teaching: Using data from course and teacher evaluations. In M. D. Svinicki & R. J. Menges, (Eds.), *Honoring exemplary teaching.* New Directions for Teaching and Learning, no. 65 (pp. 41–50). San Francisco: Jossey-Bass.

Fox, P. W., & LeCount, J. (1991, April). When more is less: Faculty misestimation of student learning. Paper presented at the annual meeting of the American Educational Research Association, Chicago, IL.

Gardiner, L., F. (1994). *Redesigning higher education: Producing dramatic gains in student learning*. ASHE-ERIC Higher Education Report No. 7. Washington, DC: School of Education and Human Development, George Washington University.

Holmes Group. (1986). *Tomorrow's teachers*. East Lansing, MI: Holmes Group.

Kusniac, E., & Finley, M. L. (1993). Student self-evaluation: An introduction and rationale. In J. MacGregor, (Ed.), *Student self-evaluation: Fostering reflective learning*. New Directions for Teaching and Learning, no. 56 (pp. 5–14). San Francisco: Jossey-Bass.

McKeachie, W. J., Pintrich, P., Lin, Y., & Smith, D. (1986). *Teaching and learning in the college classroom: A review of the research literature*. Ann Arbor: National Center for Research to Improve Postsecondary Teaching and Learning, University of Michigan.

Moore, W. S. (1994). Student and faculty epistemology in the college classroom: The Perry schema of intellectual and ethical development. In K. Prichard & R. McLaran Sawyer (Eds.), *Handbook of college teaching: Theory and applications* (pp. 45–67). Westport, CT: Greenwood Press.

Pace, C. R. (1982). *Achievement and the quality of student effort*. Washington, DC: National Commission on Excellence in Education.

Pascarella, E. T., & Terenzini, P. T. (1991). *How college affects students: Findings and insights from twenty years of research*. San Francisco: Jossey-Bass.

Pascarella, E. T., & Terenzini, P. T. (1998). Studying college students in the 21st century: Meeting new challenges. *The Review of Higher Education, 21*(2), 151–165.

Perry, W. G. (1970). *Forms of intellectual and ethical development in the college years: A scheme*. Austin, TX: Holt, Rinehart & Winston.

Perry, W. G. (1981). Intellectual and ethical development. In A. W. Chickering & Associates, *The modern American college: Responding to the new realities of diverse students and a changing society* (pp. 76–116). San Francisco: Jossey-Bass.

Pintrich, P. R., & DeGroot, E. (1990). Motivated and self-regulated learning components of classroom academic performance. *Journal of Educational Psychology, 82*, 41–50.

Shulman, L. S. (1986). Those who understand: Knowledge growth in teaching. *Educational Researcher, 15*(2), 4–14.

Shulman, L. S. (1987). Knowledge and teaching: Foundations of the new reform. *Harvard Educational Review, 57*(1), 1–22.

Silberman, M. (1996). *Active learning: 101 strategies to teach any subject*. Needham Heights, MA: Allyn & Bacon.

Stark, J. S., Shaw, K. M., & Lowther, M. A. (1989). *Student goals for college and courses*. ASHE-ERIC Higher Education Report No. 6. Washington, DC: School of Education and Human Development, George Washington University.

Sternberg, R., & Horvath, J. (1995). A prototype view of expert teaching. *Educational Researcher, 24*(6), 9–17.

Tinto, V. (1998). Colleges as communities: Taking research on student persistence seriously. *The Review of Higher Education, 21*(2), 151–165.

White, R., Gunstone, R., Elterman, E., Macdonald, I., McKittrick, B., Mills, D., & Mulhall, P. (1995). Students' perceptions of teaching and learning in first-year university physics. *Research in Science Education, 25*(4), 465–478.

Williams, T. R., & Schiralli, M. (1991). Canadian university presidents' perceptions of campus life issues. Paper presented at annual conference of the Canadian Society for the Study of Higher Education, Kingston, Ontario.

Willingham, W. W. (1985). *Success in college: The role of personal qualities and academic ability*. New York: College Entrance Examination Board.

Chapter Three

The Researcher
Generating Knowledge for Team Teaching
John M. Braxton, Marietta Del Favero

Research and teaching constitute the core functions of the academic profession (Parsons & Platt, 1973). Considerable debate focuses on the relationship between these two core functions (Braxton, 1996). Despite the arguments and empirical evidence on this relationship, we contend that the process of research conducted to advance disciplinary knowledge parallels the research tasks performed to generate or construct knowledge for teaching. Disciplinary and methodological knowledge form the foundation for this aspect of teaching (Shulman, 1987). Within the teaching team, the specialized role of the research expert is to "construct" from disciplinary knowledge the content of courses under the purview of within-discipline teaching teams. Thus, the researcher of within-discipline teaching teams performs one of the six basic functions of such teams.

The researcher role is quite congruent with prevailing patterns of attitudes, values, norms, and expectations for academic work. As a consequence, faculty members wishing to assume such a role within teaching teams will find transition to it quite unproblematic. Such congruence stems from two primary factors. First, the researcher role is firmly rooted in the nature and function of U.S. higher education. To demonstrate this assertion, we offer a brief historical overview of research activity and the rise of faculty professionalism. Second, the graduate school socialization process prepares college and university faculty members for the role of researcher within teaching teams. We describe this socialization process to reinforce this contention. The following sections of this chapter concentrate on these two factors. Third, we explore common characteristics of the faculty researcher and the world in which they work. The chapter concludes with potential issues faced by, and implications for, the researcher as a member of a teaching team.

History of Research in Higher Education

Barzun and Graff (1985) call attention to the importance of history in understanding the work and the minds of researchers. As this chapter explores the role of the research member of a teaching team, the history of research in higher education offers a compelling context for the characteristics of those who might effectively perform this specialized role. The story is one of the centrality of the research function to American higher education, and how the perception of teaching and research as two separate activities has evolved. History in this sense will aid in our understanding of the enduring value patterns into which faculty are socialized and the prevailing work patterns that have evolved.

The history of higher education in America is distinguished by its focus both on the development of an educated citizenry and on basic research in the full spectrum of disciplines. This duality has its origins in the contributions of both the English and German models of higher education. Yet, it is the prevalence of the German model, characterized by an intense research environment, the competitive race for priority in the discovery of new knowledge, and the drive to publish as the means to scholarly status, that has had the most pervasive and long-lasting effects on the academic profession. Consequently, the work of the modern professor commonly separates the research and teaching roles, affording research the number one position in a status hierarchy that is reinforced by well-ensconced faculty reward systems.

Research in American higher education claims its cultural roots largely from the influences of the land grant movement and beginning with World War II, the escalating national need for a defense structure in support of the Cold War as well as the Korean and Vietnam wars. These powerful forces came together to evolve a higher education–government alliance around the conduct of scientific research, which to this day is the foundation of the basic research enterprise in this nation. More important, however, the compelling research culture that it has spawned has become fundamental to the environment in which faculty work and has in many ways defined their attitudes and values around academic work.

Coincident with the twentieth-century restructuring of higher education to accommodate the research enterprise was the increasing professionalization of faculty. Faculty researchers, in particular, began to be viewed from both inside and outside the profession as "the specialist and expert and man of consequence in society" (Duryea, 1991, p.11). Light (1974) distinguishes those in the academic profession as a subset of all faculty, set apart by their engagement in the advancement of knowledge as a core activity. Light is specific about the criteria for judging advancement of knowledge—professional publications or scholarly reputation. The rise of research as a status-defining goal for faculty has consequently had an impact on the way in which faculty have come to view their various roles and define their careers. Most important, the stature of the research role has evolved a very visible and deliberate culture around the university research enterprise and the mind-set of the typical faculty researcher.

To prepare members of the academic profession to meet the expectations shaped by these forces, the graduate school training process in most universities concentrates on the development of the knowledge and skill necessary for research role performance. We now turn our attention to the doctoral socialization process.

Doctoral Socialization Process

Doctoral training is a powerful socialization process (Hagstrom, 1965). This process inculcates the knowledge, skills, attitudes, values, and norms important for scholarly and research role performance (Merton, Reader, & Kendall, 1957). The total learning situation becomes part of this socialization process (Toombs, 1977). Formal gateways—courses, qualifying examinations, the dissertation—and interpersonal relationships between faculty and students, and exchanges with the ambient environment, constitute the total learning situation.

This socialization process prepares individuals to engage in research and scholarly role performance. Through this process, research competencies are acquired. These seven competencies are as follows: the ability to identify, analyze, and conceptualize topics and problems of an academic discipline; the ability to analyze, synthesize, and interrelate facts and generalizations; the ability to read and understand the literature of an academic discipline; the ability to review, organize, and criticize the literature of an academic discipline; the ability to conceptualize and design a research study; the ability to evaluate research studies and their findings; and the ability to use research findings and the methods of a discipline (Braxton & Toombs, 1982; Cole & Cole, 1973; Hagstrom, 1965; Jencks & Riesman, 1968; Merton, 1973; Toombs, 1977; Reskin, 1979).

These competencies enable individual faculty members to engage in the research process that contributes to disciplinary knowledge. These competencies also equip individual faculty members to perform the research expert role within teaching teams. The level of consensus inherent in an academic discipline affects how individual faculty members engage in this research process.

The Research Process and Disciplinary Consensus

The process of designing a research or scholarly project generally entails several tasks. These tasks require one or more of the seven competencies acquired through the doctoral socialization process. These tasks are to identify a topic amenable to research or scholarly treatment, as well as current theoretical perspectives, if they are relevant, and bodies of empirical research germane to the research problem; to identify various criticisms of theoretical perspectives and empirical research associated with the research problem; to assess the quality of theory and research related to the problem identified; and to decide on which theoretical perspective to use to guide the research, as well as the appropriate research methods and techniques to study the identified topic.

To elaborate, the researcher identifies a topic for research. Such topics spring from gaps in the literature identified by the researcher through a routine reading of scholarly literature. Pertinent theoretical perspectives, if applicable to the identified topic, and empirical studies related to the identified topic are also discerned by the researcher through the reading of scholarly literature. The researcher also appraises the quality of extant theoretical perspectives and empirical studies to make decisions on the design of the research project. Such decisions are made so that the focal study will revise, extend, or break new ground in the body of literature related to the topic selected by the researcher. These decisions include the selection of a theoretical framework, if applicable, constructs to be observed or measured, appropriate methods, and data analysis procedures.

Although these tasks are arrayed in sequence, the actual enactment of each task may not occur in the delineated sequence. Moreover, the way in which each task is performed varies across different academic disciplines. More specifically, the level of paradigmatic development exhibited by an academic discipline affects the performance of each of the research tasks. Paradigmatic development refers to the extent to which members of an academic discipline agree on the importance of problems for research, theoretical orientations, and methods and techniques of research (Biglan, 1973a, 1973b; Kuhn, 1962, 1970; Lodahl & Gordon, 1972). Paradigmatic development is also interchangeable with the notion of disciplinary consensus (Braxton & Hargens, 1996; Hargens & Kelly-Wilson, 1994). Biology, chemistry, and physics are examples of disciplines exhibiting high paradigmatic development, whereas economics, English, history, political science, psychology, and sociology are examples of academic fields displaying low paradigmatic development.

The extent of disciplinary consensus affects the level of certainty associated with each of these research tasks. Scholars in high-consensus academic disciplines identify problems for research with much greater ease and certainty of their importance than their counterparts in low-consensus disciplines. The identification of theoretical perspectives on the identified problem is also more easily accomplished in high-consensus academic fields, as there may be only one rather than several theories that members of the academic discipline espouse. Because of the high level of agreement of appropriate research methods and techniques, the assessment of the quality of previous research on the problem is also greatly facilitated in disciplines exhibiting high levels of paradigmatic development. If the quality of the previous research on the problem is easily assessed, then the contribution to be made by the proposed research project is easier to judge. Consensus on the importance of problems also aids the assessment of the contribution to knowledge of the proposed piece of research. Decisions on the guiding theoretical perspective and research methods and techniques for the proposed research project are also greatly facilitated by high levels of disciplinary consensus.

Tasks of the Research Expert on the Teaching Team

Research tasks associated with teaching also parallel these tasks involved with the design of scholarly and research projects. The five research tasks for teaching pertain to the development of content for new or existing courses that come under the purview of teaching teams differentiated by teaching functions. Through the completion of these five tasks, the researcher constructs or generates knowledge for the content of courses under the purview of the within-discipline teaching team. The competencies acquired through the doctoral socialization process enable individual faculty members to accomplish these tasks. As with the tasks of design for a scholarly or research project, the academic discipline of the course also exerts an influence on the performance of each of these tasks. Each of these five tasks is described below.

Identification of Topics Related to the Focal Course

This task entails the identification of the various topics that might be included in the focal course by the research expert of the teaching team. The identification of new topics or the revision of extant topics would be the objective of this task if an existing course is being revised by the teaching team. This particular task requires a thorough and up-to-date knowledge and understanding of current disciplinary perspectives on the content of a particular course. The routine reading of current scholarly journals and books is fundamental to the enactment of this particular task. The reading of reviews of literature on topics germane to the focal course is also important to the accomplishment of this task. As a consequence, the research expert must know the key bodies of literature and core journals in his or her academic discipline. The research expert must also regularly read reviews of scholarly books.

More specifically, this task requires that the research expert develop an understanding of the structure of the various topics of a course through the reading of scholarly journals, books, and published reviews of literature. In addition, various bibliographical indexes are used by the research expert. When reading these various publications, the research expert looks for emerging and consistent themes that suggest topics and subtopics that would make up a course. The identification of topics and subtopics requires an analysis of the underlying structure of the broad area of literature being conducted by the research expert. In conducting such an analysis, the research expert would discern how the various topics relate to one another as well as how the various subtopics relate to one another and to the broader topical area. Such an analysis would identify which topics and subtopics are more important to the emerging structure of the course than others.

This task makes particular use of three research competencies developed during doctoral research training. These competencies are the ability to identify, analyze, and conceptualize topics and problems of an academic discipline; the ability to analyze, synthesize, and evaluate facts and generalizations; and the ability to read and understand the literature of an academic discipline.

The level of disciplinary consensus exhibited by the disciplinary affiliation of the research expert and the other members of the teaching team exerts a strong influence on the enactment of this particular task. This influence obtains whether the focal course is new or is being revised. High disciplinary consensus promotes the identification of topics to be included in the content of a course because academics in high-consensus disciplines agree on the importance of problems for research. Put differently, the topics selected are important to disciplinary knowledge in general and to the focal course in particular. In contrast, the identification of topics to be addressed in the content of a course in a low-consensus academic field is more problematic. The lack of agreement on the importance of problems for research makes it somewhat difficult for the research expert and the teaching team to make decisions on the topics to be covered by the focal course. An abiding concern of the research expert is to make clear to other teaching team members that the importance of the topics to the focal course is subject to discussion by the team because of low disciplinary consensus on the importance of the identified topics.

Identification of Current Theoretical Perspectives and Bodies of Empirical Research on Topics Related to the Focal Course

After potential topics for inclusion in the focal course have been identified by the research expert, the next task is to determine if any theories have been advanced to explain these various topics. Moreover, this task also entails the identification of empirical studies that either test prevailing theoretical perspectives or concentrate on topics currently without a theoretical foundation. In some cases, theories may be the topical areas, and in other cases, various dimensions or facets of the course content may make up the topical areas for a course. As with the previous task, a detailed and fine-grained understanding of the literature related to the course is needed. The regular reading of current scholarly journals and books is also requisite to this particular task.

This task also makes use of research competencies acquired through the doctoral socialization process. They include the ability to identify, analyze, and conceptualize the topics and problems of an academic discipline; and the ability to read and understand the literature of an academic discipline.

Research experts in low-consensus disciplines are more likely to discern more than one theoretical perspective to account for the various topics identified for inclusion in the focal course. In addition, they may find that some topics have not spawned any theoretical perspectives. Moreover, research experts in disciplines exhibiting low paradigmatic development may also find that some theoretical perspectives have not been the object of empirical verification.

In contrast, fewer theoretical perspectives on a given topic will likely be identified by research experts in high-consensus academic fields. The number of theoretical perspectives depends on the course of research in such disciplines. Under conditions of normal science, a singular theoretical perspective would be common (Kuhn, 1970). However, multiple theoretical perspectives are possible in topical areas that are in disarray because of anomalies identified through research that call into question the prevailing theoretical perspective (Kuhn, 1970). Nevertheless, research experts in fields having high levels of paradigmatic development are likely to discern pieces of research that test theoretical perspectives. The more central the topic to the discipline or disciplinary specialization, the greater the likelihood of a number of studies testing a given theoretical perspective.

Assessment of the Quality of Theory and Research Related to the Focal Course

This particular task is one of the most important among the various tasks performed by the research expert of the teaching team. Moreover, the expertise of the research expert is of paramount importance to this task. This responsibility entails the identification of various conceptual criticisms of theories and concepts related to the topics identified as being germane to the focal course. The research expert must engage in a close reading of the bodies of literature identified by the first two tasks to identify such conceptual criticisms. This particular task also involves the assessment of the extent of empirical backing for identified theories. Put differently, the research expert must decide how many empirical tests of a theory are needed to assert that the theory is either supported or refuted. The research expert must also make an appraisal of the research conducted to either test prevailing theories or research conducted on topics that have not spawned theoretical attention. In making such assessments, the research expert determines whether such studies have been rigorous in their methodologies and analytical techniques. Research competencies developed through doctoral research training are also used in carrying out this particular task. These competencies include the ability to review, organize, and criticize the literature of an academic discipline; the ability to conceptualize and design a research study; and the ability to evaluate research studies and their findings.

The extent of the disciplinary consensus in the research expert's academic field affects the performance of the quality assessment task. Although this particular task is challenging to research experts regardless of their disciplinary affiliation, research experts in low-consensus academic fields are likely to be more challenged by this task than their counterparts in high-consensus disciplines. Research experts in low-consensus disciplines are likely to identify criticisms of prevailing theoretical orientations and other concepts that hinge on conceptual merit rather than on empirical support. However, the research expert in low-consensus fields may also encounter empirical tests of theories that contain formulations that are amenable to such tests. The assessment of empirical research testing prevailing theories as well as other empirical studies on topics germane to the focal course are made more difficult in low-consensus disciplines because of the lack of consensus on research methods and techniques. In low-consensus academic disciplines, the methodological orientation of the research expert of the teaching team will play a pivotal role in such assessments. Research experts who subscribe to quantitative methods will employ different criteria from experts who embrace qualitative methodologies. The research expert of the teaching team bears the responsibility for informing other teaching team members of his or her methodological orientations.

Recommendations for Course Content

The advancement of recommendations for course content by the research expert to the teaching team is the culmination of the other three tasks. Without the performance of the previous tasks, such recommendations would be problematic. Moreover, this task is of critical importance given that the inclusion of topics in the content of a course serves to legitimize such topics as knowledge that is valid and worth knowing (Gumport, 1988). At base, this task requires that the research expert assess the "readiness of topics" for inclusion in a college course. Two major factors play a role in determining the readiness of a topic. First, the research expert needs to consider the importance of the topic to the academic discipline of the course in general as well as the topic's centrality to the field. All topical possibilities that have emerged from the research expert's intensive scrutiny of the field would be brought to the teaching team for consideration. Second, topics "ready" for inclusion would include theoretical perspectives that have received some degree of validation. In addition, studies refuting theoretical perspectives might also be judged as ready for inclusion. Topics that are grounded in empirical studies judged by the research expert as methodologically sound would also be ready for inclusion.

In addition to appraising the readiness of a topic, the research expert must also indicate to the teaching team any provisos that need to be communicated to students about the content recommended. For example, the research expert denotes theories or concepts that hold promise, but have seldom or never been empirically tested. The research expert will also highlight any important controversies that surround particular theories, concepts, or research conducted on a given topic.

Both the knowledge base of the academic discipline and the students, as individuals and as groups, constitute the "clients" of teaching role performance (Braxton & Bayer, 1999). Thus, a steadfast concern of the research expert must be that both the welfare of students and the academic discipline are safeguarded by the recommendations for course content made to the teaching team. More specifically, the research expert safeguards the welfare of both of these clients by making recommendations for content that allow for a range of theoretical perspectives to be covered in a course; by highlighting controversies and criticisms of theories, concepts, and research; and by including research findings that stem from studies that are methodologically sound.

The level of consensus on theoretical orientations, research methods and techniques, and the importance of problems to the discipline exhibited by an academic discipline play a significant role in the making of such recommendations by the research expert of the teaching team. As the level of disciplinary consensus of the academic field of the research expert increases, the higher the level of certainty the research expert has about the recommendations given to the teaching team. This particular task is the penultimate task of the research expert.

Organization of Course Content

This final task occurs after the teaching team has made decisions about course content based on the recommendations made by the research expert. This task entails the organization of the course content as approved by the teaching team according to conceptual or logical sequence. A fine-grained understanding of these course topics and their importance to the academic discipline are needed to accomplish this task. Moreover, the research skills of analysis and synthesis of the research expert are applied in carrying out this task—skills that stem from the research competencies acquired through doctoral study.

In addition to organizing course topics into conceptual or logical sequence, the research expert also plays a critical role in determining the level of detail concerning theories, concepts, and research findings that need to be included in course materials. This aspect of this task also involves recommendations on assigned and supplemental course readings that adequately represent the course content. Decisions regarding sequencing and level of detail in course topics are made jointly with the pedagogical expert, whose consideration of learning theory is integral to course content development.

Characteristics of the Research Expert

The design of the teaching team recognizes the disparate skills required of the various roles subsumed under the umbrella of the teaching activity in colleges and universities. In addition to specific research skills, the mix of personality traits and work habits must be considered in assembling the group of team experts. The research on the traits and characteristics of the productive faculty researcher is consistent enough that a reasonable profile can be drawn in terms of the specific traits such an individual is likely to bring to the team context. Although certainly, some individual traits can be expected to vary due to the varied personal experiences and backgrounds one brings to the team, the unique aspects of the typical researcher personality offer a profile that is useful in understanding individual researcher work habits and likelihood of success on a teaching team.

This section describes the characteristics of the effective researcher. A profile has been described that can serve as a guide for the identification and selection of personalities that are likely to fit the team researcher role and to illuminate potential issues faced by the researcher on a teaching team.

Empirical work on the skills of the productive researcher would lead us to conclude that to be effective on a teaching team, the researcher must be committed to, and active in, the research role to be successful. Following on Bess's (1998) notion of the "repackaging" of the teaching role into task clusters that are more consistent with individual faculty competencies and motivations, we believe that committed, "highly active" researchers, by virtue of their high level of satisfaction with their work as researchers (Corcoran & Clark, 1984), are those most likely to be successful as researchers on a teaching team. This section will review the characteristics of the committed and satisfied researcher as a way of demonstrating what it means to be a successful researcher and how the personal and work characteristics of these individuals lend themselves to successful performance as a teaching team member. The focus will be on two major areas—personal characteristics, and work habits and work-related skills.

The researcher personality has been described in terms of individual traits and behavior within a social space. As individuals, researchers are commonly seen as self-directed, curious, creative, and having superior stamina (Fox, 1996), ambitious (Fox, 1996; Rushton, Murray, & Paunonen, 1983), aggressive, serious-minded, intelligent, cognitively complex, dominant, and having a radical imagination and questionable emotional stability (Rushton et al., 1983). In addition, involved researchers exhibit a high need for achievement, according to Fox and to Rushton et al. These traits suggest that the researcher must be productively involved in research activity on a fairly continual basis and that the associated tasks must present challenge and provoke a sense of discovery and accomplishment. These traits suggest that in the absence of the feeling of productive work in which to focus their energies, researchers become less comfortable in their own skin, so to speak. Research productivity thus becomes an important self-image determinant, and the objective world of work is where the researcher is most comfortable.

As for behaviors within a social domain, the literature is fairly consistent with respect to active researchers' lower-than-average sociability and tendency toward solitude. Fox (1996) called attention to productive researchers' detachment in terms of social relations, including those with their immediate families. She asserts that productive researchers are apt to be frustrated by an interpersonally centered climate, resenting its distraction from their work. Fox also observed that scholarship tends to attract the "solitary mind" (p. 419). Rushton et al. (1983, p. 95) quote Terman's description of scientists as tending to be "shy, lonely, slow in social development, and indifferent to close personal relationships, group activities, or politics." A similar observation was made by Kuhn (1962) in his characterization of scientists in mature scientific communities as displaying a certain degree of insulation from the demands of the laity and everyday life.

In a slight departure from this widely held view of the researcher as somewhat of a social misfit, Bland and Schmitz (1986) describe the productive researcher as autonomous, yet simultaneously enjoying frequent meaningful contact with local colleagues. What may be construed as "meaningful contact," however, given the typical researcher personality, is likely to have sufficiently restrictive boundaries to limit the usefulness of Bland and Schmitz's counterargument to limited sociability as a common trait. Also, potentially challenging the scholar-as-a-loner view is Hoyt and Spangler's (1976) notion of research style. They defined two research styles—the collaborative style and the "lonely scholar" style. They write further that the style of the latter may be chosen by those who lack patience in collaborating with neophyte scholars. This claim can be viewed as a counterargument to the lonely researcher stereotype in that it suggests that collaborative and solitary approaches are a matter of style and therefore subject to researcher choice of work approach. Yet, whether a style choice or not, the teaching team fundamental assumption of specialization as a matter of "doing what one loves and is most comfortable with" would suggest that choice is irrelevant. What matters is the well-documented basic tendency of researchers to prefer solitary work. And as participation on a teaching team is all about specialization based on work strengths and preferences, the lonely scholar style as a common preference is salient and fundamental to understanding the researcher profile. This is all to suggest that the demands made of the lonely scholar in a collaborative work setting are atypical of the demands this person most commonly faces in the work environment.

The literature that depicts the work habits and skills of the motivated researcher also considers ability to work within an objective world of scientific data. As for disposition in such a world, the productive researcher is described consistently as one who is not easily frustrated or deterred by the task of making sense out of large amounts of often-conflicting information and who is skilled in data analysis and discovery methods. Fox's (1996) examination of the literature determined that high-producing scholars have an unusual ability to tolerate frustration and are attracted to experimentation. They enjoy abstract ideas and like information exploration, discovery, integration, and synthesis. Their cognitive styles tend to be marked by an ability to tolerate ambiguity and abstraction and by the capacity to play with ideas and stave off intellectual closure. This ability to work constructively with ideas and the "capacity for making remote associations which are useful" (Andrews, 1976, p. 337) is evidence of the creativity previously established as a required mental habit of the successful researcher. The productive researcher, according to Bland and Schmitz (1986), has in-depth knowledge in a research area and has mastered advanced methodological skills relevant to a particular area of investigation. Further, such researchers work on multiple projects simultaneously (Hargens, 1978) as a buffer against stalled work resulting from disillusionment and high levels of difficulty (Bland & Schmitz, 1986).

These characteristics strongly suggest that the researcher's greatest level of comfort and satisfaction is in the objective world of work. Consequently, researchers are less facile in their social world. In periods when discovery is stalled or frustrated, their ability to stay with a problem until some meaningful resolution is unraveled may be as much an artifact of their need to avoid removing themselves from an objective world where they find the greatest comfort and satisfaction.

Creative, productive researchers also face problems that must be overcome for them to be successful in any setting. Merton (1973) opined that scientists sometimes experience periods of difficulty in their work. He talks about "alternating periods of intense thought and almost calculated idleness" and "false starts and errors of inference" (p. 326) and self-doubt assuaged only by recognition. At the same time, establishing a public identity, from which recognition ultimately flows, can be problematic due to the exponential growth in the volume of publications. Merton also discussed the growth of teamwork and its potential for obscuring individual contributions and making it difficult for individual researchers to evaluate their own contributions. Also, the impersonal competition, characteristic of the race for priority, is no doubt a significant inducement to stress among some scientists, particularly those in what Merton characterized as "hot" fields. Simon's (1974) study of eminent scholars from a broad spectrum of high- and low-consensus fields revealed, in addition, the difficulty eminent scholars have in gaining acceptance for work considered most important. Also, researchers with higher creative ability are low in a sense of professional security, which negatively affects payoff from creative ability (Andrews, 1976). Andrews believed that this low sense of professional security creates a "security dilemma" for the organization.

In sum, the profile of the creative, active researcher is suggestive of traits that will facilitate their similarly creative and productive involvement on a teaching team. These individuals are focused on an objective world as opposed to a social world, possess high levels of cognitive ability including intelligence and ability to manage an objectified world characterized by large amounts of information, and are driven to achieve. As a teaching team member, the researcher's singular concern with work and productivity is anticipated to facilitate both individual and team success. The narrow focus of researchers allows them the latitude to explore available and relevant knowledge absent the burdens and responsibilities presented by the demands of the social environment. Unlike traditional approaches to teaching, which demand from the researcher various skills in managing the social environment for which the individual may not be equipped, the team approach provides a context in which the contributions of the researcher will be limited to those areas in which faculty possess the greatest expertise and in which they are most comfortable and derive the highest satisfaction. Problems encountered by the researcher relate to occasional low-productivity levels, self-doubt, and an intense need for recognition.

The final section considers the aforementioned traits and problems of the active researcher in the context of the demands of the researcher role and sets forth potential issues faced by the researcher on a teaching team.

Researchers as Teaching Team Members: Issues and Implications

The work of the researcher on a teaching team is fundamental to the success of the team effort and has critical implications for course content. Scholarly inquiry must be conducted with as much skill and competency as possible, so that answers to important questions on which curriculum is based can be considered reasonably reliable. The objective world and singular focus of the researcher enable work patterns that foster thorough and reliable inquiry. Researcher insulation from the larger society, according to Kuhn (1962), enables the scientist to direct attention toward problems perceived as solvable as opposed to those problems to which a high degree of social importance is attached. Consequently, focus on the research problem at hand will be stimulated, and reliable research outputs are more likely to result. At the same time, the prevailing work values previously described are indeed unique to the active researcher on a faculty, an important consideration in assembling a team with compatible personalities.

This concluding section considers the characteristics of creative, active researchers and the problems they face in the work environment and offers consideration of the potential implications that such factors might suggest for the researcher on a teaching team.

Research Interests and Work Style

Faculty seeking to assemble a teaching team must be particularly sensitive to the unique characteristics of the creative researcher. First, the productivity history of candidates for the researcher role must be understood. The focus of a candidate's research interests and current agenda are particularly important in that, together, they are suggestive of what a researcher is able to contribute in terms of content relevance. Second, serious attempts should be made in advance to assess a candidate's work habits, work styles, and particularly personality traits that may portend success in a team environment. Though, as scientists, many participate out of necessity on research teams, participation on a teaching team cannot be made mandatory, or the fundamental requirement for high motivation and drive of team participants may be compromised. This could have a negative impact on the researcher's ability to be optimally productive as a team member, and at an extreme, the instructional program and students may suffer. Researchers motivated to team participation with student learning in mind are likely to make the best team members. This particular breed of researcher can be identified as having unique appreciation for Mahoney's (1997, p. 120) aphorism, "Research seeks some resolution, and that resolution is learning." On the other hand, it should be appreciated that some researchers will be more comfortable in a functional specialty more similar to that of the pure researcher, or as a member of a research team versus a teaching team. Thus, knowledge of researcher preferences, strengths, and weaknesses relevant to teaching team goals is vital to ensuring team success.

Engagement with Knowledge Base

The researcher on the teaching team should preferably be an active researcher in the content area on which the course will be based. The ability to effectively identify current theoretical perspectives and relevant bodies of empirical literature on which to structure a course and to assess its quality requires an up-to-date knowledge of, and active engagement with, the literature. Because the identification of course content alternatives ultimately rests on the expertise of the research expert, as does the efficiency with which a team is able to operate given the fundamental nature of the researcher's contribution to the ultimate team goal, it is preferable that the research expert be actively engaged with the relevant knowledge base.

Social Requirements of Teamwork

The research expert's intense focus on the objective world and research environment to the exclusion of the social world has potential negative implications for teamwork that must be evaluated. Unlike the skill set of those faculty whose expertise in teaching makes them more adaptable to the social requirements of teamwork, the solitary work habits of the typical researcher add a dimension to the team context that must be understood in forging a productive team effort. Specifically, face-to-face interaction and collaboration, particularly in disciplines with less well developed paradigms, are likely to be necessities. Research experts whose work style is more solitary may not be used to the kind of sensitivity to the social environment that teamwork often demands. Although a solitary work style need not necessarily result in a researcher's ineligibility for participation on a research team, examination of work style should be made a prerequisite for participation to avoid extreme circumstances that may result in a problematic team environment.

Team Consensus

Team dynamics will to a great extent be influenced by the level of variation in disciplinary consensus. Where team members' specialty areas within a particular discipline are closely aligned, there is greater likelihood that work habits and approaches to inquiry will be shared. Teaching teams in low-consensus curriculums must be alert to the necessity of having to manage a potentially wide array of diverse topics to be posed by the research expert and must be sensitive to what this means for decision making related to course content. Although the sharing of similar work habits of a single disciplinary approach lessens the likelihood that sharp disagreements in addressing team goals will occur, it can nonetheless not be assumed that researchers in a disciplinary subspecialty will be of the same mind as other team members. Consequently, in selecting faculty as research experts on a teaching team, the extent of the variation in work approaches and habits among subspecialties of a single discipline should be examined to ensure greater likelihood of effective understanding and management of differences.

Need for Recognition

The researcher's intense need for recognition is a factor that cannot be ignored in assembling an effective teaching team. Researchers seek recognition from their peers in their discipline, both locally and nationally, and also from the faculty reward system that confers status in the form of salary increases and promotions. The notion of a teaching team as a venue for accomplishment and recognition for research is a new one that must ultimately be made a part of the reward system if those filling the researcher role are to remain satisfied and successful. To the extent to which the research done for the teaching team is synonymous with research submitted for publication, recognition outlets need not be an issue. However, it would be a mistake to assume this to be the case routinely, thereby putting at risk the formal recognition so important to the research expert, and potentially compromising as well the effectiveness of the teaching team.

At the disciplinary level, the professional associations provide an important venue for faculty researchers to share their work. Associations offer what is often the only formalized mechanism for networking with peers having similar interests. Given researchers' close ties to the discipline, and the role the associations play as a formal link between faculty researchers and others in their discipline, the associations are critical in establishing researchers' public identity and the recognition that flows from it. It is therefore vital for the notion of a teaching team to gain recognition and acceptance within the disciplinary associations, and within the wider disciplinary community in general, primarily as a way of ensuring appropriate consideration and recognition of the research products produced by the research expert.

Involvement in Other Research

The work of the research expert on a teaching team need not require that the scholar relinquish prior involvement in traditional research activities. Research experts can continue to engage in and publish research as in the past. In fact, the two activities can be viewed as complementary in a sense, because traditional research work in fields associated with the course focus of the teaching team can only increase the research expert's engagement with knowledge in the field, and thus the ability to apply it in teaching team research activities.

Rewards of Collaboration

The sociability characteristics of the lonely scholar notwithstanding, participation on a teaching team opens up a rich variety of communication and reflection possibilities for the research expert. Insofar as communication and reflection enrich learning and enable a viable approach to the research expert's construction of new knowledge, the team context can potentially transform the research expert's style to one that is more open to the value of collaboration and the diverse ideas it brings to the table. In addition, and contrary to the isolation of scholarship in traditional models of faculty work, being a member of a teaching team offers the research expert opportunities to experience the rewards of collaboration as a new source of professional satisfaction. The research expert may find, through participation on a teaching team, new insights and satisfactions from teaching that may not have been perceptible in the past.

Although these implications are not meant to be an exhaustive exploration of the kinds of considerations researchers might face as members of a teaching team, they offer a start for thinking about issues in assembling a productive and successful group. Without proper consideration of these potential implications, we risk compromising the success of the teaching team. Indeed, in the majority of cases, faculty researchers represent a unique personality in a teaching context. Undoubtedly, they define their world in terms of the challenge of scientific work, discovery, and concomitant research productivity. This mind-set is uniquely distinct from faculty who are more inclined toward engagement with students. And herein lies one of the major challenges of assembling a teaching team.

References

Andrews, F. M. (1976). Creative process. In D. C. Pelz & F. M. Andrews (Eds.), *Scientists in organizations* (pp. 337–365). Ann Arbor, MI: Institute for Social Research, University of Michigan.

Barzun, J., & Graff, H. F. (1985). *The modern researcher* (4th ed.). Orlando, FL: Harcourt Brace.

Bess, J. L. (1998). Teaching well: Do you have to be schizophrenic? *The Review of Higher Education, 22*(1), 1–15.

Biglan, A. (1973a). The characteristics of subject matter in different academic areas. *Journal of Applied Psychology, 57,* 195–203.

Biglan, A. (1973b). Relationships between subject matter area characteristics and output of university departments. *Journal of Applied Psychology, 57,* 204–213.

Bland, C. J., & Schmitz, C. C. (1986). Characteristics of the successful researcher and implications for faculty development. *Journal of Medical Education, 61,* 22–31.

Braxton, J. M. (1996). Contrasting perspectives on the relationship between teaching and research. In J. M. Braxton (Ed.), *Faculty teaching and research: Is there conflict?* New Directions for Institutional Research, no. 90 (pp. 5–14). San Francisco: Jossey-Bass.

Braxton, J. M., & Bayer, A. E. (1999). *Faculty misconduct in collegiate teaching.* Baltimore: Johns Hopkins University Press.

Braxton, J. M., & Hargens, L. L. (1996). Variations among academic disciplines: Analytical frameworks and research. In J. C. Smart (Ed.), *Higher education: Handbook of theory and research, 11* (pp. 1–46). New York: Agathon Press.

Braxton, J. M., & Toombs, W. (1982). Faculty uses of doctoral training: Consideration of a technique for the differentiation of scholarly effort from research activity. *Research in Higher Education, 16,* 265–282.

Cole, S., & Cole, J. R. (1973). *Social stratification in science.* Chicago: University of Chicago Press.

Corcoran, M., & Clark, S. M. (1984). Professional socialization and contemporary career attitudes of three faculty generations. *Research in Higher Education, 30,* 131–153.

Duryea, E. D. (1991). Evolution of university organization. In M. W. Peterson (Ed.), *Organization and governance in higher education* (4th ed.). ASHE Reader Series (pp. 3–16). Needham Heights, MA: Simon & Schuster Custom Publishing.

Fox, M. F. (1996). Publication, performance, and reward in science and scholarship. In D. E. Finnegan, D. Webster, & Z. Gamson (Eds.), *Faculty and faculty issues in colleges and universities* (2nd ed.). ASHE Reader Series (pp. 408–428). Needham Heights, MA: Simon & Schuster Custom Publishing.

Gumport, P. J. (1988). Curricula as signposts of cultural change. *Review of Higher Education, 12,* 49–61.

Hagstrom, W. O. (1965). *The scientific community.* New York: Basic Books.

Hargens, L. L. (1978). Relations between work habits, research technologies, and eminence in science. *Sociology of Work and Occupations, 5*(1), 97–112.

Hargens, L. L., & Kelly-Wilson, L. (1994). Determinants of disciplinary discontent. *Social Forces, 72*(4), 1177–1195.

Hoyt, D. P., & Spangler, R. K. (1976). Faculty research involvement and instructional outcomes. *Research in Higher Education, 4,* 113–122.

Jencks, C., & Riesman, D. (1968). *The American academic revolution.* New York: Doubleday.

Kuhn, T. S. (1962, 1970). *The structure of scientific revolutions.* Chicago: University of Chicago Press.

Light, D. (1974). The structure of the academic profession. *Sociology of Education, 47,* 2–28.

Lodahl, J. B., & Gordon, G. G. (1972). The structure of scientific fields and the functioning of university graduate departments. *American Sociological Review, 37,* 57–72.

Mahoney, T. A. (1997). Scholarship as a career of learning through research and teaching. In R. Andre & P. J. Frost (Eds.), *Researchers hooked on teaching* (pp. 112–124). Thousand Oaks, CA: Sage.

Merton, R. K. (1973). Behavior patterns of scientists. In R. K. Merton (Ed.), *The sociology of science* (pp. 325–342). Chicago: University of Chicago Press.

Merton, R. K., Reader, G. G., & Kendall, P. L. (1957). *The student physician.* Cambridge, MA: Harvard University Press.

Parsons, T., & Platt, G. M. (1973). *The American university.* Cambridge, MA: Harvard University Press.

Reskin, B. (1979). Academic sponsorship and careers. *The Sociology of Education, 52,* 129–146.

Ruscio, K. P. (1987). Many sectors, many professions. In B. R. Clark (Ed.), *The academic profession* (pp. 331–368). Los Angeles: University of California Press.

Rushton, J. P., Murray, H. G., & Paunonen, S. V. (1983). Personality, research creativity, and teaching effectiveness in university professors. *Scientometrics, 5*(2), 93–116.

Shulman. L. S. (1987). Knowledge and teaching: Foundations of the new reform. *Harvard Educational Review, 57*(1), 1–22.

Simon, R. J. (1974). The work habits of eminent scholars. *Sociology of Work and Occupations, 1*(3), 327–335.

Toombs, W. (1977). Awareness and use of academic research. *Research in Higher Education, 7,* 743–765.

Part Two

Direct Student Contact Roles in Classroom Settings

Chapter Four

The Lecturer
Working with Large Groups
Alenoush Saroyan

Teaching is a complex cognitive activity no matter what method or approach is used to deliver it. From the most straightforward lecture to the most sophisticated case-based instruction, it takes considerable knowledge and know-how to teach competently and well. It also takes an appropriate mix of personal, contextual, and social factors to bring out the best in individuals in the way they interpret and engage in the teaching task. If we take the lecture as an example of a popular mode of instruction in our universities and begin to tease out attributes that make it effective, we are bound to realize that such a dynamic process requires more than attending to a series of required overt behaviors. Considerable pedagogical thinking and planning and philosophical soul-searching concerning beliefs will have to precede any classroom action. The delivery itself will require particular skills, not the least of which are presentation, use of media, and time management. Then there is the aspect of on-line decision making, which calls for spontaneous reactions to unexpected events that arise during instruction. Finally, there is the notion of monitoring and evaluating both the learning and the teaching as well as the ensuing intentional reflection from which new comprehension (Shulman,

Note: This chapter is based on research funded by the Québec Fonds pour la Formation de Chercheurs et l'Aide à la Recherche and the Social Science and Humanities Research Council of Canada.

1987) is gained about the teaching process. All of these cognitive demands make the teaching task extremely challenging, particularly for most university professors, who embark on their academic careers with no formal training in pedagogy.

As the opening chapter of this book suggests, because orchestrating a successful and effective instructional event has a lot more to it than smooth delivery of instruction, we might begin to think more creatively and perhaps differently about academic task assignments. We might consider rearranging the existing bureaucratic structure of our universities to accommodate a closer match between personal dispositions and preferences, competencies, and tasks. New models of collaboration among different experts, for instance, will permit task assignments that take into account individual and group strengths and weaknesses, time and resource limitations, and overall rather than individual academic performance.

In this chapter, I examine the elements that contribute to the complexity of the teaching task in general and lecturing in particular and explore ways in which the delivery of the lecture may be optimized with the help of different kinds of experts. In the first section, I focus on task attributes: What characterizes an effective lecture? I review the theoretical underpinnings based on which different sets of characteristics have been derived. My definition of a "good lecture" is based on the principle that the teaching strategy, in this case the lecture, supports and fosters intended student learning (McKeachie, 1999). It also assumes that instructional materials, curricula, and assessment methods are "aligned" (Cohen, 1987). This means that how one teaches and what one teaches are tied in with the learning goals as well as with the way in which the learning is to be evaluated. In the first section, my point is to show that even delineating a list of task attributes, despite rich bodies of supporting literature, is not a simple undertaking. I highlight the complexity and differences in points of reference by comparing characteristics of a good lecture from the perspective of the *process-product paradigm* with that of the *expert-novice paradigm*.

In the second section, I look at another important dimension, the individual lecturer and the personal characteristics that either foster or hinder competency in delivering good lectures. I consider factors such as personality traits, conceptions and beliefs, and real and perceived social and contextual constraints that make individuals teach the way they do. The argument I present follows the approach that professors generate personal interpretations of what it means to perform well as a lecturer. It is based on this interpretation, an internal frame of reference so to speak, that they make instructional decisions and act on them. My intent is to bring to the fore the importance of taking into account personal and contextual factors at the time of assigning academic tasks, particularly courses, to individuals.

In the last section, I look at ways in which the potential of the lecture method can be maximized to promote and support those higher-order skills that are increasingly deemed as expected outcomes of postsecondary education. I look at the role of the lecturer in the proposed concept of team teaching. Having intentionally teased apart the various tasks that are involved in lecturing, I explore ways in which each of the tasks can be enhanced with expert advice and collaboration from team members, who are represented by various chapters of this book.

Introduction

Lecturing is the oldest and most widely used instructional method in university classes (McKeachie, 1999; O'Donnell & Dansereau, 1994). Biggs has called mass lecturing the default mode of instruction (1996), and Gibbs, Habeshaw, and Habeshaw (1987) have designated it as the predominant mode of instruction in traditional programs such as medicine.

A typical lecture in today's universities has some standard features and associated with them, certain advantages and disadvantages. Lecturing is an efficient way of transmitting volumes of information in classes with large student enrollments (Frederick, 1986), particularly when there are limitations in technological infrastructure and available instructional software. Moreover, it can be adapted to divergent needs and audiences (Gage & Berliner, 1991). Both of these attributes make the lecture quite viable in light of ever growing concerns about cost efficiency and student diversity in our universities. Nonetheless, they do not compensate for the shortcomings of the lecturing method. The disadvantage of the lecture method is that typically, it does not promote the *seven principles of good practice* (encouraging student-faculty contact, cooperation among students, active learning, giving prompt feedback, emphasizing time on task, communicating high expectations, and respecting diversity) (Chickering & Gamson, 1987) nor the implicit goal of university teaching—that of fostering higher-order thinking and conceptual understanding (for example, Kimmel, 1992; Puett & Braunstein, 1991). Indeed, the way many lectures are delivered invokes only a narrow range of passive cognitive functions, such as listening, interpreting, comprehending, note taking, and reflecting (Biggs, 1996). The opportunity to engender higher-order processes, such as analyzing and critiquing either the disseminator's or the recipients' interpretations of transmitted information, seldom arises, partly because of the perceived urgency to "cover" content. There is also the possibility that instructors who are assigned to lecture courses do not have the personal disposition to match the task, the motivation, or the pedagogical knowledge to plan and deliver lectures that promote deep learning. Perhaps they are even further discouraged by large enrollments and physically unsuitable teaching environments, such as huge amphitheaters with fixed benches, which pose yet another challenge in engaging the students as active participants in the learning process.

That the lecture method has survived for such a long time and that the field of education has witnessed many outstanding university lecturers speak to the potential of this popular method and suggest that under the right conditions, this method can work. But why are some lectures effective and others a complete waste of time? Is it possible to examine the model of effective lectures, tease out the pieces that make the whole, and determine what kind of advance preparation and expert advice might make it work all the time? Can a team-based approach, such as the one proposed in this book, render the lecture a more relevant and powerful medium of instruction? If so, what would it take to marry the task with the talent?

Characteristics of Effective Lectures

In addressing the questions posed above, we need to take into account the rich literature that already exists on teaching in general and lecturing in particular. The literature informs us about the various layers that contribute to the complexity of the teaching task. One aspect of this literature addresses attributes of teaching effectiveness.

Throughout the history of educational research, different paradigms have been used to define good teaching. When the process-product paradigm was in vogue (see Brophy & Good, 1986; Dunkin & Biddle, 1974), the definition of good teaching was based on low-inference teaching behaviors, which led to learning as evidenced by students' performance on tests and their evaluation of instruction. It was not long before the proponents of this paradigm began to acknowledge that teacher effects are mediated by the psychological processes or reactions of students and that teacher variables cannot be considered in isolation from student variables, such as prior knowledge, learning strategies, self-efficacy, and so forth (Doyle, 1978; Winne, 1987; Winne & Marx, 1980). More recently, with advances in cognitive psychology, the expert-novice paradigm has been used as the framework to define characteristics of pedagogical expertise and by extension effective lecturing (see, for example, Berliner, 1991; Borko & Livingston, 1989; Chickering & Gamson, 1987; Copeland, Birmingham, DeMeulle, D'Emidio-Caston, & Natal, 1994; Westerman, 1991). From each of these perspectives, attributes of effectiveness can vary—that is, the task of lecturing and the competencies associated with it might be described differently. For this reason, in any team-based approach to academic performance, establishing the group members' views as to what characterizes effective teaching would seem to be an important starting point.

The Process-Product Paradigm

Research carried out within the process-product paradigm has enriched our understanding about lecturing behaviors that are likely to correlate with or result in qualitatively and quantitatively different learning. Studies carried out within this framework have relied on student descriptions of effective lecturers as well as observations of effective teachers in action. Thus, using low-inference lecturing behavior and student outcomes as input and output variables, these studies have cumulatively contributed to a list of actions associated with good lectures (for a review, see Schonwetter, 1993).

From this body of descriptive research, we know that subject knowledge and ability to stimulate students, clarity of expression, preparation and organization, quality and frequency of feedback to students, task orientation, and pursuit of course objectives are important characteristics of effective lectures (see, for example, Centra, 1993; Feldman, 1984, 1989; Perry, Abrami, & Leventhal, 1979; Seldin, 1980). These characteristics have also been replicated in controlled, experimental studies. For instance, it has been shown that the lecturer's expressiveness, defined in terms of gestures and movement during presentation, eye contact, minimal reliance on lecture notes, and appropriate humor (Murray 1991; Perry, 1991) lead to increased student achievement (Perry, 1991), self-confidence (Schonwetter, 1993), and a larger number of completed assignments (Perry, Penner, & Kurt, 1990). We also know that clarity enables students to better integrate new material with existing knowledge because it facilitates both the storing and the retrieval of information. Clarity is attained by presenting materials in an easily understandable manner (Perry, 1991), by providing outlines and diagrams (Murray, 1991) as well as numerous and different kinds of examples, and by providing cues for transitions (Feldman, 1989). Finally, we know that good organization and material preparation lead to greater student achievement. Specific actions, such as breaking the instruction into small units (Perry, 1991) and posting headings and subheadings along the way (Feldman, 1989), and making available course and lecture outlines, notes, and handouts (Hartley & Davies, 1978), all contribute to the organization of a lecture.

The Expert-Novice Paradigm

Whereas the process-product paradigm highlights low-inference teaching behaviors that correlate highly with student achievement and course ratings, the expert-novice paradigm highlights complex cognitive processes underlying task performance. Research findings have been particularly insightful concerning the cognitive abilities that constitute expertise (Chi, Glaser, & Farr, 1988; Dreyfus & Dreyfus, 1986; Ericsson & Smith, 1991). Glaser, Lesgold, & Lajoie (1987) suggest that dimensions of expertise include knowledge organization and structure, depth of problem representation, quality of mental models, efficiency of procedures, automaticity, procedures for theory change, proceduralized knowledge, and metacognitive skills for learning. Many of the same attributes have appeared in the literature on pedagogical expertise at the elementary and secondary school levels (Berliner, 1986; Leinhardt, 1993; Shulman, 1987; Sternberg & Horvath, 1995). Expert teachers have more complex and richer knowledge schemas (Borko & Livingston, 1989), are more selective in their use of student information during planning (Housner & Griffey, 1985) and in their interactive teaching (Byra, 1992), interpret classroom situations in a more complex manner (Copeland et al., 1994), and possess a larger repertoire of instructional and management routines than novices do (Andrews, Garrison, & Magnusson, 1996; Leinhardt & Greeno, 1986; Rahilly & Saroyan, 1995). They tend to place new learning in the context of students' prior knowledge (Westerman, 1991) and see the relationship between separate units and the overall curriculum more readily (Gendron & Saroyan, 1994; Westerman, 1991).

This latter theoretical perspective provides an explanation for the effectiveness of some of the teaching actions described in the previous section. More important, however, it provides a blueprint for conceptualizing and delivering lectures in a way that is less "content driven" and more "pedagogy driven" (Saroyan & Snell, 1997). For instance, an expert lecturer, rather than organizing the lecture on the basis of clearly articulated topics, will organize it conceptually and will explicitly define the relationship between the concepts—for example, hierarchical, linear, nested, and so forth. (See Bligh, 1972, for a detailed description of different ways of organizing a lecture). Scardamalia and Bereiter (1989) highlight the significance of explicating conceptual links and suggest that understanding abstract connections is an important step in bringing about conceptual change, especially in large, heterogeneous classes. An expert lecturer would establish instructional routines and use additional handouts in order to reduce attentional demands. The lecturer would be alert to cues from students, would be able to discern student interpretations and misconceptions, and would be flexible enough to divert from plans in order to meet arising needs of students. This sensitivity—that is, being attentive to learners' needs, responses, and pedagogical concerns—appears to have an inverse relationship with the complexity of the subject matter being taught (Borko & Livingston, 1990). In university teaching, where typically the subject matter is complex, allowing or encouraging interaction may be particularly important and yet difficult to sustain because this takes time away from presumably "covering" necessary content. Being aware of and able to respond to students' needs then would be an important cognitive skill to develop in the lecturer.

The attributes discussed in the above two sections contribute partially to the elaboration of an ideal model of a lecturer. They highlight teaching actions and the cognitive processes that need to be invoked in order for the job to be done well. However, they do not capture the dynamic process of teaching, in which "multiple strands of the skill [teaching] must be accessed simultaneously and coherently at some elementary level" (Leinhardt, 1993, p. 43). A more comprehensive model of teaching would also need to take into account individual and contextual variables, such as personality traits, conceptions and beliefs, and course level or disciplinary differences. In a team-based approach, developing a shared appreciation of the complexity of the task will set the stage for collaboration among the experts.

Personal and Contextual Factors

Examining the lecture independent of the lecturer or vice versa presumes that the same person can deliver lectures on various topics in the same way. Conversely, it presumes that as long as a list of attributes are attended to, every lecture delivered by the same person will be of the same quality. There is ample evidence to make us realize that in the present system, neither of these is true, as many factors can hinder good teaching. We know for instance that the degree of familiarity with the lecture topic and knowing how to teach it are two such factors. Shulman (1986) refers to these as *content* and *pedagogical content knowledge*. He defines the latter in terms of those pedagogical interventions that are specific to the domain and the context. Although he sees a place for general pedagogy— that is, pedagogy that is transferable from teaching one subject to the next—he argues that the more important dimension in teacher knowledge is pedagogical content knowledge. This knowledge is contained within the subject matter and is not transferable from one teaching situation to the next. In contrast, general pedagogy is generic and can be used across courses and disciplines. The same idea is discussed by Sternberg and Horvath (1995) when they refer to *content-specific* and *content-nonspecific pedagogical knowledge.*

In addition to the degree of familiarity with the subject at hand, personal and contextual factors also influence the way in which the teaching task is interpreted and carried out. These attributes are discussed in the following section.

Personality Traits

Of the factors that have a strong impact on the way a lecture is delivered, one is personality. The literature on this topic has provided insight into at least two aspects. The first is that individuals who are considered to be good lecturers share certain traits, as do those who are considered to be poor lecturers. The second is that the same individuals perform differentially across different types of courses. Murray, Rushton, and Paunonen (1990) looked at personality traits and instructor performance across courses in the field of psychology. They found that *extroversion* and *liberalism* were two factors that received high scores among the traits of all instructors that were rated as good. Similarly, they found that instructors that were rated poor across courses received low scores on extroversion and somewhat high scores on *neuroticism.* Qualities such as being friendly, lighthearted, colorful, and charismatic were considered to be manifestations of extroversion, whereas aesthetic sensitivity, flexibility, and nonauthoritarianism were expressions of liberalism. Neuroticism, on the other hand, was associated with fearfulness and cautiousness.

These researchers also found that instructors who performed well in large, lower-level lecture classes scored high on the extroversion and neurosis factors but received low scores on *negative affect*—that is, they were friendly, warm, and approachable, had a flair for the dramatic, and were fair and reasonable in relations with students but showed no element of neurotic worrying. The researchers asserted that "perhaps an individual with these characteristics enjoys the stimulation of speaking before a large audience, but nonetheless is compulsive enough to attend to the myriad of details involved in organizing and orchestrating a large lecture course" (Murray et al., 1990, p. 258).

The results of several other empirical studies show that individual differences cannot be ignored when thinking about the various requisites of effective lecturing in light of the complexity of the task. One study, for instance, found that what individuals do in their classes is closely linked with their psychological typing (Brown, Bakhtar, & Youngman, 1984). The five different types of lecturers identified in this study were oral, exemplary, information provider, amorphous, and self-doubter. Oral lecturers were depicted as being dependent on their verbal skills more than on their notes or audiovisual support. Exemplary lecturers were organized according to a set of objectives; stayed away from providing detailed information; emphasized, repeated, and summarized frequently; and used media effectively. Information providers remained attached to their notes and more often than not presented unnecessary details. Amorphous lecturers and self-doubters emerged as having an unstructured approach to lecturing and not being able to keep to the topic. As a result, they seldom achieved their instructional goals.

Diversity in lecturing style was also reported in another study that looked at a series of lectures and identified individual differences in lecturing styles that were subsequently referred to as content driven, context driven, and pedagogy driven (Saroyan & Snell, 1997). The content-driven lecture was planned around disseminating content, and the means of this dissemination was didactic lecturing. The instruction consisted of hardly any activities that could enhance cognitive processing and storing of a large amount of factual information. The context-driven lecture aimed at conveying key information about a limited number of topics and communicating the affective factor surrounding the topic of instruction. This type of lecture relied on the context of instruction to promote instructional goals that clearly extended beyond providing information. The pedagogy-driven lecture attempted to promote and foster the learning of useful principles by means of a wide range of pedagogical tools and ensured that the opportunity to apply the knowledge was provided during the lecture.

Contextual Variables

Another factor that has a strong impact on the way a lecture is delivered is the context of instruction. Marsh (1981) and Murray (1980), for instance, found a relatively low correlation of student ratings across different courses taught in the same year. They concluded that college teaching effectiveness may, to some extent, be context dependent. "In other words, instructors may be differentially suited to different types of courses rather than uniformly effective or ineffective in all types of courses" (p. 251). Husbands's (1997) analysis of student course ratings yielded similar results. He found that course level, size of enrollment, the number of other lecturers involved in team teaching (the traditional meaning of the term) the course, and the quality and aspects of course organization were among the variables that influenced course ratings. More specifically, he found that undergraduate students rated courses overall lower than graduate students; in classes with large enrolment (over two hundred), instructors were less likely to improve their teaching; and when four or more individuals collaborated, teaching results were better than when teaching in twos and threes. He concluded that although "there are no lecture-specific characteristics that lead some lecturers as individuals to have more dispersed lecturing ratings across different courses on which they lecture . . . some course specific characteristics do clearly aggravate or facilitate the lecturer's task in producing [desirable teaching]" (p. 67).

Murray et al. (1990) also found that certain personality traits correlated positively and significantly with teacher ratings in one level but not another. For instance, sociability and extroversion showed to be important factors at the undergraduate level; whereas orderliness, compulsiveness, and endurance emerged as important factors at the graduate level.

Finally, the study conducted by Brown and Bakhtar (1988) found that lecturing styles correlated with the disciplines: oral lecturers were more common in the humanities, exemplars were more common in biomedical sciences, and information providers and amorphous lecturers more common in science and engineering. Self-doubters appeared to be distributed across all disciplines.

Moreover, the study found that years of experience was not an active variable in shaping the lecturing style.

The findings of the above-cited studies are both alarming and useful. They are alarming in light of current practices concerning course allocation in most institutions. At best, the system takes into account personal preferences. More often than not, however, there is little conscious effort to allocate responsibilities based on the individual's knowledge of pedagogy, competence, personality, previous experience, or willingness to try new ways and means of instruction. If we only consider the number of inexperienced faculty who are assigned to teach large lecture classes every year and the amount of anxiety these assignments create, and if we consider the actual learning that occurs in these classes, we are bound to detect some of the inadequacies of the present system that have a direct impact on the quality of teaching and learning in our universities.

The findings of these studies are useful in light of the proposed concept of team teaching because they show that without extra preparation and support, few teachers will have the necessary range of personality traits to excel in all types of courses. Together, the proposed team of experts can help discover the conditions under which one teaches most effectively. This may have to do with matching the personality to the type of instructional context, more extensive pedagogical preparation, practice in the delivery of instruction, deeper grasp of the subject to be taught, and the like. A flexible and supportive university structure would make it possible for the team to operationalize the abstract ideas presented in this book at least on a very small scale and learn from the experience for wider implementation.

Conceptions and Beliefs

The broader literature on teacher thinking introduces yet another layer to the complexity of the teaching task. Rather than highlighting behavioral and cognitive attributes of effective teaching and lecturing or personality traits, this perspective sheds light on personal conceptions and beliefs and the way they influence task interpretation and performance. In this context, beliefs are defined as implicit and explicit espoused theories of teaching and learning. They are revealing because they are the best indicators of task interpretation, decisions, and subsequent actions (Ayer, 1968; Argyris, 1976; Bandura, 1986; Dewey, 1933).

One relevant dimension of this literature to the topic at hand is that it underscores the complexity of teaching and shows that gaining competency in lecturing, for instance, takes much more than acquiring a set of behaviors and cognitive skills. It shows that for any fundamental change to occur in one's practice, it is necessary to first make a change at the conceptual level (Kember, 1997; Murray & MacDonald, 1997; Saroyan, Amundsen, & Li, 1997). This assertion supports the notion of a team-based approach to task performance because a group of experts are more likely to contribute to the development of the lecturer than any individual can in isolation and without collegial input.

Another relevant dimension is that it clearly shows that attributes of effectiveness may vary from the individual's point of view, depending on what one interprets the teaching task to be. This means that what one assumes one's role to be as a teacher and the way one defines the meaning of learning will influence the way in which one plans and delivers a lecture. For instance, if one believes that teaching is disseminating expert knowledge, then one is most likely to dedicate the instructional period to transmitting information. In contrast, if one views teaching as facilitating learning, then the lecture is likely to include a variety of activities that support and foster intended learning and that engage students in active participation.

Kember's (1997) review of the literature pertaining to conceptions of teaching in higher education is not exhaustive but is sufficiently comprehensive to provide a coherent perspective of what is meant by beliefs or conceptions. He used a 5x5 matrix to delimit conceptions of teaching along five dimensions (teacher, teaching, student, content, and knowledge) and five meanings of instruction (imparting information, transmitting structured knowledge, teacher-student interaction, facilitating understanding, and conceptual change). After having reviewed thirteen articles, he depicted his synthesis of the conceptions of teaching in a two-level categorization model. At one level, he showed the distinction between a teacher-centered, content-oriented way of instruction and a student-centered, learning-oriented way of instruction. At the second level, he depicted a developmental continuum, at one end of which he placed teaching as imparting knowledge and at the other, teaching as promoting conceptual change and intellectual development. Variations of these two extremes were placed in between.

Among the articles reviewed by Kember (1997), the article by Pratt (1992) proposed one of the more elaborate models representing conceptions of teaching. This model is specific to adults and teachers of adults, which by definition would include university teachers and is discussed in terms of the relationship between the teacher, the learner, the content, the context, and the ideal version for society. Using the five conceptions depicted in this model, it is possible to see how the meaning of effectiveness might vary from each perspective.

The first and second conceptions are teacher centered and are identified as engineering or delivering content and modeling ways of being. The dominant elements in both are the teacher and the content, although in the latter, the meaning of content seems to be broader and inclusive of values, practices, disciplinary norms, and culture, all of which are overtly communicated during instruction. The relationship between teacher and content is one of authority over and concern for what is to be taught and learned. From the perspective of an engineering conception, a good lecture would imply a tight control over material to be taught, meticulous planning and organization, smooth delivery, efficient coverage, subject matter competency, and successful time management. From the perspective of the conception of apprenticeship, a good lecture, in addition to the attributes listed above, would also represent the practicing of craft knowledge.

The remaining three conceptions are all learner centered. This means that the significance of content is greatly overshadowed by the importance given to the relationship between the teacher and learner and the ideal. Of these, one conception is developmental. It implies that the goal of teaching is more to cultivate the intellect of the learner than to disseminate knowledge. From this perspective, the important characteristics of a good lecturer would be to show consideration for students' prior knowledge and their threshold of understanding and thinking, to demonstrate sensitivity for individual differences and appropriate compensation for it throughout instruction, to be able to stimulate interest and curiosity, and to communicate enthusiasm about the subject matter to the students. Moreover, because from this perspective the intent is not to communicate a finite set of facts but rather to create an environment that will generate self-learning and facilitate personal construction of knowledge, a good lecture would include relevant planned activities for students that would foster intellectual growth. The conception of nurturing or facilitating personal agency stresses the importance of developing the learner's self-concept, worthiness, and a capacity to feel in control of life's events. From this perspective, a good lecturer would be characterized as caring for and being respectful of the learner and maintaining a fine balance between being challenging, supportive, and directive. A good lecturer would also be characterized by the ability to create an environment of mutual trust and a climate of both cooperation and independence. This last conception, which appears to be more a function of the individual rather than the educational context, is that of social reform or seeking a better society. That which characterizes a good lecturer, from this perspective, would be tolerance and acceptance of different viewpoints and a focus on macro rather than micro concerns.

Task, Talents, Expert Collaboration

So far, I have discussed task and talent attributes and contextual factors that may influence the effectiveness of the lecture. I have suggested that for a lecture to be effective, it needs to be clear and well organized and that specific actions undertaken by the instructor, such as attending to students' needs, providing timely and frequent feedback, and being dynamic, contribute to the effectiveness of a lecture. I have also suggested that cognitive processes such as depth and organization of knowledge, automaticity, and proceduralized routines characterize expert performance. In addition to behavioral and cognitive capabilities, I have referred to personality traits and conceptions and beliefs and ways in which they might influence task interpretation and performance. Finally, I have talked about the significance of contextual factors in task performance. Here I have referred to course level, discipline, and course type and their interaction with the task at hand as well as with personal attributes. I hope that by this point, the reader has reaffirmed a deep appreciation of the complexity of the teaching task in general and lecturing in particular.

The purpose of teasing apart these various and complex layers has been to draw a clearer picture of the magnitude of the responsibilities that a lecturer has to attend to in a seemingly straightforward teaching method. More important, this partitioning, provided that it does not profoundly alter the nature of the task, makes it possible to attend to each demand separately. Along the same lines, Leinhardt (1993) has suggested that the "entire interwoven collection of knowledge salient to teaching must be pulled apart into more manageable pieces without disrupting the fabric" (p. 43). In the context of her discussion, she has proposed several common axes along which the teaching task can be separated. Among them, one is to divide it between generic teaching knowledge and subject matter content knowledge (or in Shulman's [1987] terms, pedagogical content knowledge), or between management and subject matter. Another is along common academic subdivisions of learning theory—subject matter content, methods, and management.

The analysis presented in the first two sections of this chapter has taken into account Leinhardt's (1993) proposed dimensions. This way of partitioning does provide the opportunity for the lecturer, the pedagogue, and the researcher to collaborate closely in order to conceptualize the course and prepare for its delivery. The role of the pedagogical expert in this process is fairly clear. Earlier on, I mentioned that before attempting to partition the elements that constitute an effective lecture, my assumption was that instructional materials, curricula, and assessment methods are aligned (Cohen, 1987). The realization of this assumption will be one of the major contributions of the pedagogue who, in collaboration with the lecturer, will at the outset delineate the learning outcomes, the appropriate content of instruction, the relevant classroom activities and interventions, and finally the means and ways of assessment. The researcher can contribute to this process by selecting content and representing it conceptually and by providing the group with recent literature and advances in the field.

Nevertheless, teaching is a dynamic process: at any given time, one is drawing on several strands of skills to simultaneously and spontaneously manage the class, respond to student needs, implement plans, disseminate knowledge, and facilitate learning. It would take more than a prepared script to address the heavy demands of lecturing, and for this reason, I have intentionally steered clear of being prescriptive with regard to what it takes to be an expert lecturer. What is clear is that in a team-based approach, any pedagogical preparation for the lecturer would have to be based on a shared philosophical thinking and belief system among group members. This mutual understanding is bound to evolve as the group works and grows together. The role of the mentor could be significant in mediating discussions along these lines.

I have chosen this quotation from Gage and Berliner (1984) to end this chapter, hoping that it will not in any way diminish the complexity of lecturing by reducing it to a stage performance. I hope that it can serve as a guide to determine who is best suited to animate and showcase the fruit of collaborative work in the lecture hall: "Just as plays and movies require casting, and not every actor is suitable for every role, so teaching methods require matching with the strengths and weaknesses of the teacher. If a teacher's personality is unsuited for lecturing, it will be much more worthwhile for that instructor to choose a method other than lecturing than to try to learn to use the method effectively" (p. 482).

References

Andrews, J., Garrison, D., and Magnusson, K. (1996). The teaching and learning transaction in higher education: A study of excellent professors and their students. *Teaching in Higher Education, 1*(1), 81–103.

Argyris, C. (1976). *Reasoning, learning, and action.* San Francisco: Jossey-Bass.

Ayer, A. (1968). *The origins of pragmatism: Studies in the philosophy of C. S. Peirce and W. James.* Old Tappan, NJ: Macmillan.

Bandura, A. (1986). *Social foundations of thought and action: A social cognitive theory.* Englewood Cliffs, NJ: Prentice Hall.

Berliner, D. (1986). In pursuit of the expert pedagogue. *Educational Researcher, 15*(7), 5–13.

Berliner, D. (1991). Educational psychology and pedagogical expertise: New findings and new opportunities for thinking about training. *Educational Psychologist, 26*(2), 145–155.

Biggs, J. (1996). Enhancing teaching through constructive alignment. *Higher Education, 32,* 347–364.

Bligh, D. (1972). *What's the use of lectures?* (3rd ed.) Harmondsworth, England: Penguin.

Borko, H., & Livingston, C. (1989). Cognition and improvisation: Differences in mathematics instruction by expert and novice teachers. *American Educational Research Journal, 26,* 473–498.

Borko, H., & Livingston, C. (1990). High school and mathematics review lessons: Expert-Novice distinctions. *Journal for Research in Mathematics Education, 21,* 372–387.

Brophy, J. E., & Good, T. L. (1986). Teacher behavior and student achievement. In M. Wittrock (Ed.), *Handbook of research on teaching* (3rd ed., pp. 328–375). Old Tappan, NJ: Macmillan.

Brown, G., & Bakhtar, M. (1988). Styles of lecturing: A study of its implications. *Research Papers in Education, 3*(2), 131–153.

Brown, G. A., Bakhtar, M., & Youngman, M. B. (1984). Toward a typology of lecturing styles. *British Journal of Educational Psychology, 54,* 93–100.

Byra, M. (1992). Preservice teachers' preactive and interactive decisions: Within group differences. Pittsburgh: University of Pittsburgh.

Centra, J. A. (1993). *Reflective faculty evaluation.* San Francisco: Jossey-Bass.

Chi, M.T.H., Glaser, R., & Farr, M. J. (Eds.). (1988). *The nature of expertise.* Hillsdale, NJ: Erlbaum.

Chickering, A. W., & Gamson, Z. F. (1987). Seven principles for good practice in undergraduate education. *American Association for Higher Education Bulletin,* pp. 3–7.

Cohen, S. A. (1987). Instructional alignment: Searching for a magic bullet. *Educational Researcher, 16*(8), 16–20.

Copeland, W. C., Birmingham, C., DeMeulle, L., D'Emidio-Caston, M., & Natal, D. (1994). Making meaning in classrooms: An investigation of cognitive processes in aspiring teachers, experienced teachers, and their peers. *American Educational Research Journal, 31*(1), 166–196.

Dewey, J. (1933). *How we think.* Lexington, MA: Heath.

Doyle, W. (1978). Paradigms for research on teacher effectiveness. In L. S. Shulman (Ed.), *Review of research in education* (Vol. 5). Itasca, IL: Peacock.

Dreyfus, H. L., & Dreyfus, S. E. (1986). *Mind over machine.* New York: Free Press.

Dunkin, M. J., & Biddle, B. J. (1974). *The study of teaching.* Austin, TX: Holt, Rinehart & Winston.

Ericsson, K. A., & Smith, J. (Eds.). (1991). *Toward a general theory of expertise: Prospects and limits.* New York: Cambridge University Press.

Feldman, K. A. (1984). Class size and students' evaluation of college teachers and courses: A closer look. *Research in Higher Education, 5,* 243–288.

Feldman, K. A. (1989). Instructional effectiveness of college teachers as judged by teachers themselves, current and former students, colleagues, administrators, and external (neutral) observers. *Research in Higher Education, 30*(2), 137–194.

Frederick, P. (1986). The lively lecture. *College Teaching, 34*(2), 43–50.

Gage, N. L., & Berliner, D. C. (1984). *Educational psychology* (3rd ed.). Boston: Houghton Mifflin.

Gage, N. L., & Berliner, D. C. (1991). *Educational psychology* (4th ed.). Boston: Houghton Mifflin.

Gendron, M. J., & Saroyan, A. (1994, July). Pedagogical expertise of professors. Paper presented at the 19th International Conference on Improving University Teaching, College Park, Maryland.

Gibbs, G., Habeshaw, S., & Habeshaw, T. (1987). Improving student learning during lectures. *Medical Teacher, 9*(1), 11–20.

Glaser, R., Lesgold, A., & Lajoie, S. (1987). Toward a cognitive theory for the measurement of achievement. In R. Ronning, J. Glover, J. Conoley, & J. Witt (Eds.), *The influence of cognitive psychology on testing* (pp. 41–85). Hillsdale, NJ: Erlbaum.

Hartley, J., & Davies, I. K. (1978). *Contributions to an educational technology.* (Vol. 2). London: Kogan Page.

Housner, L. D., & Griffey, D. C. (1985). Teacher cognition: Differences in planning and interactive decision making between experienced and inexperienced teachers. *Research Quarterly for Exercise and Sport, 56*(1), 45–53.

Husbands, C. (1997). Variations in students' evaluations of teachers' lecturing in different courses on which they lecture: A study at the London School of Economics and Political Science. *Higher Education, 33,* 51–70.

Kember, D. (1997). A reconceptualization of the research into university academics' conceptions of teaching. *Learning and Instruction, 7*(3), 225–275.

Kimmel, P. (1992). Abandoning the lecture: Curriculum reform in the introduction to clinical medicine. *The Pharos, 55*(2), 36–38.

Leinhardt, G. (1993). On teaching. In R. Glaser (Ed.), *Advances in instructional psychology* (pp. 1–54). Hillsdale, NJ: Erlbaum.

Leinhardt, G., & Greeno, J. G. (1986). The cognitive skill of teaching. *Journal of Educational Psychology, 78,* 75–95.

Marsh, H. W. (1981). The use of path analysis to estimate teacher and course effects in student ratings of instructional effectiveness. *Applied Psychological Measurement, 6,* 47–60.

McKeachie, W. (1999). *Teaching tips* (10th ed.). Lexington, MA: Heath.

Murray, H. G. (1980). *Evaluating university teaching: A review of research.* Toronto: Ontario Confederation of University Faculty Associations.

Murray, H. G. (1991). Effective teaching behaviors in the college classroom. In J. C. Smart (Ed.), *Higher Education: Handbook of Theory and Research, 7(4).* New York: Agathon.

Murray, H. G., Rushton, J., & Paunonen, S. V. (1990). Teacher personality traits and student instructional ratings in six types of university courses. *Journal of Educational Psychology, 82*(2), 250–261.

Murray, K., & MacDonald, R. (1997). The disjunction between lecturers' conceptions of teaching and their claimed educational practice. *Higher Education, 33*(3), 331–349.

O'Donnell, A., & Dansereau, D. (1994). Learning from lectures: Effects of cooperative review. *Journal of Experimental Education, 61*(2), 116–125.

Perry, R. P. (1991). Perceived control in college students: Implications for instruction in higher education. In J. C. Smart (Ed.), *Higher Education: Handbook of Theory and Research, 7(4).* New York: Agathon.

Perry, R. P., Abrami, P., & Leventhal, L. (1979). Educational seduction: The effect of instructor expressiveness and lecture content on student ratings and achievement. *Journal of Educational Psychology, 71,* 107–116.

Perry, R. P., Penner, K. S., & Kurt, S. (1990). Enhancing academic achievement in college students through attributional retraining and instruction. *Journal of Educational Psychology, 82,* 262–271.

Pratt, D. D. (1992). Conceptions of teaching. *Adult Education Quarterly, 42*(4), 203–220.

Puett, P., & Braunstein, J. (1991). The endocrine module: An integrated course for first-year medical students combining lecture-based and modified problem-based curricula. *Teaching and Learning in Medicine, 3*(3), 159–165.

Rahilly, T., & Saroyan, A. (1995, April). A job well done: Experienced and inexperienced professors' critical incidents of teaching. Paper presented at the annual meeting of the American Educational Research Association, San Francisco.

Saroyan, A., Amundsen, C., & Li, C. (1997). Incorporating theories of teacher growth and adult education in a faculty development program. *To Improve the Academy, 16,* 93–115.

Saroyan, A., & Snell, L. S. (1997). Variations in lecturing styles. *Higher Education, 33,* 85–104.

Scardamalia, M., & Bereiter, C. (1989). Conceptions of teaching and approaches to core problems. In M. Reynolds (Ed.), *Knowledge base for beginning teachers* (pp. 37–45). Oxford: Pergamon Press.

Schonwetter, D. (1993). Attributes of effective lecturing in the college classroom. *The Canadian Journal of Higher Education, 23*(2), 1–18.

Seldin, P. (1980). *Successful faculty evaluation programs.* Crugers, NY: Coventry Press.

Shulman, L. S. (1986). Paradigms and research programs in the study of teaching: A contemporary perspective. In M. Wittrock (Ed.), *Handbook of research on teaching* (3rd ed., pp. 3–36). Old Tappan, NJ: Macmillan.

Shulman, L. S. (1987). Knowledge and teaching: Foundations of the new reform. *Harvard Educational Review, 57*(1), 1–22.

Sternberg, R., & Horvath, J. (1995). A prototype view of expert teaching. *Educational Researcher, 24*(6), 9–17.

Westerman, D. A. (1991). Expert and novice teacher decision making. *Journal of Teacher Education, 42*(4), 292–305.

Winne, P. H. (1987). Why process-product research cannot explain process-product findings and a proposed remedy: The cognitive mediational paradigm. *Teaching and Teacher Education, 3*(4), 333–356.

Winne, P. H., & Marx, R. W. (1980). Matching students' cognitive responses to teaching skills. *Journal of Educational Psychology, 72,* 257–264.

Chapter Five

The Discussion Leader
Fostering Student Learning in Groups
Richard G. Tiberius, Jane Tipping

As noted in the Preface, the premise of this book is that faculty working in teams can take advantage of the individual teacher's strengths and interests and thus produce more efficient and effective instruction than a single faculty member playing multiple roles. The purpose of this chapter is to examine one of the team member roles—the discussion leader—and to explore the nature of the tasks to be performed and the temperaments or dispositions of the player of this role that would lead to high satisfaction, continuing motivation, and commitment.

Extreme differences in the abilities and interests of faculty are familiar to all of us who conduct instructional development sessions for teachers. Talents and interests underlie such differences. We assume that a teacher who has the talents and motivation to become an excellent discussion leader might not ordinarily also be an effective lecturer, mentor, evaluator, or curriculum designer. Talents and motivations found to be specific to certain teaching formats are likely to result in more successful teaching when faculty are assigned to tasks that match them.

The purpose of this next section is to specify the principal competencies needed by teachers who conduct discussion classes. We have drawn from three literatures in pursuit of this goal—the body of practical wisdom about small group teaching; recent contributions from cognitive science on the nature of human competencies; and learning theories that emphasize the cognitive, social, and cultural contexts (rather than the strictly behavioral). Although these three approaches are relatively isolated from one another— they have their own vocabularies, goals, and methods—they each contribute to a coherent and detailed picture of the requirements of the discussion leader. Our purpose is to develop that picture in the following pages.

Practical Wisdom on Small Group Teaching

The body of writing that has now become the classical literature on small group teaching was generated in the early 1970s. (See, for example, Abercrombie, 1971; Bligh, 1971; McGregor, 1967; McLeish, Matheson, & Park, 1973; Miles, 1973; McKeachie & Kulik, 1975; Rudduck, 1978; Mill, 1980.) Rereading sources such as Miles today is revealing. It leaves the impression that virtually everything that we are teaching about learning in small groups today comes out of that early literature. This early work attempted to uncover the wisdom embedded in the actions of expert practitioners. They used methods that Argyris, Putnam, and Smith (1985) and Schön (1995) would describe as action research—observation, reflection-on-action, and self-reflection—although they did not use these terms nor the rigorous methods of action science that are used today.

Legitimate Goals of Discussion Learning

The early work defined the important learning goals of class discussion. Discussion provides needed practice in using terms and concepts correctly, in constructing arguments, and in thinking on one's feet. Discussion enables students to place themselves within the spectrum of student opinion, ideas, and abilities. Students can make valuable inferences about their own ability in a subject by observing others grapple with the same concepts. They come to know whether their views on a topic are conservative, radical, or middle-of-the-road by listening to others' opinions and values. Discussion sessions are uniquely suited to learning the skills of group interaction, such as sensitivity and tolerance of others' views, building group cohesiveness, establishing and following group rules, resolving group conflicts, cooperative learning skills, and active learning.

When properly led, a discussion can facilitate the independence of the learners from their teacher. Discussion fosters active involvement in learning (Bonwell & Eison, 1991). Active involvement and increased responsibility for their learning helps students build self-confidence and a sense of competency. Interaction helps the thinking process by facilitating connections between the material and the learners' most salient ideas and thoughts (Simpson & Galbo, 1987).

Teachers also learn from class discussion. By listening to student discussion, teachers learn important information about their students' knowledge gaps and experiences, information that will enable teachers to guide the group and to provide useful corrective feedback (Tiberius, 1990).

Functions and Activities of the Discussion Leader

The early work also described the activities or functions of the discussion leader that are necessary to encourage the desired learning goals (see Exhibit 5.1). A distinction was made between functions that supported the group *work* and functions that encouraged and maintained good group *process* (see Jacques, 1991, for a summary of work and process functions). Work-oriented functions included leadership activities that directly support the learning objectives of the group, such as clarifying the topic and maintaining focus. Process-oriented functions included those that indirectly support the learning objectives, such as maintaining and encouraging a safe and comfortable psychological climate. The problem with these functions of the discussion leader, for our purposes, is that they were not framed in terms of teacher competencies, that is, qualities or abilities or types of intelligence (Gardner, 1993). The leadership function of *summarizing,* for example, does not identify a skill or talent, such as *sensitivity to others,* which would enable a leader to know when is the optimal time to make the summary. Nor does the function include the cognitive skill of *ability to form a useful summary.* Cognitive theory has defined more precisely some of these categories of human ability.

Exhibit 5.1. Task Requirements of
an Effective Discussion Group Leader.

Encourage and Maintain Discussion.

Encourage a climate of acceptance to promote freedom of expression.

Choose topics that provide stimulus for discussion.

Choose a topic of interest to the group and define it clearly.

Create an informal atmosphere.

After getting the group going, serve primarily as a guide.

Keep the Discussion on Topic.

Summarize when appropriate.

Clarify the topic.

Clarify the goals.

Promote Sharing Among Learners.

Set ground rules.

Encourage members to listen to one another and hear the viewpoints of others.

Encourage balanced interaction among the learners.

Encourage Participation and Involvement.

Listen to students actively.

Provide opportunities for practice or rehearsal.

Provide opportunities for self-expression.

Encourage Awareness of Group Process.

Role model good group process.

Point out process issues to the group.

Deal with Group Difficulties.

Deal with disruptive students.

Reduce destructive conflict and competition.

Help students who lack motivation.

Deal with uncooperative students.

Note: Abstracted from the early work on small group teaching.

Recent Contributions from Cognitive Science on the Nature of Human Competencies

Cognitive theorists such as Collins, Brown, and Newman (1989) and Bereiter and Scardamalia (1993) have developed classification systems of cognitive competencies, which we have combined to form a system consisting of five categories (see Exhibit 5.2). Knowledge is subdivided into *informal knowledge* and *textbook knowledge*;

Exhibit 5.2. General Competencies Required to Teach Effectively and Specific Competencies for Teaching Discussion Groups.

---

1. Knowledge: "Knowing That"

Informal knowledge. This subcategory includes the "common sense" background knowledge such as cultural assumptions about normal behavior in various teaching settings that teachers rarely think about deliberately while teaching. This includes knowledge of the culture of the students and knowledge of the norms of the students.

Formal knowledge. This subcategory includes the formal knowledge "about" teaching; for example, knowing important facts and concepts about small groups, about discussion groups, or about characteristics of learners. This category includes knowledge of the subject matter that enables the discussion leader to view the subject from many perspectives; knowledge of discipline-specific learning strategies; knowledge of learning theory, such as attribution theory, self-efficacy, and constructivism; and knowledge of techniques such as those presented by cooperative learning.

2. Diagnostic Strategies

This category includes the skills that enable teachers to find out when to use a particular strategy, to recognize patterns, and to obtain diagnostic information. This category includes "teaching scripts" and the ability to assess individual needs and to provide reinforcement.

3. Heuristic Strategies

This category includes the "tricks of the trade," the wise moves that under most conditions will help achieve the learning objectives or useful remedies for the common presenting problems of the group. This category includes skills of group leadership—setting ground rules, summarizing, and so forth; skills of the subject matter; skill in arranging and conducting cooperative learning situations;

interpersonal intelligence—the ability to understand other people, including their emotions, motivations, desires, moods, temperaments, and the way that they operate in the world; and intrapersonal intelligence—the ability to form an accurate awareness of one's own feelings and to use that knowledge to act effectively in the world.

4. Self-Regulatory Strategies

This category includes the skills that enable teachers to control their responses to events occurring while they are teaching, so that they can engage in diagnostic strategies and reflect on optimal interventions before responding. These skills may be held explicitly but are often held implicitly. Teachers are not aware of using them and would have difficulty explaining what they were doing if asked. This category includes skill in managing emotions.

5. Intuition, Feelings, and Impressionistic Knowledge

This category includes the collection of intuitions, feelings, and impressions that predispose a teacher to react in one way rather than in another in response to some event in the class or in interaction with the student. Such predispositions implicitly contribute to a teacher's understanding of students and ability to intervene. They are part of expert knowledge.

---

skills are subdivided into *self-regulatory behavior, diagnostics,* and *interventions;* and attitudes are divided into *intuition, feelings,* and *impressions.* The following is a brief description of each of these categories as they are applied to the skills needed by discussion group leaders to fulfill the major roles of their task. A formal taxonomy is useful not only because it enables us to classify the known competencies of the discussion leader but also because it enables us to search for competencies that are known to be important in expert human performance although they are not apparent to practitioners themselves. An example of this is *tacit knowledge* (Polanyi, 1967).

Knowledge

As mentioned, the two types of knowledge used by the discussion leader are informal knowledge and formal knowledge, also called textbook knowledge.

Informal Knowledge

Teachers already possess more knowledge about discussion groups before taking any formal education in the subject than they will ever acquire by formal study. The information that they have is informal. It is not found in a textbook on discussion group teaching. Informal knowledge represents what is obvious—a vast store of background information learned from life experience with groups. We are largely unaware of this knowledge. We have absorbed it by virtue of our experience living among people. Informal knowledge of small groups is not deliberately applied to group situations the way formal rules are; instead, it operates "through perception itself, determining the way situations are apprehended" (Bereiter & Scardamalia, 1993, p. 52).

Although all of us possess most of the informal knowledge that we need to function effectively in our own social groups, this knowledge is "situated" (Lave & Wenger, 1991; Brown, Collins, & Duguid, 1989) in the specific context of our social groups. Leadership roles and formal educational settings frequently represent very different contexts from the social groups of one's childhood. Moreover, educational groups often consist of people of different cultures who hold different conceptions of group process, such as a learning group that is dysfunctional because of a clash of cultures, perhaps caused by sexist attitudes among some of the members. Group leaders who fail to detect the offensive language, because such behavior is normative in their culture, cannot address it. Discussion group leaders require informal knowledge about the normative behavior of groups in the culture in order to "read" their groups correctly.

Formal Knowledge or Textbook Knowledge

Formal knowledge is knowledge *about* teaching—for example, knowing the characteristics of well-functioning groups, or knowing about the characteristics of learners, leadership theory, or the stages of group development. This kind of knowledge is usually not learned informally in the course of participation but by reading, by attending lectures, and by other deliberate learning activities. The use of formal knowledge is illustrated by the case of a teacher who discovers that the introduction of a new member in her group has caused a disruption. This teacher would be better equipped to deal with the situation if she understood that normal group development includes phases of power struggle and inclusion-exclusion issues.

Self-Regulatory Strategies, Metaknowledge, or Metacognition

Bereiter and Scardamalia (1993, p. 60) describe self-regulatory knowledge as "knowledge that controls the application of other knowledge." They offer two examples of self-regulatory strategies—the baseball player who is able to remain calm during the World Series and the writer who uses a strategy of pouring everything out in a rough draft before editing. Self-regulatory strategies are vital to discussion leaders as well. The discussion leader who counts to ten and then attempts to clarify the situation whenever a group member challenges his or her authority is using a self-regulatory strategy. Parker Palmer (1998) writes about dealing with the "student from hell," the one student in a class who fails to respond to your efforts. Even one such student can have a terribly destructive impact on the teacher's attitude and class climate if the teacher is not in touch with her or his feelings about such students and has not developed methods of controlling trigger responses to such behavior. Self-regulatory strategies are essential for teachers who are dealing with group difficulties. When disruptive behaviors push our buttons, we may respond with trigger reflexes that are not always appropriate to the learning situation.

Diagnostic Strategies—Knowing When to Do What

Diagnostic strategies help teachers choose the right teaching strategy to use at the right time. They provide teachers with the necessary information to arrive at an accurate perception of the group. Teachers who are skilled at perceiving their groups use an array of interventions for gathering information. In addition, they often invest time in the creation of a safe psychological climate that fosters disclosure and openness, a climate that encourages frank and timely feedback. A misreading of the group that leads to an application of the wrong remedy may worsen the situation, even if the remedy were perfectly executed. To mistake an angry student for a shy one or a reflective group for a bored one can lead to remedies that worsen the dysfunction. Effective discussion leaders make accurate interpretations of group behavior.

Heuristic Strategies

Heuristic strategies consist of the so-called "tricks of the trade," or useful moves that under most conditions will help the group achieve its learning objectives. In addition to setting ground rules, other examples of useful strategies include clarifying the topic and keeping the group on track. Heuristics also consist of remedies for addressing the common presenting problems of the group. Examples of these include disruptive students, unclear objectives, and lack of interest. Effective teachers acquire the ability to carry out some of these useful functions, and they acquire a repertoire of strategies to handle frequently arising problems. Because heuristic skills are tied closely to language, the likelihood that teachers will actually use a strategy goes up sharply when they have specific phrases at their command. So the ability to use these strategies depends not only on an understanding of the strategy itself but also on possession of the verbal skills that enable one to execute the strategy.

Impressionistic Knowledge—Feelings and Impressions

This category includes the collection of intuitions, feelings, and impressions that predispose a teacher to react in one way rather than another in response to some event in the class or some interaction with a student. Such predispositions implicitly influence a teacher's understanding of students and ability to intervene. They are part of expert knowledge. Some predispositions may affect teacher perceptions and decisions in unproductive ways. For example, teachers who have difficulty yielding authority, who have a high need for drama, or who are not flexible enough to deal with changing structures are not best suited to leading discussions (Jacques, 1991).

Feelings and impressions are associated with knowledge and operate in the background. Feelings are important in educational groups, not only because they influence perceptions, actions, and the climate of the group but also because strong feelings tend to make events more memorable (Bereiter & Scardamalia, 1993). For our purposes, the most important function of impressionistic knowledge is that it provides the basis for intuition. "An attribute often ascribed to brilliant researchers, designers, and trouble-shooters, usually amounts to a strong impression that something is interesting, promising, or amiss" (Bereiter & Scardamalia, 1993, p. 58). Impressions and feelings are clearly vital qualities for discussion group leaders (Goleman, 1995).

These five categories provide a structure that can organize the practical wisdom about discussion group leaders, the so-called "functions" of the discussion group leader. In writing this chapter, when we assigned the practical functions to one or another of these five generic categories of competence (see Exhibit 5.2), we found that almost all of the functions turned out to be skills, especially the heuristic and diagnostic strategies. Knowledge is also mentioned in this early work, but there is not very much specific guidance about what the leader needs to know. There is even less discussion of the kind of emotional intelligence (Goleman, 1995) that falls under self-regulatory strategies and under impressionistic knowledge in our taxonomy. In the following section, we turn to recent theories of learning that can fill the gaps in the taxonomy.

Theories of Learning That Emphasize the Cognitive, Social, and Cultural Context

We will focus on theories that treat teaching and learning as an interactive process. These theories help us identify the kinds of specific competencies that are required of interactive teaching situations, such as leading discussions. In the last decade, there has been an explosion of interest in classroom interaction, driven by the growing acceptance of the concept of learning as an active process. We can now draw some guidance not only from evolving practice but also from these learning theories applied to classroom learning. In this section, we will review some of these learning theories and practices with an eye toward identifying specific teacher skills and motivations, framed in terms of human aptitudes and abilities.

Attribution Theory

Teachers who possess the appropriate skills and interest can use class discussion to enhance students' motivation to learn by helping them acquire positive attributional styles—what students perceive as the causes for academic achievement or failure. A healthy style, characterized by students who attribute their success to ability and effort, is self-reinforcing and reflects high self-esteem and a sense of efficacy (Weiner, 1986, 1992; Eccles et al., 1983). Such students are more effective at using their intellectual and emotional skills to tackle new tasks than are students who do not make the connection between achievement and their own efforts and talents (Borkowski & Thorpe, 1990; Carr, Borkowski, & Maxwell, 1991).

The dynamics of attribution for failure are more complicated. Students who attribute failure to lack of native ability are at risk for lowered self-esteem. In addition, they may become discouraged and withdraw effort because there is nothing they can do to change their native ability (Abramson, Garber, & Seligman, 1980). Attributing their failure to controllable causes such as effort is healthy in that it can help preserve students' self-esteem and optimism. Over the long run, however, attributing failure to effort may discourage students from seeking help or from realistically assessing their ability. Or it may drive them to lower their effort (the underachiever solution) in order to maintain self-worth (Weiner, 1992).

What can teachers do, within the context of the discussion group, to help students develop healthy attributional styles? And what competencies do teachers require for these roles? Teachers may be able to influence students' attributional styles by fostering appropriate peer influence among their students. In two studies, students attained higher grades after watching videos of upper-class students testifying to their academic improvement over the years (Wilson & Linville, 1982; VanOverwalle, Segebarth, & Goldschstein, 1989). The authors attributed the improvement in scores to an increase in the tendency of the students to attribute their failures to transient causes such as effort rather than stable ones such as their ability. These experiments suggest that students can encourage one another to give positive explanations for their academic success or failure. To foster frank exchanges between students, teachers require the traditional skills of facilitating small group interaction (see Exhibit 5.2, under Heuristic Strategies). For the purposes of encouraging frank interchange, a facilitation skill that would be particularly useful is the ability to forge a trusting relationship with students, what Tiberius and Billson (1991) have called the *teacher-learner alliance*. Within such a relationship, the student will feel safe enough to disclose perceived weaknesses, and the teacher will be able to reassure the student without becoming paternalistic or artificial. Salovey and Mayer (1990) have defined a domain of intelligence, called *handling relationships,* a further specification of Gardner's (1993) personal intelligences, which describes this ability very well (see Exhibit 5.2, under Heuristic Strategies).

Another way in which teachers may be able to influence college students' attributional styles is "through natural exchanges of conversation between faculty and students" (Stage, Muller, Kinzie, & Simmons, 1998, p. 18). Extrapolating from work involving younger students, Stage et al. argued that "as students struggle to interpret their academic performance, faculty can redirect students' disclaimers of ability for success and, likewise, their claims of low ability for failure" (p. 18). Pascarella, Edison, Hagedorn, Nora, & Terenzini (1996) noted that after less than one year, effective teaching practices actually increased students' internal attribution of success. To detect destructive attribution patterns and intervene positively, teachers require good perceptual skills and rapport with their classes (see Exhibit 5.2). Of course, a knowledge of attribution theory would also be helpful. It would enable teachers to be more conscious of attribution patterns in their classrooms (see Exhibit 5.2, under Formal knowledge).

A third way in which teachers may be able to influence college students' attributional styles is through teachers' feedback on student performance. Teachers who have a good relationship with students can build students' confidence by helping them realize that they have the intellectual capacity to cope with the material. The teacher also provides a model of these constructive interaction patterns for the group to emulate. Unfortunately, teachers can also prime the downward attributional self-esteem spiral by unjustified praise and sympathy for poor performance (Graham, 1990). Interpersonal perceptual skills and relational skills and talents are essential for the teacher who wishes to use feedback and modeling to influence attributional style.

One of the most powerful methods by which discussion group leaders can build the self-confidence and positive attributions within the group is to help students succeed at the learning task. Teachers can take advantage of the rich opportunities to individualize the material by connecting with the motivational orientations and learning styles of different members of the group, a strategy that is prohibitive in large groups. In a small group, not everyone has to interpret the material in the same way or learn by the same method. The discussion format can foster negotiation and individualization of learning. The teachers who are able to encourage individualization of the material in the group have a multifaceted understanding of their disciplines. This kind of flexible understanding of the subject matter cannot be assumed present in every teacher who has engaged in scholarship in a field or has lectured on the subject, as both scholarship and formal presentations can be narrowly focused. What we are suggesting is that the discussion leader has a special requirement to be able to understand the perspective of the subject that each student may hold so that the teacher can help the student make personal connections with the material (see Exhibit 5.2, under Formal knowledge).

Teachers can also create a positive atmosphere by assisting students "in identifying and practicing the use of discipline-specific strategies that are most likely to bring academic success" (Stage et al., 1998, p. 18). Another valuable teacher quality, therefore, is knowledge of discipline-specific learning strategies that may help learners who have specific misconceptions or difficulties mastering the subject matter (see Exhibit 5.2, under Formal knowledge).

These last two characteristics, a broad understanding of the various ways in which a student might view the subject and a repertoire of strategies for matching intervention, are often combined in expert teachers. Highly experienced teachers have developed packages of information consisting of examples, explanations, and questions designed to overcome specific student learning problems or to foster particular learning objectives. These packages or *scripts* (Putnam, 1987; Shulman, 1987; Irby, 1992) enhance efficiency because they provide teachers with the flexibility to teach interactively in response to students' questions (see Exhibit 5.2, under Diagnostic Strategies and Formal knowledge).

Self-Efficacy Theory

Another learning theory that should be helpful in identifying specific competencies for teachers of discussion is self-efficacy theory, because of its emphasis on interaction and social context. Self-efficacy is defined as the set of beliefs about one's capabilities to perform at a designated level (Bandura, 1994). Students' level of self-efficacy influences their behavior, emotions, thinking, and motivation to learn. High self-efficacy is correlated with academic and even social success in college (Pajares, 1996; Stage et al., 1998). A positive sense of self-efficacy may initiate a healthy spiral, beginning with an acceptance of academic challenges, moving to success at those tasks, and then to the development of a more positive sense of self-efficacy. Repeated failures can initiate a downward spiral.

In a review of the self-efficacy literature, Stage et al. (1998) define three ways in which faculty can foster learning environments that enhance self-efficacy: "(1) Construe ability as an acquirable skill, (2) de-emphasize competitive social comparisons and highlight self-comparison of progress and personal accomplishment, and (3) reinforce an individual student's ability to exercise some control over the learning environment" (p. 30). We are comfortable assuming that most teachers, because of the nature of their profession, will view ability as an acquirable skill; but we are not comfortable assuming that this belief guides their teaching style. Many college teachers have inherited practices from their own learning experiences that are unexamined with regard to the implications for their students' sense of self-efficacy. Teachers who have no appreciation of the implications of self-efficacy for their classroom may unwittingly engage in practices that increase destructive competition among students. The old schoolroom device of sending the weakest student to the blackboard to struggle in front of the class is only a step away from common contemporary college classroom practices that foster competition. We recommend that the discussion group leader have some understanding of the theory of self-efficacy and of its implications for practice (see Exhibit 5.2, under Formal knowledge).

Stage et al.'s (1998) second suggestion by which teachers could create learning environments that enhance self-efficacy is through de-emphasis of competitive social comparisons in favor of self-comparison. Fortunately, the tools for creating positive environments are available. Several new books mark the arrival of cooperative learning at the college level (Millis & Cottell, 1998; Bosworth & Hamilton, 1994). With dozens of techniques readily available for fostering group work, teachers can now construct cooperative arrangements that highlight self-comparison of progress and personal accomplishment and that therefore build self-efficacy. But teachers need more than an awareness of these techniques, as we have argued before. They need practice in the skills of arranging and conducting cooperative learning (see Exhibit 5.2, under Heuristic Strategies).

The third method that Stage et al. (1998) suggest for enhancing self-efficacy is the reinforcement of the individual student's ability to exercise some control over the learning environment. The development of this kind of skill, like the development of teaching scripts, depends on the acquisition of diagnostic skill. The skillful teacher assesses the individual student's level of ability and applies reinforcements that are specific (see Exhibit 5.2).

Constructivist Theory

Finally, constructivist learning theory is helpful in identifying specific competencies for teachers of discussion because of its emphasis on social context and interaction. According to the constructivists, learning is an active process in which each learner constructs his or her own understanding of reality by interpreting and transforming the environment (Lave & Wenger, 1991; Steffe & Gale, 1995). Further, knowledge is not viewed as a thing that can be transmitted to students. Students construct knowledge by making meaning out of their environment. The teacher's role is to facilitate learning by helping students make connections between the subject matter (its concepts, facts, and procedures) and both their previous experiences and the real context in which the knowledge will be used. *Social constructivism,* which extends the context of learning to the social and the cultural, is particularly relevant to discussion group teaching.

The roots of social constructivism can be traced to Vygotsky's (1978) theory of the social construction of understanding. Social constructivists emphasize the need for students to talk about the subject matter with one another, to compare ideas and perspectives, and to learn from one another cooperatively in the process of constructing meaning (Barr & Tagg, 1995; Meyers & Jones, 1993). The classroom climate that supports such interaction is characterized by dialogue rather than performance and control, by cooperative and reciprocal interaction, by mutual respect, by shared responsibility for learning, by effective communication, by a willingness to negotiate and to understand one another, and by a sense of security within the process (Tiberius & Billson, 1991).

The consequences of social constructivism for teachers are profound. Teachers require a number of skills and talents to be able to create what Tiberius and Billson (1991) call an *alliance* with their students. They need to be able to form trustful, open, and secure relationships that involve a minimum of control. They need to communicate in a reciprocal manner. They need to know how to form cooperative learning arrangements. And they need to make sufficiently accurate perceptions of others to diagnose the behavior of dysfunctional groups. In addition to several of the competencies already mentioned, two of Gardner's (1983) types of intelligence would be very helpful to teachers according to social constructivist theory—*interpersonal intelligence* and *intrapersonal intelligence* (Gardner, 1983). Interpersonal intelligence includes the abilities to understand other people—their emotions, motivations, desires, moods, temperaments—and the way that they operate in the world (Gardner, 1983; Salovey & Mayer, 1990). Intrapersonal intelligence includes the abilities required to form an accurate awareness of one's own feelings and to use that knowledge to act effectively in the world (Gardner, 1983; Salovey & Mayer, 1990) (see Exhibit 5.2, under Self-Regulatory Strategies).

For example, effective teachers share authority if they wish to create an atmosphere in which students feel free to speak (Jacques, 1991). Sharing authority depends on a teacher's sensitivity to students' reactions. The teachers who are able to detect when they are overwhelming or boring will have a great advantage in adjusting their interventions.

Another example is that effective teachers possess strategies for self-regulation and methods of cooling down or regaining control. These strategies prevent what Goleman (1995) calls the "emotional hijacking" of the cortex (see Exhibit 5.2, under Self-Regulatory Strategies). When a teacher's perception of threat triggers controlling behavior that stifles class discussion, the effective teacher is able to refrain from this behavior.

Requisite Personal Characteristics and Dispositions

The previous sections have dealt with the substantial complexity of the role of the discussion leader as part of the teaching team. It is necessary now to turn to the characteristics of the person who may be disposed to select this subrole and to find satisfaction and fulfillment in its performance.

The opportunity to develop a high level of skill in a particular form of teaching solves one of a teacher's most worrisome problems, the feeling of incompetence. The sense of mastery and institutional reward are powerful motivators, but teachers will not sustain a career interest in teaching if it is not personally satisfying. Teachers who are suited to discussion leading or small group teaching will enjoy achievement of mastery of these skills. Training will confirm their view and reinforce their talents. Exhibit 5.2 suggests the kind of competencies that would constitute a natural talent for discussion leading. High emotional intelligence (Goleman, 1995), particularly self-awareness and impulse control, empathy and social deftness, and the ability to understand the emotions of others, would be a good start. This means that faculty whose dispositions allow them to be sensitive to nuances of student emotions in class and to attend to them with skill will find the interactions in discussion groups both a challenge to their teaching and a source of satisfaction when they are successful.

The discussion leader, in our view, is also highly tolerant of ambiguity in situations. Thus, in the relatively unstructured setting of a discussion group, this teacher would not feel the need to intervene excessively or to overly control the direction of the dialogue. Indeed, another quality that would be compatible with discussion leadership is the ability to give away authority and control. Highly controlling people will have an uphill struggle to be effective discussion group leaders (see Jacques, 1991). The inclination to trust the group process, to allow the group to unfold in its own way without constraining it, is another important personal characteristic needed for discussion leaders. Faculty members who find satisfaction in the egalitarian atmosphere and the give-and-take of discussions among students who are struggling to understand the content of the session, as well as to discover personal identities in their developing lives, will take pleasure in seeing these students find for and by themselves the personal understandings and meanings with which they are comfortable. The discussion leader will enjoy playing the role of facilitator of such processes.

Finally, effective discussion leading requires a strong ego that can be exposed in settings where prevailing wisdom is challenged (indeed, where challenges to written authority—for example, in books, as well as in discussion leader knowledge and evaluation power—are encouraged). The effective discussion leader is, therefore, a willing learner, who takes pleasure in questioning his or her own acquired pieties and enjoys discovering new truths in conjunction with others—even when those others are inexperienced and naive. Surely, this is a difficult role to play—and one quite different from those expected of other members of the teaching team described in other chapters.

Conclusion

Our inquiry has identified a formidable set of competencies, including skills, talents, and motivations, that would help discussion leaders influence the learning outcomes and the learning habits of students. Our list surely does not exhaust the useful competencies of a discussion leader. However, our purpose is to develop a sufficiently detailed list to enable comparisons among the competencies required by discussion group leaders and those required by teachers of other formats. Our belief, reinforced by an examination of Exhibit 5.2, is that expertise in leading discussions is composed of a set of specific competencies. And although these competencies may equip teachers for other types of small group teaching in addition to discussion leading, they may not help teachers deliver dramatic and captivating lectures. Our inquiry has supported the view that leading small group discussion, and likely other forms of small group teaching, is a bona fide specialization.

Effective discussion group leadership requires the same high standard of expertise that characterizes other professional domains, such as medicine and engineering. We are assuming that teaching is neither less important nor less complex than medicine or engineering. The appropriate definition of "expertise" for the craft of teaching is the one described by Bereiter and Scardamalia (1993). Bereiter and Scardamalia's definition of expertise goes beyond the knowledgeable and smooth functioning achieved by those who have mastered a high level of ability in their activity. By their definition, experts are those who, after they have achieved the ability to perform intuitively and with little effort, continually reinvest the dividend of time and energy, which they have gained from intuitive and effortless performance, into reflection toward ever more subtle and challenging teaching problems. According to this definition, the list of competencies outlined in Exhibit 5.2 is not a minimal set of requirements but a set of goals for the expert who continually strives to achieve them.

The best news about individual specialization—in this case in the domain of leading discussions—is that it provides an opportunity for certain faculty members to select a narrower range of tasks that are especially well matched to their native talents and interests and precludes their required attention to tasks for which they have little native prowess and little interest. Teachers who are particularly suited to leading discussions or small group teaching will enjoy achievement of mastery in these skills. Employment of those skills will reinforce their talents and confirm their commitment.

Needless to say, there are many impediments to the implementation of the newly conceived team approach to teaching described in this book. These are addressed by the discussion in Chapters Nine and Ten by James Bess. Despite the barriers, we think that team collaboration will become a serious alternative to individual instruction in the future. The vast majority of college and university teachers, including the authors of this chapter, must share their teaching time with research, service, and both institutional and community obligations. The usual remedy that the modern world gives to the problem of explosive growth of knowledge is specialization. Each of us can sustain only a limited number of areas in our lives in which we function as experts (Bereiter & Scardamalia, 1993). Each of us has a limited supply of time and energy. As Bereiter and Scardamalia point out, we do not adopt an expert approach to taking out the garbage or brushing our teeth. On reflection, if we aspire to a high level of teaching competence, limited faculty time turns out to be an argument in favor of specialization and team teaching.

The growth of individual specialization and cooperative team teaching is difficult to predict. What is certain, in our view, is that there is going to be increasing pressure for cooperative teaching structures that benefit from the advantages of specialization. The pressure comes from our exploding knowledge, as it does in every other sphere of human life. As educational research continues to deliver useful techniques, the pressure on faculty to learn them will grow. Our modern world is becoming a learning society because it is changing so quickly that all workers must continually learn to keep up with innovations in their fields. The experts who work in high technology or medicine are respected by modern society because they are assumed to have acquired the latest advances from science. Our admittedly optimistic view of educational research is that it will identify knowledge, skills, and personal characteristics that will enable teachers to help learners with an immensely increased power in the future. These advances in education will have implications for the way teaching is organized. Teachers, like everyone else, will have to specialize in order to acquire and maintain expertise, and they will have to collaborate with other teachers in order to specialize. Our prediction is that faculty members will find team teaching more fulfilling and enjoyable than their current modes of performing the teaching role.

References

Abercrombie, M.L.J. (1971). *Aims and techniques of group teaching* (4th ed.). Guildford, Surrey, United Kingdom: Society for Research into Higher Education, University of Surrey.

Abramson, L., Garber, J., & Seligman, M. (1980). Learned helplessness in humans: An attributional analysis. In J. Garber & M.E.P. Seligman (Eds.), *Human helplessness: Theory and applications*. Orlando: Academic Press.

Argyris, C., Putnam, R., & Smith, M. C. (1985). *Action science: Concepts, methods, and skills for research and intervention*. San Francisco: Jossey-Bass.

Bandura, A. (1994). Self-efficacy. In V. S. Ramachaudran (Ed.), *Encyclopedia of Human Behavior* (Vol. 4). Orlando: Academic Press.

Barr, R. B., & Tagg, J. (1995). From teaching to learning: A new paradigm for undergraduate education. *Change, 27*(6), 13–25.

Bereiter, C., & Scardamalia, M. (1993). *Surpassing ourselves: An inquiry into the nature and implications of expertise.* Chicago: Open Court.

Bligh, D. A. (1971). *What's the use of lectures?* (3rd ed.) Harmondsworth, England: Penguin.

Bonwell, C. C., & Eison, J. A. (1991). *Active learning: Creating excitement in the classroom.* ASHE-ERIC Higher Education Report No. 1. Washington, DC: School of Education and Human Development, George Washington University.

Borkowski, J. G., & Thorpe, P. K. (1990). Self-regulation and motivation: A life-span perspective on underachievement. In D. H. Schunk & B. J. Zimmerman (Eds.), *Self-regulation of learning and Performance: Issues and educational applications.* Hillsdale, NJ: Erlbaum.

Bosworth, K., & Hamilton, S. J. (Eds.). (1994). *Collaborative learning: Underlying processes and effective techniques.* New Directions for Teaching and Learning, no. 59. San Francisco: Jossey-Bass.

Brown, J. S., Collins, A., & Duguid, P. (1989). Situated cognition and the culture of learning. *Educational Researcher, 18*(1), 32–42.

Carr, M., Borkowski, J., & Maxwell, S. (1991). Motivational components of underachievement. *Developmental Psychology, 27,* 108–118.

Collins, A., Brown, J. S., & Newman, S. E. (1989). Cognitive apprenticeship: Teaching the crafts of reading, writing, and mathematics. In L. Resnick (Ed.), *Knowing, learning and instruction: Essays in honor of Robert Glaser.* Hillsdale, NJ: Erlbaum.

Eccles, J. S., Adler, T., Futterman, R., Goff, S., Kaczala, C., Meece, J., & Midgley, C.(1983). Expectancies, values, and academic behavior. In J. Spence (Ed.), *Achievement and achievement motives.* New York: Freeman.

Gardner, H. (1983). *Frames of mind: The theory of multiple intelligences.* New York: Basic Books.

Gardner, H. (1993). *Multiple intelligences: The theory in practice.* New York: Basic Books.

Goleman, D. (1995). *Emotional intelligence: Why it can matter more than IQ.* New York: Bantam Books.

Graham, S. (1990). Communicating low ability in the classroom: Bad things good teachers sometimes do. In S. Graham & V. Folkes (Eds.), *Attribution theory: Applications to achievement, mental health, and interpersonal conflict.* Hillsdale, NJ: Erlbaum.

Irby, D. M. (1992). How attending physicians make instructional decisions when conducting teaching rounds. *Academic Medicine, 67*(10), 630–638.

Jacques, D. (1991). *Learning in Groups* (2nd ed.). London: Kogan Page.

Lave, J., & Wenger, E. (1991). *Situated learning: Legitimate peripheral participation.* New York: Cambridge University Press.

McGregor, D. (1967). *The professional manager.* New York: McGraw-Hill.

McKeachie, W. J., & Kulik, J. A. (1975). Effective college teaching. In F. N. Kerlinger (ed.), *Review of research in education.* Itasca, IL: Peacock.

McLeish, J., Matheson, W., & Park, J. (1973). *The psychology of the learning group.* London: Hutchinson University Library.

Meyers, C., & Jones, T. B. (1993). *Promoting active learning strategies for the college classroom.* San Francisco: Jossey-Bass.

Miles, M. B. (1973). *Learning to work in groups: A program guide for educational leaders.* New York: Teachers College, Columbia University.

Mill, C. R. (1980). *Activities for trainers: 50 useful designs.* San Diego: Pfeiffer.

Millis, B. J., & Cottell, P. G. (1998). *Cooperative learning for higher education faculty.* Phoenix: Oryx Press.

Pajares, F. (1996). Self-efficacy beliefs in academic settings. *Review of Educational Research, 66*(4), 543–578.

Palmer, P. J. (1998). *The courage to teach: Exploring the inner landscape of a teacher's life.* San Francisco: Jossey-Bass.

Pascarella, E. T., Edison, M., Hagedorn, L. S., Nora, A., & Terenzini, P. T. (1996). Influences on students' internal locus of attribution for academic success in the first year of college. *Research in Higher Education, 37,* 731–756.

Polyani, M. (1967). *The tacit dimension.* New York: Doubleday.

Putnam, R. T. (1987). Structuring and adjusting content for students: A study of live and simulated tutoring of addition. *American Educational Research Journal, 24,* 13–48.

Rudduck, J. (1978). *Learning through small group discussion: A study of seminar work in higher educaiton.* Guilford, Surrey: Society for Research into Higher Education, University of Surrey.

Salovey, P., & Mayer, J. D. (1990). Emotional intelligence. *Imagination, Cognition, and Personality, 9*(3), 185–211.

Schön, D. A. (1995). The new scholarship requires a new epistemology. *Change, 27*(6), 26–34.

Shulman, L. S. (1987). Knowledge and teaching: Foundations of the new reform. *Harvard Educational Review, 57*(1), 1–22.

Simpson, R. J., & Galbo, J. J. (1987). Interaction and learning: Theorizing on the art of teaching. *Interchange, 17*(4), 37–51.

Stage, F. K., Muller, P. A., Kinzie, J., & Simmons, A. (1998). Creating learning centered classrooms: What does learning theory have to say? ASHE-ERIC Higher Education Report No. 4. Washington, DC: School of Education and Human Development, George Washington University.

Steffe, L. P., & Gale, J. (Eds.). (1995). *Constructivism in education.* Hillsdale, NJ: Erlbaum.

Tiberius, R. G. (1990). *Small group teaching: A trouble-shooting guide.* Toronto: Ontario Institute for Studies in Education/University of Toronto Press.

Tiberius, R. G., & Billson, J. M. (1991). The social context of teaching and learning. In R. J. Menges & M. D. Svinicki (Eds.), *College teaching: From theory to practice.* New Directions for Teaching and Learning, no. 45, San Francisco: Jossey-Bass.

VanOverwalle, F., Segebarth, K., & Goldschstein, M. (1989). Improving performance of freshmen through attributional testimonies from fellow students. *British Journal of Educational Psychology, 59,* 57–85.

Vygotsky, L. S. (1978). *Mind in society: The development of higher educational processes.* (M. Cole, Ed.). Cambridge, MA: Harvard University Press.

Weiner, B. (1986). *An attributional theory of motivation and emotion.* New York: Springer-Verlag.

Weiner, B. (1992). Attributional theories of human motivation. In B. Weiner (Ed.), *Human motivation: Metaphors, theories, and research.* Thousand Oaks, CA: Sage.

Wilson, T., & Linville, P. (1982). Improving the academic performance of college freshmen with attributional techniques. *Journal of Personality and Social Psychology, 42,* 367–376.

Part Three

Facilitating Roles

Chapter Six

The Mentor
Facilitating Out-of-Class Cognitive and Affective Growth
Michael W. Galbraith, Patricia Maslin-Ostrowski

Mentoring is an old idea with relevance and meaning in today's world of higher education. The term *mentor* has a long and distinguished history. In Homer's *Odyssey,* Odysseus is preparing to begin an epic voyage. He entrusts his son Telemachus to his friend Mentor, who guides Telemachus in the passage from boyhood to manhood. Mentor, an Ithacan elder, often has his body taken over by Athena, the Greek goddess of war, wisdom, and craft. Therefore, when Mentor's body was taken over by Athena, he was given the goddess's most glorious qualities as he guides Odysseus's son. It was wisdom personified. Mentor's role in this story is instructive, "for he is a classic transitional figure, helping the youth achieve his manhood and confirm his identity in an adult world" (Daloz, 1986, p. 19). When we think about a mentor, it is synonymous with a wise teacher, guide, and friend. It is the mentor who often makes the difference between success and failure through a life journey.

Mentoring is assuming national importance as a vital component in the personal, educational, and professional experiences of higher education learners. Mentoring is cited as a significant element in understanding the growth and development of men and women (Bova, 1995; Daloz, 1986; Levinson, Darrow, Klein, Levinson, & McKee, 1978). It has also been a topic of discussion related to enrichment possibilities in the student personnel and development functions in higher education (Gaskill, 1993; Jacobi, 1991).

Mentoring has found its place in higher education settings as a means of improving the instructional process, student and faculty relations, professional enhancement, and faculty development (Bova, 1995; Cohen, 1995a; Evanoski-Orsatti, 1988; Galbraith & Cohen, 1995, 1997; Galbraith & Zelenak, 1991; St. Clair, 1994; Wunsch, 1994).

To a large extent, the personal, educational, and professional significance of mentoring will depend on the ability of the mentor to develop and maintain a relevant interpersonal relationship with the mentee (Cohen, 1995a). Although most higher education institutions expect faculty to mentor students, the mentor role does not fit the individual talents and interests of all professors. Students might be better served if the mentoring role were identified as one of several on a teaching team of faculty, with each role played by individuals with the requisite attributes and personality.

Mentoring should not be confused with advising. Mentoring exceeds the role of advising. Whereas advising is typically a short-term process with a focus on giving information and guidance to the learner, mentoring is a more intricate long-term one-on-one relationship that goes well beyond providing information. Ideally, mentoring relationships foster in learners the ability to identify and test assumptions about themselves and the world around them. A natural complement to the goals of teaching, true mentoring is a complex process between professor and college learner that supports a mutual enhancement of critically reflective and independent thinking. Mentors help facilitate the cognitive and affective growth of students.

In this chapter, we first examine the connections between mentoring and instruction in the higher education environment. Next, we explore various definitions and themes of mentoring, present a profile of the complete mentor, and discuss the associated six interrelated functions. We next suggest some desired attributes of the "good" mentor and mentee. Finally, roles and phases of mentorship are examined. As this chapter will show, the mentor role may not be as simple as it seems at first glance and is best reserved for faculty with the appropriate temperament and skills. Consistent with the premise of this book, if university and college departments use a team model to organize professors, it is essential that each team include members who specialize in mentoring students.

Connecting Mentoring and Instruction

The primary goals of mentoring are directed toward enhancing personal and professional growth through the development of the learner's self-concept and self-efficacy efforts. Where does mentoring fall in relation to undergraduate and graduate teaching perspectives? Pratt and Associates (1998) provide a detailed analysis of five teaching perspectives—*transmission, apprenticeship, developmental, nurturing,* and *social reform*—through an examination of indicators of commitment, which include actions, intentions, and beliefs. It is their contention that once these indicators are examined, a specific perspective on teaching emerges. They make it clear that a teaching perspective is not the same as a teaching style. Rather, a teaching perspective gives direction to the teaching style or process. It is in the nurturing perspective that we find mentoring most closely linked and assimilated.

Both mentors and teachers with a nurturing perspective believe that learning is most affected by a student's self-concept and self-efficacy. As Pratt (1998a) suggests, "Learners must be confident that they can learn the material and that learning the material will be useful and relevant to their lives" (p. 49). He goes on to say, "A nurturing relationship is neither permissive nor possessive. . . . it is professional and demanding, characterized by a high degree of reciprocal trust and respect, and always seeks a balance between caring and challenging" (p. 49). As in mentoring, the goal of one who subscribes to the nurturing perspective is to help people become more confident, critically reflective, and self-sufficient learners. The mentoring and nurturing perspectives share the guiding principle "that mastery of content is considered secondary to the way in which mastery is achieved" (T'Kenye, 1998, p. 161). The major role from these two perspectives is to facilitate healthy interpersonal development in conjunction with learning encounters.

Nurturing instructors and mentors have much in common. In fact, professors who have the nurturing perspective may be good candidates for the position of faculty team mentor. T'Kenye (1998) points out that "many qualities associated with nurturing education are traditionally thought of as 'feminine': empathy, sensitivity to others' emotional needs, practice of 'intuitive' understanding of others' emotional states, and an ability to offer support during emotional crisis and so forth" (p. 163). Although we would argue with T'Kenye's traditional and narrow interpretation of feminine, these same qualities (feminine and masculine) are found in the mentoring role. What Pratt (1998b) suggests about the primary responsibilities of the nurturing educator also holds true for the mentor role, such as fostering a climate of trust and respect, engaging empathetically with individual needs, promoting and enhancing learners' self-esteem, guiding students through content to build confidence, promoting success in learning, providing encouragement and support, encouraging expressions of feelings, reinforcing effort as well as achievement, focusing evaluation on individual growth or progress, and challenging learners while also caring about them. This description closely mirrors the behavioral functions of the complete mentor that will be described later in the chapter. Nurturing is concerned with the emotional wholeness of the learner, and mentoring finds that to be primary as well. Mentoring and the nurturing perspective are concerned about *power with* not *power over* in the teaching and learning process. Pratt (1998b) states that although this "may not be easy, it also means never doing for learners what they can do for themselves" (p. 246). The challenge is to find a balance between caring and challenging and believing in learners, and then helping them achieve what they must achieve.

Definitions and Themes of Mentoring

The literature offers numerous definitions of mentoring, yet a single, widely accepted operational definition is absent. Jacobi (1991, p. 505) suggests that this "definitional vagueness is a continued lack of clarity about the antecedents, outcomes, characteristics, and mediators of mentoring relationships despite a growing body of empirical research."

Definitions of Mentoring

Mentoring is a process of intellectual, psychological, and affective development based on meetings of relative frequency scheduled over a reasonably extended time frame. Meetings can take place face-to-face and electronically. Mentors accept personal responsibility as competent and trustworthy nonparental figures for the significant growth of other individuals. Galbraith and Zelenak (1991, p. 126) suggest that mentoring is "a powerful emotional and passionate interaction whereby the mentor and protégé experience personal, professional, and intellectual growth and development." They contend that mentoring is a unique one-to-one teaching and learning method that incorporates the basic elements of collaboration, challenge, critical reflection, and praxis.

In the field of higher education, other definitions are presented. For example, Blackwell (1989, p. 9) writes, "Mentoring . . . is a process by which persons of superior rank, special achievements, and prestige instruct, counsel, guide, and facilitate the intellectual and/or career development of persons identified as protégé." Lester and Johnson (1981) further define mentoring as "a one-to-one learning relationship between an older and a younger person that is based on modeling behavior and extended dialogue between them" (p. 119). According to Moore and Amey (1988), mentoring is a form of professional socialization with the intent of the relationship to develop and refine the protégé's skills, abilities, and understanding. Another way of thinking about mentoring is "not in terms of formal roles, but in terms of the character of the relationship, and the functions it serves" (Levinson et al., 1978, p. 98). Finally, Daloz (1986) points out that mentoring has to "do with growing up, with the development of identity" (p. 19).

The ideal mentoring relationship can be characterized as a series of mentor-mentee dialogues noted for collaborative critical thinking and planning, mutual participation in specific goal setting and decision making, shared evaluation regarding the results of actions, and joint reflection on the worth of areas identified for progress. The premise of mentoring as one-to-one developmental learning is that an important professor-student relationship will be formed that enables mentees to take appropriate risks, deal better with stress and uncertainty, develop more self-confidence, make more informed decisions, and thus allow for more likely attainment of current and future personal, educational, and professional objectives.

Mentoring as a concept is a "philosophical vision as well as a pragmatic approach" (Cohen & Galbraith, 1995, p. 13) to guiding learner development. Mentors, as proactive role models in an evolving interpersonal transaction, directly attempt to assist their mentees in benefiting from the great variety of educational possibilities available. As realistic advocates for mentee development, mentors are accessible and consistent sources of positive influence who demonstrate a sincere effort to promote worthwhile, reasonable, and attainable change.

Themes of Mentoring

A cursory review of the above definitions suggests that there are similar themes imbedded in them. After reviewing the many different definitions of mentoring, Golian and Galbraith (1996) identified the following set of common themes, which suggest that mentoring:

- Is a process within a contextual setting
- Involves a relationship between a more knowledgeable and experienced individual (perhaps older) and a less experienced individual
- Provides professional networking, counseling, guiding, instructing, modeling, and sponsoring
- Is a developmental mechanism (personal, professional, and psychological)
- Is a social and reciprocal relationship
- Provides an identity transformation for both mentor and protégé [p.100]

They acknowledge that numerous definitions do not recognize the essence of a good mentoring relationship, such as the necessity of a reciprocal and developmental process for both the mentor and mentee. Mentoring is not about just giving advice on professional and career advancement and opportunities. It is about dialogue, caring, authenticity, emotion, passion, and identity. The complexity and demands of the role may help explain why all professors cannot commit to a mentoring relationship and add to the argument that this is a role best assumed by those who possess the desired mentor attributes.

The Complete Mentor

Although mentoring has been part of our culture for centuries, few scholars have designed valid and reliable instruments to measure mentor effectiveness. Cohen (1993, 1995a) has accomplished this by developing the Principles of the Adult Mentoring Scale, which is based on a composite profile of the complete mentor role. It is a self-assessment instrument designed primarily for use by professionals who have consciously assumed mentoring responsibilities in their relationships with learners.

The scale assesses the mentor functions and behaviors that experts in postsecondary education agree are most likely to be significant in relationships between mentors and mentees, such as faculty and students. Departments and faculty teams are encouraged to use this instrument for the selection of team mentors and to establish a foundation for mentoring training. The scale evaluates fifty-five specific mentor interpersonal behaviors relevant to establishing and maintaining an evolving mentoring relationship. The primary purpose of the scale scores is to "help mentors better locate themselves on the map of their mentoring relationship, so they can contribute as much as possible to the meaning of the journey for the mentee" (Cohen, 1995b, p. 23). As a baseline reference point, the scale offers faculty the opportunity to compare and contrast privately their current or probable mentoring style with the behavioral profile of an effective mentor.

The mentor role is based on a "synthesis of those mentoring behaviors in the adult and higher education literature that are considered essential for the development of meaningful mentor-mentee relationships" (Cohen, 1995b, p. 17). Mentoring is viewed as a blend of six interrelated behavioral functions, each with a distinct and central purpose. They are *relationship emphasis*—to establish trust, *information emphasis*—to offer specific advice, *facilitative focus*—to introduce alternatives, *confrontive focus*—to challenge, *mentor model*—to motivate, and *mentee vision*—to encourage initiative (Cohen, 1995a). An explanation of each of the six functions, which are collectively labeled the *complete mentor role,* are presented next, along with specific behaviors that the mentor would perform.

Relationship Emphasis

In this first function, the mentor conveys through active, empathetic listening a genuine understanding and acceptance of the mentee's feelings. The purpose is to create a psychological climate of trust that allows mentees (who perceive mentors as listening and not judging) honestly to share and reflect on their personal experiences (positive and negative) as adult learners in education or the workplace.

In the relationship emphasis, the mentor practices responsive listening (verbal and nonverbal reactions that signal sincere interest), asks open-ended questions related to expressed immediate concerns about actual situations, and provides descriptive feedback based on observations rather than inferences of motives. The mentor also uses perception checks to ensure understanding of feelings and offers nonjudgmental, sensitive responses to assist in clarifying emotional states and reactions.

As trust develops and students reveal more of themselves, mentors must remember to respect the confidentiality of the relationship. The team member cannot in good conscience reveal to other faculty private conversations with mentees. Mentors may, however, guide students to share information as appropriate with other members of the faculty team. Being a team member with a good pulse on student needs, the professor mentor may discuss with colleagues salient student issues without breaching confidentiality.

Information Emphasis

The mentor, when practicing this function, directly requests detailed information from and offers specific suggestions to mentees about current plans and progress in achieving personal, educational, and career goals. The purpose is to ensure that the advice offered is based on accurate and sufficient information of individual mentees' differences.

When emphasizing information, the mentor asks questions aimed at ensuring factual understanding of the student's present educational and career situation, reviews relevant background to develop an adequate personal profile, and asks probing questions that require concrete answers. In addition, the mentor poses directive-type questions about present problems and solutions that should be considered, makes restatements to ensure factual accuracy and interpretive understanding, and relies on facts as an integral component of the decision-making process.

Facilitative Focus

When practicing the facilitative focus of the role, the mentor guides mentees through a reasonably in-depth review of their interests, abilities, ideas, and beliefs relevant to academia. The purpose is to assist mentees in considering alternative views and options while reaching their own decisions about attainable personal, academic, or career goals.

As a facilitator, the mentor poses hypothetical questions to expand individual views, uncovers the underlying experiential and information basis for assumptions, and presents multiple viewpoints to generate a more in-depth analysis of decisions and actions. In addition, the mentor examines the seriousness of commitment to goals, analyzes reasons for current pursuits, and reviews recreational and vocational preferences.

Confrontive Focus

In this function, the mentor respectfully challenges mentees' explanations for or avoidance of decisions and actions relevant to their development as learners in the educational setting. The purpose is to help mentees attain insight into unproductive strategies and behaviors and to evaluate their need and capacity to change.

From the confrontive perspective, the mentor uses careful probing to assess psychological readiness of the student to benefit from different points of view and openly acknowledges concerns about possible negative consequences of constructive and critical feedback on the relationship. The mentor also employs a confrontive verbal stance aimed at the primary goal of promoting self-assessment of apparent discrepancies, focuses on the most likely strategies and behaviors for meaningful change, and sparingly provides feedback for impact. Finally, the mentor offers comments before and after confrontive remarks to reinforce belief in the potential for student growth beyond the current situation.

Mentor Model

The mentor shares with mentees appropriate life experiences and feelings as a role model in order to personalize and enrich the relationship. The purpose is to motivate students to take necessary risks, make decisions without certainty of successful results, and continue to overcome difficulties in their own journey toward educational and career goals.

The mentor draws on personal experiences as well as experiences with other mentees in order to share thoughts and genuine feelings that emphasize the value of learning from unsuccessful or difficult experiences (perhaps portrayed as trial and error leading to self-correction, not as growth-limiting failures). The mentor also provides a direct, realistic assessment of the mentee's ability to pursue goals; expresses a confident view of appropriate risk taking as necessary for personal, educational, training, and career development; and makes statements that clearly encourage mentees to take action to attain their stated goals.

Mentee Vision

In this final function, the mentor stimulates mentees' critical thinking with regard to envisioning their own future and developing their personal and professional potential. The purpose is to encourage students to function as independent adult learners, to take initiatives to manage change, and to negotiate constructive transitions through personal life events.

The mentor in this context makes statements that require the mentee to reflect on present and future educational, training, and career attainments. The mentor also asks questions aimed at clarifying positive and negative perceptions, reviews individual choices based on a reasonable assessment of options and resources, and expresses confidence in carefully thought-out decisions. In addition, the mentor discusses and shows respect for students' capacity to determine their own future and encourages them to develop their talents and pursue dreams.

The six mentoring functions, as detailed by Cohen (1995a), are summarized by Golian and Galbraith (1996) as:

- Building and establishing relationships
- Providing information and support
- Facilitating change
- Challenging and confronting ideas
- Modeling
- Visioning

The discussion of these six functions shows that the role of mentor goes well beyond that of giving information and advice. It is that and so much more.

Attributes of the Good Mentor and Mentee

Colleges and universities benefit from strong professor and student mentoring relationships in that they contribute to a supportive and open academic climate. It is unrealistic, however, to believe that all professors are capable of being effective mentors, and it is equally unreasonable for a university to expect each professor to assume the role of mentor. A better plan is to recruit faculty (from within the ranks or to look for the necessary attributes when hiring new faculty) who demonstrate the desired mentor profile to serve as the team's designated mentors. It is also true that not all students are effective mentees. Rather, there is a constellation of characteristics and dispositions that each partner in the mentoring relationship must have or cultivate for it to be successful, and these are described next.

Desired Mentor Attributes

The good mentor possesses respect for the mentee; strong communication skills; and a capacity to encourage, motivate, and develop others. In addition, the professor as mentor would respect differences in opinions and challenge ideas not people, plus have a genuine interest in helping others flourish in the college and university setting. Good mentors also demonstrate a wide range of professional skills and an awareness and access to resources, along with the willingness to share these with mentees. Beyond such attributes, the mentor must have the will to invest time and effort in developing an effective professor and learner relationship (Cohen, 1995a; Daresh & Playko, 1992; Galbraith & Cohen, 1995). This means that the good mentor must have a disposition toward nurturing and relationship building. Along these lines, one could say that the personality traits are consistent with those of the counselor, psychologist, and critically reflective educator. Clearly, not all professors possess the personality traits or psychological dispositions to be a mentor. It is naive to assume that because one can be a good professor, he or she can also be a good mentor. Of course, mentors need not be psychologists or counselors; however, it is advantageous if they are reflective educators.

Desired Mentee Attributes

In the mentoring partnership, it is essential that the mentee possess certain characteristics and dispositions for it to be successful. Effective characteristics and attributes include a desire and a willingness to work toward an academic goal, to learn new things, and to be open to different points of view. These seem to be reflective of what many entering graduate students already possess; however, this may not reflect the average freshman. This means that students at the undergraduate level will require special attention and support from mentors, especially during the freshman year, as they learn to be mature persons, which will simultaneously assist in the development of the disposition needed to engage in a mentoring relationship.

Given that students will not arrive at college, for the most part, with the maturity level needed to be good mentees, it is incumbent on the mentor to guide students as they grow and develop; for example, to provide support as they learn the attitudes, values, and skills of relating well to diverse groups of people. If the mentor professor recognizes that a mentee must be willing to accept help and seek advice from the professor, be cooperative, and carry out mutually determined obligations and activities, the mentor can assist the student in developing these characteristics. Finally, it is essential that the mentee receive encouragement to work hard and juggle several tasks at once (Daresh & Playko, 1992; Golian & Galbraith, 1996; Kram, 1985; Shea, 1994).

Roles and Phases of Mentorship

The literature describes the role of the mentor in various ways (Cohen, 1995a; Daloz, 1986, 1998; Galbraith & Cohen, 1995, 1996, 1997; Galbraith & Zelenak, 1991; Golian & Galbraith, 1996; Murray, 1991). Kram (1985) and Cohen (1995a) also suggest that the mentorship experience comprises several phases.

Roles of Mentorship

Within the mentorship process, a mentor often assumes multiple roles to bring about the enhancement of the mentee's professional, personal, and psychological development. At different times, the mentor may be a role model, advocate, sponsor, adviser, guide, developer of skills and intellect, listener, host, coach, challenger, visionary, balancer, friend, sharer, facilitator, and resource provider. Along with these roles comes a responsibility to consider the psychological dimensions of the relationship, for example, accepting, confirming, counseling, and protecting. The role that best describes the mentor may be decided as a result of how well the mentor understands the total mentorship process. Clearly, the mentor role does not suit all people, including professors.

Phases of Mentorship

There has been little investigation of mentoring phases or stages from a conceptual and theoretical perspective, except for the work of Kram (1985) and Cohen (1995a). Kram examined the phases of a mentor relationship from the perspective of psychological and organizational factors that influence career and psychological functions performed. She suggests that developmental relationships vary in length but generally proceed through four predictable, yet not entirely distinct, phases.

The *initiation phase* is the period in which the relationship is conceived and becomes important to both mentor and mentee. This phase may last for a time span of six months to one year. From the undergraduate perspective, this would occur during the freshman year. Given the apparently overwhelming challenge of college to most freshmen on entrance, one can imagine the mentor on the team finding himself or herself in great demand. Yet, all students, undergraduate and graduate level, learn best in a supportive environment, and having a designated mentor on the team will give students much easier access to faculty. The mentor team member would be willing, able, and desirous of this kind of interaction with students, instead of faculty whose academic preparation and research makes them offer "limited office hours."

The second phase, called the *cultivation phase,* lasts from two to five years. For the undergraduate, this then might take place during the sophomore and junior years, or even longer. During this phase, the positive expectations that emerged during the initiation phase are continually tested against reality. The mentor and mentee discover the real value of relating to each other and clarify the boundaries of their relationship.

Phase three, *separation,* is marked by significant changes in the relationship and might happen during or soon after a student's senior year. It is a time when the mentee experiences new independence and autonomy, as well as turmoil, anxiety, and feelings of loss. The separation phase lasts from six months to two years. Mentors on teams that are teaching college seniors or students at the end of their graduate course work will represent a new resource to students feeling the anxiety of departure from the comfort of their college or university years and seeing the uncertainty of their postgraduate experience.

The final phase is *redefinition.* In this phase, the relationship takes on significantly different characteristics and becomes either a more peerlike friendship or one that is characterized by hostility and resentment. In general, during the redefinition phase, both the mentor and mentee recognize that a shift in developmental tasks has occurred and that the previous mentorship process is no longer needed or desired.

Getting out of sync with the developmental phases of the mentoring relationship could result in a less-than-positive experience for both mentor and mentee. Although everyone will not experience the phases at the same rate, it is essential that they go through all of them, and in sequence.

If one accepts the stage theory of mentoring, it is obvious that the time commitment required precludes this being accomplished in a single semester. Mentoring is not a short-term relationship. It does not fit the higher education model of taking a series of courses with different professors if the expectation is for all faculty to mentor all students. One course in one semester does not provide sufficient time to move through the total process.

It is, however, reasonable to expect that if the mentor team members are given the responsibility for teaching entry-level required courses, then they may begin to establish a relationship with future mentees early in the students' academic careers. This would be accomplished, in part, through active listening and questioning that establishes a psychological climate of trust. This lays the foundation for a more engaging mentoring relationship. Without this kind of connection, the likelihood of a meaningful mentor-mentee experience is limited.

Although mentoring relationships evolve over an extended period of time, advising can be effective in the short-term because the emphasis is more on information than on relationship and nurturing. On the other hand, if the team members chosen to be mentors are given the companion assignment of department advisers, they would have a better chance of getting to know students both in and out of the classroom. This would allow them to cultivate relationships further and continue building a foundation of trust. Advising may be transformed into mentoring. An additional benefit to this team approach is that students would get some of their needs met through the department mentor—for example, advising, career planning, and even some counseling needs—rather than having to seek out help from strangers located across the campus community.

Concluding Thoughts

Good mentoring is a distinctive and powerful process that enhances intellectual, professional, and personal development through a special relationship characterized by highly emotional and often passionate interactions between the mentor and mentee. Although we can assume that all professors in higher education engage in some level of instructional activity, it cannot be concluded that all are actively involved in mentoring, nor should they be. The complete mentor role does not fit all individuals: some faculty are less inclined toward developing close relationships with students and with nurturing the students' development. Not all faculty are capable of or willing to take on this role and if required to do so would be inadequate or "incomplete" mentors. That is why the faculty team concept has the promise of improving the quality of education. If only faculty who are well matched to this role become the team mentors, students will be better served.

Even if all professors are not mentors, understanding the role of the complete mentor can be a template for the good instructor. The essence of mentoring is grounded in the concept of one-on-one teaching. If one is engaged in mentoring, one is engaged in teaching. Thus, in addition to having the responsibility of mentoring students, the team mentor could also be asked to share his or her expertise regarding the mentor role with colleagues. The functions of the effective mentor, which include building a relationship, providing information, being facilitative and challenging, serving as a role model, and co-constructing a vision, are not far removed from what good teachers do. If one also examines the role of a skillful instructor, it will become clear that there is high correlation between the two roles (Brookfield, 1990, 1995; Daloz, 1986). Regardless of the academic discipline or subject, the instructional process can be enhanced by understanding and incorporating aspects of the complete mentor role.

Instructors as mentors, according to Daloz (1998), provide a balance of support and challenge such that our learners feel safe to move. From ancient times to contemporary life, mentors have challenged students to have a vision that places their journey in a larger context and invokes purpose in their lives. Mentoring is a special role that should only be assigned to professors who embrace it. Mentors support their students, challenge their students, and help their students construct a vision to further their educational journey. Complete mentors work in a truly responsive and interactive way with learners, which allows for a profound affirmation of both teaching and learning in the higher education environment. The faculty team model would permit the mentor-mentee relationship to flourish.

References

Blackwell, J. E. (1989). Mentoring: An action strategy for increasing minority faculty. *Academe, 75,* 8–14.

Bova, B. (1995). Mentoring revisited: The Hispanic woman's perspective. *Mountain Plains Adult Education Association Journal of Adult Education, 23,* 8–19.

Brookfield, S. D. (1990). *The skillful teacher.* Jossey-Bass: San Francisco.

Brookfield, S. D. (1995). *Becoming a critically reflective teacher.* San Francisco: Jossey-Bass.

Cohen, N. H. (1993). *The development and validation of the principles of adult mentoring scale for faculty mentors in higher education.* Unpublished doctoral dissertation, Department of Curriculum, Instruction, and Technology Education, Temple University.

Cohen, N. H. (1995a). *Mentoring adult learners: A guide for educators and trainers.* Malabar, FL: Krieger.

Cohen, N. H. (1995b). The principles of adult mentoring scale. In M. W. Galbraith & N. H. Cohen (Eds.), *Mentoring: New strategies and challenges.* New Directions for Adult and Continuing Education, no. 66. San Francisco: Jossey-Bass.

Cohen, N. H., & Galbraith, M. W. (1995). Mentoring in the learning society. In M. W. Galbraith & N. H. Cohen (Eds.), *Mentoring: New strategies and challenges.* New Directions for Adult and Continuing Education, no. 66. San Francisco: Jossey-Bass.

Daloz, L. A. (1986). *Effective teaching and mentoring.* San Francisco: Jossey-Bass.

Daloz, L. A. (1998). Mentorship. In M. W. Galbraith (Ed.), *Adult learning methods* (2nd ed.). Malabar, FL: Krieger.

Daresh, J. C., & Playko, M. A. (1992, April). A method for matching leadership mentors and protégés. Paper presented at the annual meeting of the Association for Supervision and Curriculum Development, New Orleans.

Evanoski-Orsatti, P. (1988). The role of mentoring in higher education. *Community College Review, 8*(2), 22–27.

Galbraith, M. W., & Cohen, N. H. (Eds.). (1995). *Mentoring: New strategies and challenges.* New Directions for Adult and Continuing Education, no. 66. San Francisco: Jossey-Bass.

Galbraith, M. W., & Cohen, N. H. (1996). The complete mentor role: Understanding the six behavioral functions. *Mountain Plains Adult Education Association Journal of Adult Education, 24*(2), 2–11.

Galbraith, M. W., & Cohen, N. H. (1997). Principles of the adult mentoring scale: Design and implications. *Michigan Community College Journal, 3*(1), 29–50.

Galbraith, M. W., & Zelenak, B. S. (1991). Adult learning methods and techniques. In M. W. Galbraith (Ed.), *Facilitating adult learning.* Malabar, FL: Krieger.

Gaskill, L. R. (1993). A conceptual framework for the development, implementation, and evaluation of formal mentoring programs. *Journal of Career Development, 20,* 147–160.

Golian, L. M., & Galbraith, M. W. (1996). Effective mentoring programs for professional library development. In D. Williams & E. Garten

(Eds.), *Advances in library administration and organization.* Greenwich, CT: JAI Press.

Jacobi, M. (1991). Mentoring and undergraduate academic success: A literature review. *Review of Educational Research, 61*(4), 505–532.

Kram, K. E. (1985). *Mentoring at work: Developmental relationships in organizational life.* Glenview, IL: Scott, Foresman.

Lester, V., & Johnson, C. (1981). The learning dialogue: Mentoring. In J. Fried (Ed.), *Education for student development.* New Directions for Student Services, no. 15. San Francisco: Jossey-Bass.

Levinson, D., Darrow, C., Klein, E., Levinson, M., & McKee, B. (1978). *The seasons of a man's life.* New York: Ballantine.

Moore, K. M., & Amey, M. J. (1988). Some faculty leaders are born women. In M.A.D. Sagaria (Ed.), *Empowering women: Leadership development strategies on campus.* New Directions for Student Services, no. 44. San Francisco: Jossey-Bass.

Murray, M. (1991). *Beyond the myths and magic of mentoring.* San Francisco: Jossey-Bass.

Pratt, D. D. (1998a). Alternative frames of understanding: Introduction to five perspectives. In D. D. Pratt & Associates (Eds.), *Five perspectives on teaching in adult and higher education.* Malabar, FL: Krieger.

Pratt, D. D. (1998b). Analytical tools: Epistemic, normative, and procedural beliefs. In D. D. Pratt & Associates, *Five perspectives on teaching in adult and higher education.* Malabar, FL: Krieger.

Pratt, D. D., & Associates. (1998). *Five perspectives on teaching in adult and higher education.* Malabar, FL: Krieger.

St. Clair, K. L. (1994). Faculty-to-faculty mentoring in the community college: An instructional component for faculty development. *Community College Review, 22,* 23–35.

Shea, G. F. (1994). *Mentoring: Helping employees reach their full potential.* New York: American Management Association.

T'Kenye, C. (1998). The nurturing perspective: Facilitating self-efficacy. In D. Pratt & Associates, *Five perspectives on teaching in adult and higher education.* Malabar, FL: Krieger.

Wunsch, M. A. (Ed.). (1994). *Mentoring revisited: Making an impact on individuals and institutions.* New Directions for Teaching and Learning, no. 57. San Francisco: Jossey-Bass.

Chapter Seven

The Integrator
Linking Curricular and Cocurricular Experiences
Thomas W. Grace

If higher education is to remain vital and congruent with the rapidly changing interests of our society, there is a need for a reassessment of the conventional model of faculty practice, a reconceptualization of the academic administrative structure that incorporates "a campuswide, collaborative effort around teaching" (Boyer, 1990, p. 80), and an academy that relates to the world beyond. The reader of this book is presented with just such an innovative, yet pragmatic, approach to the teaching-learning process. In this alternative model, departmental faculty members, each of whom assumes a designated functional role, are organized into a collaborative team that approaches both students and the process of learning from a holistic, integrated perspective.

A key member of this faculty team model is the curriculum-cocurriculum (C-C) integrator, an individual whose responsibility it is to build personal and administrative bridges between the faculty team and noncurricular entities, including both administrative units within the institution and nonuniversity agencies. First and foremost, it is the function of the integrator to facilitate opportunities for the faculty team to place students in meaningful, supervised learning experiences, such as internships or other positions, in these nonacademic offices and agencies. Second, by virtue of the relationships that the integrator has formed with these nonacademic administrators, he or she serves as a communication conduit through which information about how a student's cocurricular experiences may be affecting academic performance (or vice versa) and may exchange this information with administrators and the faculty team members. The integrator also acts as a problem-solving advocate to assist students, individually or in general, whose classroom work is being negatively affected by nonacademic situations. Finally, the integrator aids the other team members in identifying how the unique personal characteristics of a particular student may be influencing that student's classroom experience and then designing related strategies, curricular and otherwise, to optimize the student's learning process through the development of an out-of-class curriculum (Blake, 1979).

Unlike the other members, whose responsibilities are described by the other chapter authors, the function of the integrator is one that is not readily associated with the faculty role as it currently exists. Because the integrator is an entirely new position, one that is somewhat of a hybrid of a faculty member and a student affairs administrator, the rationale for its inclusion on the faculty team may not be as obvious as it is for the other team members. Furthermore, the integrator's functional responsibilities figuratively and literally epitomize the linkage between the curricular and cocurricular domains of the undergraduate student experience, two aspects of higher education that have been "at odds" for well over a century. In fact, it is the manner in which the faculty role has evolved in relation to this debate that makes the integrator position necessary. Thus, a discussion of the rationale for, the role of, and the personal characteristics that are needed to effectively perform the function of the integrator must begin with a consideration of the historical context.

The Segregated Academy

Throughout the history of higher education in America, there has been substantial disagreement as to whether the goals and priorities of the institution should extend beyond an emphasis on the student's cognitive domain—that is, academic and intellectual development—to include also a concern for the student's affective development—that is, intrapersonal and interpersonal growth. That students do experience some degree of affective (for example, social, moral, and psychological) change during college has never been the focal point of this debate (Chickering & Reisser, 1993; Astin, 1993). Rather, the disagreement has primarily centered on the extent to which the institution, and in particular members of the faculty, have a responsibility to be concerned about and involved with the nonacademic experiences of their students (Carpenter, 1996).

Since the colonial era, when practically every aspect of student activity was supervised, there has been almost a total disengagement by faculty from the cocurricular lives of students. This withdrawal process began gradually during the Enlightenment, or the utilitarian movement, of the latter part of the eighteenth century, and flourished as the faculty role shifted to a greater emphasis on scientific research and scholarship during the nineteenth century (Knock, 1985). To fill the void, a new administrative infrastructure was created and assigned the duties of managing the expanding institutional bureaucratic structure, student behavior, and extracurriculum. By the 1930s, the relationship between faculty and students was so dramatically altered that faculty members at most institutions had yielded virtually all responsibility for the burgeoning student activities, clubs and organizations, residence halls, and intercollegiate athletics (Rentz, 1996).

Today, most undergraduates exist within a dichotomous campus paradigm in which there are two distinct and unequal worlds. The preeminent curricular domain, in which formal learning and cognitive development take place, has come to be viewed as the exclusive purview and responsibility of faculty members. It has been left to administrative personnel, especially those in student affairs, to assume the authority for the subordinate cocurriculum, in which the "less important" personal and affective development is thought to be facilitated (Baxter Magolda, 1996).

The administrative infrastructure, especially at larger universities, has evolved into a complex and decentralized set of distinct and administratively segregated domains, which frequently seem to have conflicting or competing goals and priorities. An almost total bifurcation of the academic and nonacademic components has become characteristic of many institutions. The differences in training, vocabulary, orientation, power, and status that separate these two constituencies have led, in many instances, to defensiveness, a general sense of mistrust, poor communication, and even "turf wars" between faculty and student affairs administrators (Blake, 1979). "This sometimes dysfunctional relationship has become one of the greatest sources of dynamic tension on the campus today." (Garland & Grace, 1993, p. 59).

So too has a corresponding gulf emerged between faculty and students. With respect to scope, dynamics, and duration, most student-faculty relationships are carried out entirely within the context of the one or two courses in which the student is enrolled that are taught by that particular faculty member. In most cases, when the course is over, the relationship either diminishes or ceases altogether. The sort of personal bonding that "is needed to give any life or spirit to education never develops" (Douglas, 1992, p. 41). The limited context of the relationship between today's faculty members and their students does not afford faculty members the opportunity to learn a great deal about the unique characteristics or the cocurricular experiences of their students, so that they might apply that knowledge in integrated learning strategies. Experts have found "this conflict between scholarly productivity and other campus duties to be especially conspicuous at institutions that define themselves as emerging" (Boyer, 1987, p. 123).

In recent years, a growing body of scholars has begun to challenge the wisdom of this conceptual and organizational dichotomy, contending that such a perspective is a divisive, misleading, and unrealistic paradigm for understanding and optimizing student learning. An expanding body of research evidence indicates that many valued educational outcomes, including academic performance, retention, and overall level of education attained, are clearly associated with nonclassroom experiences both prior to and during college (Chickering & Reisser, 1993). Factors such as the nature of the students' living situation; involvement in campus activities; degree of social and academic integration; utilization of student support services; and interactions with faculty (in and out of the classroom), administrators, peers, and family members have each been shown to contribute significantly to academic and cognitive outcomes (Astin, 1993; Pascarella & Terenzini, 1991). Whereas classroom learning serves to enhance the student's conceptual knowledge and potentially leads to new insights and perspectives, cocurricular learning "is an intensification of the processes of learning by experience, encouraging personal development commensurate with intellectual sophistication. In contrast to the classroom's encouragement of individualized challenges to accepted ideas, the campus context fosters cooperative effort within the imposed structures of community living" (Blake, 1979, p. 283).

Unfortunately, despite this renewed awareness of the learning process as a function of the relationship between curricular and cocurricular experiences, blending theory and practice has proven to be elusive. Although there are notable exceptions, such as at Harvard, the University of Pennsylvania, the University of Michigan, and several other institutions, the potential of faculty with respect to assuming a leadership role in establishing collaborative learning initiatives is one that has largely gone unrealized at many colleges and universities. Clark Kerr, author and former president of the University of California, once stated that the ideal university was "as British as possible for the sake of the undergraduates, as German as possible for the graduate and research personnel, and as American as possible for the sake of the public at large" (1963, p. 36). Yet, many would contend that only a weak semblance remains of the legacy of the British residential college on which the American college was founded. Overcoming those gaps is essential if the faculty team is to be able to implement integrated learning strategies. By transcending the artificial and conceptual boundaries of the administrative fiefdoms and establishing formal partnerships and informal connections with other institutional and nonuniversity units and constituencies, the integrator is the one who serves as the catalyst in this process. There are several areas in which collaborative efforts between faculty and nonacademic administrators to link the curricular and cocurricular aspects of the students' lives could prove to be extremely beneficial.

Linking Curricular and Cocurricular Experiences

This section describes some of the key areas in which the integrator can be an effective link between the two important domains of student experience.

Individualized Learning Strategies

Transformative learning does not occur entirely within a singular isolated domain, such as a classroom. It is an integrated and evolving process that is a function of overlapping and mutually influential academic and nonacademic experiences that are inherently interconnected (Rhoads & Black, 1995). "[L]ife outside the classroom is an important venue that provides ample opportunity to synthesize and integrate material introduced in the formal academic program (classes, laboratories, studios), to test the value and worth of these ideas and skills, and to develop more sophisticated, thoughtful views on personal, academic, and other matters" (Kuh, Douglas, Lund, & Ramin-Gyurnek, 1994). For example, the student who is studying about race relations in a class undoubtedly will bring to that class prior and concurrent relevant life experiences, knowledge, attitudes, and beliefs. The student is constantly filtering and interpreting what is heard in the class through this personal and ever evolving cognitive structure, making decisions about the "value" and "validity" of the material. In turn, the student is using classroom experiences to interpret and understand the meaning of subsequent nonclassroom experiences.

The implementation of cooperative learning strategies must be preceded by an assessment of each student's background, interests, motivation, learning style, and intent to use the information offered in a particular class. The integrator assists the faculty team assessment specialist in identifying those psychosocial characteristics and nonclassroom experiences that affect the student's learning process and in personalizing learning strategies and designing class sessions for optimal impact (Donald, 1997; Anaya, 1996).

What is happening on the national, regional, or local level may directly or indirectly have an impact on the lives of students in ways that we do not always anticipate or readily observe. As all faculty team members must do, the integrator must be familiar with social, political, economic, and technological trends and events that may prove to be sources of stimulation, or conversely stress or dysfunction, on any institutional constituency and must share that information with colleagues, so that this information may be incorporated, as appropriate, into individualized classroom activities (Michman, 1983).

Career Development

The significance of the relationship between curricular and cocurricular experiences is particularly evident in relation to the career development of students. According to an annual national survey of college freshmen that is conducted by the University of California at Los Angeles Higher Education Research Institute, the percentage of respondents who have reported "to be able to get a better job" as their primary reason for attending college has grown to over 70 percent during the past few years. Over 47 percent of the respondents on one such survey indicated that they had selected their specific college based on their belief that it was an institution whose graduates get good jobs (*Chronicle of Higher Education,* Aug. 28, 1998).

Given this career emphasis, connecting the classroom and major to career choice may be a natural priority for the faculty team. The placement of students in meaningful internships and practicums allows them to become physically and psychologically invested in activities that are related to, or concerned with, the nature of the material being covered in a course or in a set of courses associated with a major and ultimately a career (Baxter Magolda, 1992). These experiences can provide students with valuable insight into areas of potential vocational interest, allow them to test those career options, help them clarify related priorities, and serve to instill in them a sense of community responsibility and citizenship (Simpson & Frost, 1993). In doing so, however, we must be careful not to instill so great a sense of vocationalism in our students that they value only material or experiences that have an apparent connection to their career interests and disregard other classroom or nonclassroom activities.

To facilitate the career development of students through practical experiences, the integrator has the responsibility for establishing an array of diverse and meaningful placement opportunities, so that students might be placed in positions congruent with their learning interests and needs. The integrator also orients students, trains the on-site supervisors, and in conjunction with other team members coordinates the process of matching each student to a site. A successful internship program requires cooperative relationships among the faculty, the agency or office at which the student is placed, and the institutional office (for example, student employment or community service) that is dedicated to securing and placing students in part-time positions. The site supervisor must know that there is someone at the college or university, such as the integrator, with whom to discuss problems or issues concerning a student's progress. Conversely, the student relies on the integrator for support and guidance in resolving difficulties or making decisions associated with the placement. Finally, the integrator advises other faculty team members, such as the pedagogy specialist, on the progress and activities of each student intern and that information is, in turn, formally integrated into the planned classroom learning experiences (Duley, 1981).

The faculty may enhance the value of the practical experience through guided discussions, mentoring, the review of student journals, and other writing assignments that encourage students to apply or consider knowledge obtained in class in the context of their practical out-of-class experience. The use of such strategies requires creativity, organization, collaborative supervision, and active sharing among faculty team members (Ender & Carranza, 1991; Duley, 1981). The integrator facilitates this process by assisting the other faculty team members in developing a seminar that provides students with the opportunity to relate their classroom and practical experiences, to jointly fashion the meaning of what they have encountered through *relational knowing* (Baxter Magolda, 1992).

Facilitating Academic Performance and Retention

It has been postulated that student retention is a function of both social and academic integration, the extent to which a student feels psychologically connected and actively engaged with each of those components of the educational experience (Tinto, 1987). Neither integration nor attrition is a singular event. It is, instead, "a progressive series of engagements, failures to engage, or disengagements with a multitude of academic and social elements on campus" within both the cocurricular and curricular domains (Garland & Grace, 1993, p. 75). Students who engage in informal interactions with faculty and who are involved in integrative initiatives such as residential academic college programs, discipline-based organizations and activities, and internship experiences are much more likely to establish a connection and sense of commitment on both the institutional and departmental levels (Pascarella & Terenzini, 1991). Enhancing a student's sense of assimilation within an academic unit is an especially important microgoal at large universities, where the student's perceptions of the psychological size of such an institution can make it seem overwhelming and can inhibit connection at the macro or institutional level (Chickering, 1969).

Our efforts to understand better how our students' cocurricular experiences may have an impact on their academic achievement and retention, and vice versa, are further complicated by the increasing complexity of the college population (Ramirez, 1993). As colleges and universities have reached out to new populations, many faculty members find that they now encounter a much more heterogeneous group of students than in years past, accentuating the relationship gap between faculty and students. There is far greater diversity among today's students in terms of age, race, socioeconomic status, culture, social experiences, academic preparedness, relationships with faculty, commitment, goals for learning, and attitudes toward the educational process and the institution than was the case among students of even a generation ago (Simpson & Frost, 1993). These new students bring a vastly different set of cocurricular experiences and personal characteristics to the campus and in particular a varied set of expectations that strongly influence their academic endeavors.

Such disparities extend beyond the obvious differences in gender, race, or age. For example, one particularly relevant difference seems to be in the manner and style in which today's college students learn as compared with the learning and teaching style preferred by most college faculty members. Many present faculty members, as products of their own college experience, tend to use more global, abstract, and conceptual strategies and perspectives in their teaching approaches. As current college students overwhelmingly seem to learn best through concrete and experiential approaches, there is potential for a teaching-learning gap. Students tend to prefer practical examples and have a need to understand the application of the material to their world and goals: essentially, students learn more effectively when they can associate and understand connections between what is happening in the classroom and what is happening in their lives (Schroeder, 1993).

Even the very notion of the "college experience" has been transformed by the advent of distance learning initiatives, leading to the phenomenon of the *virtual classroom*. Some faculty members no longer teach in actual rooms but rather through technological features, including on-line or televised sessions, Web sites, e-mail, and teleconferences. There is an entirely new student subpopulation in higher education whose college experience is manifested primarily through on-line course work sessions, message boards, and Web site visits. Obviously, developing relationships with students who are rarely, if at all, actually physically on campus presents significant challenges to faculty members and administrators. The impact of technology is prompting a reexamination of the very essence of the traditional student-faculty relationship (Hall, 1991).

For those seeking to better understand college students, their development, the impact of the college environment on them and their impact on the environment, or the teaching and learning process, the institution is the laboratory. Although student affairs administrators often do not possess the research expertise of the faculty team, it is not unusual in this time of diminished funds and compartmentalization for these nonacademic administrators to enjoy far greater access to student populations and more extensive technical and monetary resources than their faculty counterparts. It is the integrator who, through his or her network of campus relationships and in conjunction with the faculty team researcher, is able to arrange the sort of cooperative projects that benefit both the faculty team and the sponsoring nonacademic office. Thus, the administrators benefit from the faculty team researcher's expertise in gathering important information, and the faculty team gains access to the students and staff and fiscal support.

The reluctance of many faculty to become involved in cocurricular matters, in conjunction with the failure of nonacademic administrators to solicit faculty input, has led to inefficiency, redundancy, inconsistent policies and procedures, and ineffectiveness in responding to campuswide conditions that affect student learning. It is desirable for all faculty members to extend themselves to administrators, demonstrate an interest in serving on campuswide committees, and become stakeholders in resolving institutional stumbling blocks. But it is the integrator who serves as the point person in this process by personally serving on task forces and— through knowledge of the institutional committee structure and relationships with key administrators—encouraging the appointment of other faculty team members to critical university-wide committees. Examples of issues that require this sort of collaborative attention include the development of mission statements, admission criteria and practices, protocol for transfer between departments and colleges and other academic units at the institution, retention and attrition initiatives, efforts to promote diversity and multiculturalism, new student orientation, student conduct policies and procedures, leave-of-absence policies, and the incorporation of technology into curricular and cocurricular activities (Gardiner, 1994).

Advocacy and Problem Resolution

The virtues of out-of-classroom experiences as serving to complement classroom endeavors notwithstanding, such involvement is not entirely without a downside. The relationship between involvement in out-of-class activities, learning, and personal growth is probably "curvilinear rather than linear" (Whitla, 1981, p. 14). Students who devote the majority of their time to out-of-class activities, or are not involved at all, benefit less than students who are involved at moderate levels (Whitla, 1981). Most of those who have attended college can recall classmates who became so caught up in the social life of the institution that they forsook academic responsibilities, and their academic performance suffered to the extent that they were forced to leave the institution. Certainly, overinvolvement in one area of one's life seems to result in underinvolvement in other areas. Although moderate involvement in educationally purposeful activities contributes to learning, excessive participation can lead to deterioration in academic accomplishment.

Other cocurricular experiences may have a devastating impact on the curricular accomplishments of students. "Attending college is a major life transition for late adolescents or young adults that includes a number of potentially stressful events such as relocation, separation from family members, and development of new peer relationships" (Damush, Hays, & DiMatteo, 1997, p. 181). Related intrapersonal and interpersonal crises, albeit an inherent part of the developmental process, can prove to be detrimental to a college student's academic well-being. In some instances, a problem can be so debilitating that it results in academic paralysis (Grayson, 1989).

Perhaps one of the most critical causes of academic decline is the use of alcohol and illegal drugs by students. A study conducted by the Harvard School of Public Health indicated that such behavior is on the rise on campuses across the nation. Over 19 percent of students reported engaging in some form of binge drinking on a regular basis (Wechsler, 1996). Similar patterns with respect to the use of illegal drugs greatly concern faculty and administrators, for the abuse of alcohol and drugs is clearly associated with deteriorating academic performance and inappropriate social behavior. Compounding the problem is the fact that the user of the substance is not the only person whose personal or academic life may be compromised or disrupted. Over 60 percent of the respondents in the Harvard study indicated that they had been negatively affected by behavior of another student who was using alcohol or drugs.

Faculty team members who are attempting to assist a particular student with any of the aforementioned problems may discover that the sharing of information, on a case-by-case basis and with the permission and participation of the student and the implementation of holistic interventions with other faculty or administrators who have contact with that student or who are the campus officials-experts on related matters, is an effective way of aiding that student (Caplan, Caplan, & Erchul, 1994). It is the integrator who is primarily responsible for facilitating the formal (and perhaps even more important, the informal) communication between faculty and campus administrators that is needed to facilitate awareness and intervention in relation to any critical issues that may be affecting students, individually or in general.

In some instances, the integrator serves as a passive mediator by contacting the appropriate college or university office or administrator and arranging for the student to obtain needed services and information (Crego, 1996). In other cases, relying on familiarity with campuswide cocurricular events, activities, or administrative deadlines that may be affecting a great many students, the integrator can make other faculty team members aware of those events. For example, it may be important for faculty members to know the date that financial aid awards are issued or the period during which students must designate roommates for the following year. Nonacademic administrators have long known that these times are particularly stressful, and frequently nonproductive, periods in the lives of many students.

The act of assisting a student in recognizing and coming to terms with a personal, interpersonal, or even an academic performance issue is the first step in facilitating the resolution of the problem. Recognition in and of itself, however, is rarely a sufficient response. The integrator, who is expected to be knowledgeable about such matters, shares with the other team members information about institutional and off-campus resources to which a student who requires support might appropriately be referred. The integrator also assists the mentor's efforts to encourage a student's willingness to take advantage of such services, through actions such as securing an appointment, arranging personal contacts between the student and the agency, or following up to be sure that the student made and kept the appointment (Winston, 1996). In those rare instances when a campus agency is conducting a mandatory evaluation and information from that session will be used to make decisions regarding a student's position in the department, the integrator may serve as the official to whom the agency reports, with the permission of the student, the results of the evaluation.

Overcoming the Legacy of Separation

Spanning a gulf that has been growing for over a century requires the integrator not only to have a vision but also to possess a certain set of formal and informal knowledge, technical skills, political savvy, interpersonal and communication skills, and personality traits that bring that vision to life. The distance, both literal and figurative, between student and academic affairs has undoubtedly fueled a great many mutual misconceptions about their respective roles and perspectives. In fact, "Studies examining attitudes of student affairs staff and faculty have revealed that while both demonstrated an equivalent concern for students' development, neither constituency believed the other to be as concerned or capable of facilitating that outcome" (Garland & Grace, 1993, p. 59).

In developing and nurturing collegial relationships with student affairs administrators, the integrator must recognize and overcome the suspicion of motives, conflicting priorities, and pervasive turfism that has too often divided these components. It is essential for the integrator and the other faculty team members to be willing to embrace nonacademic administrators as equal partners rather than relating to them as subordinates whose role is to support the supremacy of the faculty's goals. And it will be incumbent on the integrator to initiate these interactions.

Characteristics of the Curriculum-Cocurriculum Integrator

This section examines some of the necessary attributes of the team member who will assume the integrator role.

A Requisite Base of Knowledge and Skills

Given the range of responsibilities, it is apparent that the integrator must be someone who has a varied set of knowledge and skills. Although it may not be essential for the integrator to be, or have experience as, a faculty member, at the very least the person filling the role must be familiar with the nature of the teaching and learning process and the academic environment. The integrator must be able to relate to faculty members, students, and nonacademic administrators and in doing so retain a sense of self and purpose in a role that many on campus, even other faculty team members, may not immediately understand or regard as being an integral part of the academic process.

The integrator must have and must use knowledge of the theory and practice of student development—the process and likely outcomes of the psychosocial, cognitive, and affective growth of students—in order to assist other team members in connecting what appears to be random and to organize what appears to be "chaotic" with respect to student behavior (McEwen, 1996). Theories and models of student development, such as those by Marcia (1966), Chickering and Reisser (1993), Kohlberg (1976), Josselson (1987), and Perry (1970), can help the integrator better anticipate and understand the nature of the typical issues and dilemmas with which their students will be challenged, often to the degree of being preoccupied. The work of Gilligan (1982), Cross (1991), Helms (1990), Cass (1979), Poston (1990), and Atkinson, Morten, and Sue (1993) can aid faculty in comprehending how gender and racial, cultural, and sexual orientation are influential factors in the developmental process. Models such as those by Moos (1986), Pace and Stern (1958), Kuh et al. (1991), and Hage and Aiken (1970) provide insight as to how the interaction among various environmental and individual factors stimulates or suppresses the overall cognitive and affective development of students and implicitly facilitates or impedes their academic progress. Finally, the integrator should look to the work of Schlossberg, Waters, and Goodman (1995) for insight concerning the issues and experiences of nontraditional students.

Similarly, the integrator will need to be conversant with theories and models of social cognition and learning psychology. These models clarify the manner in which unique individual cognitive factors affect the education process, including differences in learning strategies (Brown & Campione, 1990), cognitive styles (Kolb, 1984), field dependence (Witkin, Moore, Goodenough, & Cox, 1977), processing styles (Myers, 1980), reasoning (King & Kitchener, 1994), and the construction of meaning (Baxter Magolda, 1992).

It is imperative for the integrator to be familiar with the dynamics of the retention and attrition process. Given what is known about the importance of noncurricular factors on retention and attrition, there may be no more significant and obvious point of intra-institutional collaboration between faculty and student affairs administrators than in identifying and addressing the sources of attrition at the college or university. The integrator will rely on the work of Astin (1993), Pascarella (1984), and Tinto (1987) for models describing how the interaction among mutually influential individual and institutional characteristics ultimately contributes to student persistence.

Although formal training is not essential, the integrator must have at least a working knowledge of database management programs and network strategies. Because so much of the role involves the sharing of information among faculty and administrators, time management becomes an issue of practicality. The use of a shared database allows those persons who are designated as having a legitimate need to know (as allowed by the Family Educational Rights and Privacy Act) to readily exchange information about students. Although the inclusion of medical or counseling information in such a data file would be inappropriate, other general sources of information, such as disciplinary reports, campus police incident reports, or staff administrative reports, might be shared with those persons who have been authorized to have such information. With the necessary security measures and devices in place, these sources of information would be made available only to those persons who have the training and responsibility to use such information.

Finally, the integrator must have superior interpersonal and communication skills. He or she must demonstrate an understanding of and respect for the role and function of campus administrative offices and resources, work to identify and articulate common goals and priorities, and assuage any concerns that collaboration equates with loss of autonomy or that shared information will somehow be used inappropriately. Collaboration is essentially a function of relationships. If the integrator is perceived as being insincere or disingenuous in any of these matters, the administrators with whom he or she is seeking to collaborate will remain guarded, reticent to share information, and hesitant to enter into cooperative initiatives.

It follows that as the integrator is successful in establishing personal relationships with students and colleagues, a great deal of anecdotal and subjective information will be conveyed to that faculty member. There are likely to be inconsistencies, discrepancies, and apparent irrelevancies among the many pieces of information to which the integrator is privy. The integrator not only must be knowledgeable with respect to the legal and ethical issues associated with possessing information but also must be able to discern the relationship among seemingly divergent pieces of information, synthesize that information into a holistic perspective of the student, and assist the faculty team members in applying it in a manner that facilitates the student's learning process and personal well-being. Essentially, the integrator must have a convergent cognitive style (Kolb, 1984).

Motivation and Personal Characteristics

There are those who contend that the attributes of successful faculty members are in direct contrast to those traits that are embodied by successful student affairs administrators (Blake, 1979). It follows that those who serve as integrators must first resolve the philosophical and organizational gaps within themselves before they can be effective in that role. They must be empowered by a holistic educational philosophy, viewing collaborative initiatives with nonacademic administrators as opportunities to operationalize their belief that cognitive and affective development are interrelated components of each student's existence rather than separate and mutually exclusive domains.

It is primarily through relationships that the integrator operationalizes this philosophical belief. Because the role is one that is driven by relationships, the person who views speaking informally with students, attending meetings, or engaging in casual exchanges with colleagues as distracting and inefficient uses of time will not be drawn to, or effective in, this new role. Rather, the role must be filled by an individual who is relationship oriented, who is personally and professionally invigorated by connecting with others in a collaborative manner.

The sort of person who enjoys trying creative and innovative activities may be more suited to the integrator role than the person who is most comfortable working within an established set of expectations. Although the process of creation is one that requires coordination and effort, it can also prove to be professionally revitalizing. By breaking down existing organizational barriers, faculty team members are allowed to enter into new relationships with potentially rewarding opportunities for personal and professional enrichment beyond the bounds of their academic department or discipline (Pazandak, 1989). But the integrator must first be someone who is capable of looking past traditional faculty relationships and reaching out to new constituencies within and outside the academy. As such, the integrator must be somewhat of a risk taker.

The integrator must, above all else, be a facilitator who is able to build coalitions among skeptical colleagues and must be willing to facilitate both action and compromise in terms of goal setting, intervention design, and implementation. The sense of "us versus them" that pervades the relationship between academic and nonacademic staff must be replaced with unified priorities and mutual investment and recognition. The integrator cannot demand the cooperation of a colleague but can only solicit and persuade. When managing change in a paradoxical environment, patience is indeed an essential virtue (Barr & Gloseth, 1990).

Those familiar with the Myers-Briggs Type Indicator (MBTI) might recognize the aforementioned personality characteristics of one who is "driven" by an internal "vision" that is brought to fruition by melding a seemingly disparate set of elements through relationships with others. Specifically, the characteristics associated with ENFJ (extroverted, intuitive, feeling, judging) Myers-Briggs Type might well be indicative of the type of person who would be effective in this capacity (Myers, 1980). The ENFJ is a highly artic-ulate person who exhibits a phenomenal capacity for working with people, generally drawing out their best. The ENFJ also has an intuitive ability for perceiving relationships among seemingly unconnected elements and is comfortable utilizing his or her the-oretical and pragmatic expertise to address related issues. Although some ENFJ tendencies, such as the need for recognition, could compromise the collaborative process, these are not insur-mountable obstacles if recognized and addressed.

Given the intensity of the role and the natural evolution of pro-fessional and personal priorities, it is anticipated that the average person will be effective in the integrator role for only a limited period, perhaps no longer than four or five years. Career devel-opment theory suggests that the selection and performance of a job is not merely a "trait factor" issue—whether the person pos-sesses the necessary and prerequisite skills and knowledge—but is also a function of whether the nature of the job is congruent with the values, maturation, motivation, and self-concept of the person who assumes the position (Super, 1957). As one's personal and professional interests naturally mature, the person who assumes the role of integrator may eventually need to move on to new chal-lenges to remain vital and invigorated. This may not be the culmi-nating experience for many individuals and as such may be a role that is best performed early in one's career, or perhaps late in one's career, when one's mark in the discipline has already been made.

A Full Circle

If, as the emerging research contends, all that takes place on a campus does indeed have curricular implications, then: "A college or university must have not only integrity in the curriculum, but also integrity between the curriculum and the college's ecology"

(Kuh et al., 1991 p. 373). But a totally integrated learning community will not be created instantaneously, for an institutional environment is not subject to immediate manipulation. Rather, it will be the product of a gradual "de-evolution" of a century of institutional divisions, the removal of administrative and personal barriers, and a unified mission based on holistic learning (Garvin, 1993). Thus, in some ways, the integrator is not a new position at all. As a generalist who is person centered rather than discipline based, the integrator is an updated version of the colonial college faculty member whose intimate involvement in the cocurricular lives of students made integrated approaches to learning the rule, rather than the exception.

References

Anaya, G. (1996). College experiences and student learning: The influence of active learning, college environments and cocurricular activities. *The Journal of College Student Development, 37*(6), 611–622.

Astin, A. W. (1993). *What matters in college? "Four critical years" revisited.* San Francisco: Jossey-Bass.

Atkinson, D. R., Morten, G., & Sue, D. W. (1993). *Counseling American minorities: A cross-cultural perspective* (4th ed.). Dubuque, IA: W. C. Brown.

Barr, M. J., & Gloseth, A. E. (1990). Managing change in a paradoxical environment. In M. J. Barr & M. L. Upcraft (Eds.), *New futures for student affairs.* San Francisco: Jossey-Bass.

Baxter Magolda, M. (1992). *Knowing and reasoning in college: Gender-related patterns in students' intellectual development.* San Francisco: Jossey-Bass.

Baxter Magolda, M. (1996). Cognitive learning and personal development: A false dichotomy. *About Campus, 1*(3), 16–21.

Blake, E. S. (1979). Classroom and context: An educational dialectic. *Academe, 65*(5), 280–292.

Boyer, E. L. (1987). *College: The undergraduate experience in America.* Princeton, NJ: Carnegie Foundation for the Advancement of Teaching.

Boyer, E. L. (1990). *Scholarship reconsidered: Priorities of the professoriate.* Princeton, NJ: Carnegie Foundation for the Advancement of Teaching.

Brown, A. L., & Campione, J. C. (1990). Communities of learning and thinking, or a context by any other name. In D. Kuhn (Ed.), *Developmental perspectives on teaching and learning thinking skills.* Basel, Switzerland: Karger.

Caplan, G., Caplan, R. B., & Erchul, W. P. (1994). Caplanian mental health consultation: Historical background and current status. *Consulting Psychology Journal: Practice and Research, 46,* 2–12.

Carpenter, D. S. (1996). The philosophical heritage of student affairs. In A. L. Rentz & Associates, *Student affairs practice in higher education* (pp. 3–27). Springfield, IL: Thomas.

Cass, V. C. (1979). Homosexual identity formation: A theoretical model. *Journal of Homosexuality, 4,* 219–235.

Chickering, A. W. (1969). *Education and identity.* San Francisco: Jossey-Bass.

Chickering, A. W., & Reisser, L. (1993). *Education and identity* (2nd ed.). San Francisco: Jossey-Bass.

Chronicle of Higher Education. (1998, August 28). [entire almanac issue]. *XLV*(1).

Crego, C. A. (1996). Consultation and mediation. In S. R. Komives, D. B. Woodward, & Associates, *Student services: A handbook for the profession* (3rd ed., pp. 361–379). San Francisco: Jossey-Bass.

Cross, W. E. (1991). *Shades of black: Diversity in African-American identity.* Philadelphia: Temple University Press.

Damush, T. M., Hays, R. D., & DiMatteo, M. R. (1997). Stressful life events and health-related quality of life in college students. *Journal of College Student Development, 38*(2), 181–190.

Donald, J. G. (1997). *Improving the environment for learning: Academic leaders talk about what works.* San Francisco: Jossey-Bass.

Douglas, G. H. (1992). *Education without impact: How our universities fail the young.* New York: Birch Lane Press.

Duley, J. S. (1981). Learning through field experience. In O. Milton & Associates, *On college teaching: A guide to contemporary practices.* San Francisco: Jossey-Bass.

Ender, S. C., & Carranza, C. (1991). Students as paraprofessionals. In T. K. Miller, R. B. Winston, & Associates, *Administration and leadership in student affairs: Actualizing student development in higher education* (pp. 533–561). Muncie, IN: Accelerated Development.

Gardiner, L. F. (1994). *Redesigning higher education: Producing dramatic gains in student learning.* ASHE-ERIC Higher Education Report No. 7. Washington, DC: Graduate School of Education and Human Development, George Washington University.

Garland, P. H., & Grace, T. W. (1993). *New perspectives for student affairs professionals: Evolving realities, responsibilities, and roles.* ASHE-ERIC Higher Education Report No. 7. Washington, DC: School of Education and Human Development, George Washington University.

Garvin, D. A. (1993). Building a learning organization. *Harvard Business Review, 41*(4), 78–91.

Gilligan, C. (1982). *In a different voice.* Cambridge, MA: Harvard University Press.

Grayson, P. A. (1989). *College psychotherapy.* New York: Guilford Press, 8–28.

Hage, J., & Aiken, M. (1970). *Social change in complex organizations.* New York: Random House.

Hall, J. (1991). *Access through innovation: New colleges for new students.* American Council on Education. Old Tappan, NJ: Macmillan.

Helms., J. E. (1990). *Black and white racial identity: Theory, research, and practice.* Westport, CT: Greenwood Press.

Josselson, R. (1987). *Finding herself: Pathways to identity development in women.* San Francisco: Jossey-Bass.

Kerr, C. (1963). *The uses of the university.* Cambridge, MA: Harvard University Press.

King, P. M., & Kitchener, K. S. (1994). *Developing reflective judgment: Understanding and promoting intellectual growth and critical thinking in adolescents and adults.* San Francisco: Jossey-Bass.

Knock, G. H. (1985). Development of student services in higher education. In M. J. Barr, L. A. Keating, & Associates, *Developing effective student service programs* (pp. 15–42). San Francisco: Jossey-Bass.

Kohlberg, L. (1976). Moral stages and moralization: The cognitive-developmental approach. In T. Lickone (Ed.), *Moral development and behavior: Theory, research, and social issues* (pp. 31–35). Austin, TX: Holt, Rinehart and Winston.

Kolb, D. A. (1984). *Experiential learning: Experience as the source of learning and development.* Englewood Cliffs, NJ: Prentice Hall.

Kuh, G. D., Douglas, K. B., Lund, J. P., & Ramin-Gyurnek, J. (1994). *Student learning outside the classroom: Transcending artificial boundaries.* ASHE-ERIC Higher Education Report No. 8. Washington, DC: School of Education and Human Development, George Washington University.

Kuh, G. D, Schuh, J. H., Whitt, E. J., Andreas, R. E., Lyons, J. W., Strange, C. C., Krehbiel, L. E., & MacKay, K. A. (1991). *Involving colleges: Successful approaches to fostering student learning and development outside the classroom.* San Francisco: Jossey-Bass.

Marcia, J. E. (1966). Development and validation of ego-identity status. *Journal of Personality and Social Psychology, 3,* 551–559.

McEwen, M. L. (1996). Theories of student development. In S. R. Komives, D. B. Woodward, & Associates, *Student services: A handbook for the profession* (3rd ed., pp. 164–187). San Francisco: Jossey-Bass.

Michman, R. D. (1983). *Marketing to changing consumer markets: Environmental scanning.* New York: Praeger.

Moos, R. H. (1986). *The human context: Environmental determinants of behavior.* Malabar, FL: Krieger.

Myers, I. B. (1980). *Gifts differing.* Palo Alto, CA: Consulting Psychologists Press.

Pace, C. R., & Stern, G. G. (1958). An approach to the measurement of psychological characteristics of college environments. *Journal of Educational Psychology, 49*, 269–277.

Pascarella, E. (1984). College environmental influences on students' educational aspirations. *Journal of Higher Education, 55*, 544–595.

Pascarella, E. T., & Terenzini, P. T. (1991). *How college affects students: Findings and insights from twenty years of research.* San Francisco: Jossey-Bass.

Pazandak, C. H. (Ed.). (1989). *Improving undergraduate education in large universities.* New Directions for Higher Education, no. 66. San Francisco: Jossey-Bass.

Perry, W. G. (1970). *Forms of intellectual and ethical development in the college years: A scheme.* Austin, TX: Holt, Rinehart and Winston.

Poston, W.S.C. (1990). The biracial identity development model: A needed addition. *Journal of Counseling and Development, 69*, 152–155.

Ramirez, B. C. (1993). Adapting to new student needs and characteristics. In M. J. Barr (Ed.), *The handbook of student affairs administration* (pp. 427–438). San Francisco: Jossey-Bass.

Rentz, A. L. (1996). A history of student affairs. In A. L. Rentz & Associates, *Student affairs practice in higher education* (pp. 28–53). Springfield, IL: Thomas.

Rhoads, R. A., & Black, M. A. (1995). Student affairs practitioners as transformative educators: Advancing a critical cultural perspective. *Journal of College Student Development, 36*(5), 413–421.

Schlossberg, N., Waters, E. B., & Goodman, J. (1995). *Counseling adults in transition* (2nd ed.). New York: Springer.

Schroeder, C. C. (1993). New students: New learning styles. *Change, 25*(4) 21–26.

Simpson, R. D., & Frost, S. F. (1993). *Inside college: Undergraduate education for the future.* New York: Insight Books.

Super, D. E. (1957). *The psychology of careers.* New York: HarperCollins.

Tinto, V. (1987). *Leaving college: Rethinking the causes and cures of student attrition.* Chicago: University of Chicago Press.

Wechsler, H. (1996). Alcohol and the American college campus: A report from the Harvard School of Public Health. *Change, 28*(4), 20–25.

Whitla, D. K. (1981). *Value added and other related matters.* Washington, DC: National Commission on Excellence in Education. (ED 228 245)

Winston, R. B. (1996). Counseling and advisement. In S. R. Komives, D. B. Woodward, & Associates. *Student services: A handbook for the profession* (3rd ed., pp. 335–360). San Francisco: Jossey-Bass.

Witkin, H. A., Moore, C. A., Goodenough, D. R., & Cox, P. W. (1977). Field dependent and field independent cognitive styles and their educational implications. *Review of Educational Research, 47*, 1–64.

Chapter Eight

The Assessor
Appraising Student and Team Performance
Bruce W. Speck

Because the purpose of this chapter is to discuss evaluation in the classroom context, I begin with my experience as a university teacher and a researcher on grading for two reasons. The first reason is that my experience reinforces a major theme of this book: one teacher cannot perform well every task that teaching requires, including assessment, which demands a certain set of capabilities that, quite frankly, may be hard to find in any one person. The second reason is that my experience early in my career exemplifies, I surmise, the typical apprenticeship of innumerable graduate students preparing for professorial positions and can serve as a cautionary tale about the need for training in assessment for all professors.

A Cautionary Tale About Classroom Assessment Practices

Many, many years ago, as a doctoral student, I was given the opportunity to teach, unencumbered by instruction in the art of teaching. In my role as a university English teacher, i constructed various tests, quizzes, and writing tasks—again, unencumbered by instruction in assessment. When I began to evaluate students' work, I found that the inchoate assessment measures I had in my head (and that I used to construct a particular assignment or test) were continually being called into question by what students actually produced. This was particularly true when I evaluated their written work. For example, the problem of matching my hopes and dreams for a "good" piece of writing with students' actual prose was particularly painful when the writing assignment I had created yielded a piece of writing that did not fit my concept of the assignment. At the same time, I had to admit that students' "misinterpretations" of any of my assignments were often legitimate, given my instructions. Instead of clear specifications, I had created assignments (and even quiz and test questions) with elastic boundaries. My ability to evaluate students' work according to the specifications of my assignments was subverted, and I was the agent of subversion.

Had my experience been unique, I would have chalked up my failures to inept personal communication skills and perhaps joined a foreign legion for assignment-addicted teachers. Unfortunately, my plight was not unique. Even senior professors that I knew and sought out for grading advice wondered about the mystery of grading, devising various idiosyncratic systems in an attempt to bring order out of chaos. Alas, those professors were not unique either. Throughout my career as an academic, particularly as coordinator of a writing-across-the-curriculum program, I have heard professors from a variety of disciplines wonder how to evaluate students' performance, asking questions arising from many years of grading experience. Although I was able to provide some tentative answers for these colleagues, I must admit that I was perplexed about grading myself. In fact, I did not carefully and critically examine grading until I undertook a bibliographical project that gave me the opportunity to read extensively the literature about grading students' writing (Speck, 1998a). My conclusions from reading the literature are sobering. We do not have a theory of grading student writing (Speck & Jones, 1998); we have no standard definition of good writing that will stand up in court (Purves, Gorman, & Takala, 1988; Purves & Hawisher, 1990; Quellmalz, Capell, & Chou, 1982; Raymond, 1982; Sloan, 1975), even a court of peers; we grade idiosyncratically (Charnley, 1978; Dulek & Shelby, 1981; Edwards, 1982; Garrison, 1979; Ober, 1984; Rachal, 1984; Sneed, 1986; Wilkinson, 1979), so much so, in fact, that we have the flexibility to give the same paper different grades—sometimes widely different grades—when we are presented the opportunity to do so. I use the pronoun *we* because the literature implicates all teachers who grade students' writing, regardless of discipline. In fact, those who should be the most knowledgeable about grading writing—professors of English—are the ones most often studied as assessors of university students' writing, and the ones who in fact demonstrate idiosyncratic grading behaviors. So those outside the English profession who supposedly have even less expertise in analyzing written discourse would, it would seem, fare much worse in their grading practices.

The problems associated with grading students' writing are emblematic of grading other types of student performance, not the least so because grading of any type is inherently subjective. One necessary accommodation, then, is to maintain whatever subjective professional judgment that is legitimate while making plain to students whatever can be made plain (Speck, 1998b). Although this balancing act of revealing what can be revealed while maintaining the integrity of what must remain mysterious can be achieved at some level by the individual classroom teacher, the grading enterprise, to achieve the promise of equity, requires a level of professional training that is perhaps too demanding for professors who are also required to perform a host of other teaching tasks. The assessor, as a member of the professorial teaching team, therefore, can provide a solution to the problems associated with classroom grading. My task then is to provide a prototype, an ideal assessor who, when flesh and blood are added, will, despite human limitations, be a functional member of the professorial teaching team, able to provide assessment direction at the outset of any teaching-learning endeavor. Before discussing that prototype, I provide a brief theoretical discussion to set the stage for exploring the assessor's role in the team proposed in this book.

Theoretical Considerations

Terenzini (1989) cites a major problem associated with any discussion of assessment in higher education when he says, "One of the most significant and imposing obstacles to the advancement of the assessment agenda at the national level is the absence of any consensus on precisely what 'assessment' means" (p. 646). The problem is no less acute at the classroom level, as I discovered when, after reviewing literature on classroom grading, I found no stable definition of grading. In an attempt to make sense out of evaluative methods, Gardner (1977) identified five evaluative frameworks and explained when any particular framework would be an appropriate assessment measure. By contextualizing evaluative frameworks, Gardner emphasized the need for those who evaluate educational outcomes to be sensitive to the fit between framework-methodology and assessment opportunity. The assessor that I have in view not only needs to match method and assessment opportunity but also needs to be conversant with a variety of evaluative frameworks.

The definitional problem and the methodological problems are complicated by two other issues. One is the nature of faculty work. For instance, Paulsen and Feldman (1995), in recapitulating Boyer (1990), promote an expanded view of traditional scholarship, a view "that encompasses and encourages diversity in the creative talents of faculty, allows for different disciplinary perspectives, and promotes the development of mission statements expressing more distinctive and differentiated priorities" (p. 636). One outcome of the expanded view is that "evaluation and reward structures" can be changed "to reflect the diversity of institutional missions, disciplinary contexts, and special interests and talents of individual faculty" (p. 638). In other words, assessment can be tailored to particular contexts, a theme Gardner articulated. The impact on generalizability of tailoring assessments is not clear, however, and the assessor will need to consider assessment methods that will promote both institutional mission and individual professors' concerns without invalidating the generalizability of assessment results to the larger context of higher education as a whole.

Krahenbuhl (1998) points to another scheme for charting individual professors' work. He notes that although faculty responsibilities follow a pattern of knowledge generation, transmission, and application, "There is, however, significant variation among faculty members in the relative effort devoted to each area and in the specific activities that constitute their work" (p. 21). Thus, each faculty member's responsibilities can be charted as a unique profile. Such a profile has a profound impact on evaluation, not only of the faculty member's level of achievement in meeting his or her responsibilities but also of the interrelationship of those responsibilities as they impinge on one another. What, for instance, is the relationship among knowledge generation, transmission, and application as they relate to classroom teaching? And once those relationships are established, how are they evaluated to determine the level at which a professor's classroom teaching has been affected and effective? These are difficult assessment questions that the assessor will need to grapple with when considering how to evaluate professorial performance as it relates to institutional mission, classroom performance, and student outcomes.

The second issue that complicates assessment concerns is student outcomes. What exactly are the goals of higher education concerning students? In Astin's (1990) talent development model, the role of assessment changes when the goal of higher education is to develop each student's talent. "Rather than being used to promote institutional resources and reputation, assessment is used to place students in appropriate courses of study and to determine how much talent development is actually occurring by repeated assessments over time" (p. 470). Although such an assessment goal has virtue, it presupposes not only repeated assessments over time but also a breadth of assessments that are not characteristic of classroom assessment as it is now practiced by individual instructors (though increasingly outcomes assessment centers are appearing on many campuses). For instance, Pascarella, Whitt, and Nora (1996) report, after analyzing data from the National Study of Student Learning, "A wide variety of curricular, instructional, out-of-class, and organizational climate variables . . . affect how students learn and grow. This finding indicates a need to blur the boundaries between 'academic' and 'student' affairs" (p. 191). Though this finding fits nicely with the premise that teaching requires a team of experts, not only from academic disciplines but also from allied fields, assessment of teaching outcomes is complicated; and the assessor will need to consider ways to evaluate the interwoven strands of student experiences. At present, those strands of experiences may not be knitted together when classroom academic performance is evaluated. The assessor will need to investigate multifarious considerations that impinge on classroom academic performance—no small task, but one that can be aided by members in a professorial teaching team. Thomas Grace, in the previous chapter, echoes this perspective and sketches some scenarios to accomplish these ends.

Student outcomes, however, are a bit more complex and include educating for citizenship (Soder, 1996; Terenzini, 1994) and developing critical thinking skills (Terenzini, Springer, Pascarella, & Nora, 1995), among others. If, as Pascarella and Terenzini (1998) predict, "The demographic, institutional, economic, and technological changes that will reshape the study of college impacts on students over the next decade may well be 'revolutionary'" (p. 163), then assessment of outcomes will take on new importance. In fact, the assessor will need to address changes that portend a revolution in studying the impact of diverse variables on educational outcomes. In short, assessment is a complex task that requires, at least, a professional assessor as a member of the professorial teaching team. How will the assessor function as a team member?

What Will the Assessor Do?

To develop a prototype of the assessor, I begin by speculating on what the assessor will actually do. How will the assessor function in a professorial teaching team? The assessor I envision has a sixfold task—to work with the other team members to determine what should be evaluated, to design evaluations, to manage the evaluation process, to evaluate the data derived from the process, to report those data to the team and to the wider academic community, and to use the data to create a body of research about effective teaching and learning.

Work with the Other Team Members to Determine What Should Be Evaluated

In accordance with the principle that evaluation should be central to the planning stages of a teaching-learning endeavor, the assessor should work with the other team members to determine what should be evaluated. The answer to the question about what should be evaluated has two prongs, because the assessor not only assists team members in developing evaluations to measure student learning but also develops instruments to measure team members' performance. Certainly, the two prongs are related, but they are not synonymous. For instance, a lecturer may give an excellent performance, and the audience may give the lecturer high marks for effectiveness; but the learning outcomes may be nonexistent (Naftulin, Ware, & Donnelly, 1973; Marsh & Ware, 1982). As Angelo and Cross (1993) point out, "Teaching without learning is just talking" (p. 3). What is perceived to be a good teaching performance does not necessarily translate into effective learning performance, so one of the assessor's tasks is to stimulate the team to think about the relationship between effective teaching and effective learning and to suggest ways to measure teaching and learning and the relationship between the two. In performing this task, the assessor will participate in plenary meetings with the professorial teaching team and in individual or subgroup meetings. During those meetings, the assessor will

- Consult with the researcher team member to determine what the team wants to learn about its teaching performance and students' learning, so that the assessor can develop instruments that will provide data for the researcher to analyze.
- Talk with the pedagogy expert to determine what types of pedagogical tools can be used for any particular teaching-learning task and what is the best way to evaluate those tools and their learning outcomes.
- Confer with the lecturer to discuss ways to evaluate his or her performance and the consequent student learning, particularly in relation to audience analysis, learning styles, and interactive strategies to enrich the lecture format.
- Interact with the discussion leader (and pedagogical expert) to develop ways to evaluate both individual and group learning.
- Discuss with the mentor ways to evaluate individualized instruction and the quality and usefulness of professional advice.
- Confer with the integrator about the relationship among variables outside the classroom (peer group support, family support, extracurricular activities, study habits, financial exigencies, drug abuse, and so forth) and discuss ways to measure those variables and relate them to experts' performance and students' learning.
- Evaluate the assessment practices and determine whether the data the researcher uses are valid and reliable.

Clearly, the assessor cannot conduct all the assessments at once, so in consultation with the team, the assessor will need to focus on a specific task and the associated learning goals. For instance, the team may decide to evaluate the effectiveness of a particular laboratory procedure. This could entail the assessor working with the researcher to determine how to collect data for the procedure, including asking the researcher what the literature already says about the effectiveness of the laboratory procedure; working with the pedagogy expert to examine the laboratory procedure and determine whether it should be modified in light of the literature review that the researcher prepares; working with the lecturer (and pedagogy expert) to incorporate techniques derived from the researcher's literature review and from the discussion leader's experience conducting labs; working with the discussion leader to ensure that the procedures outlined in the lecture are reinforced in the lab; working with the integrator to collect data about things outside the class that might interfere with the lab (a rock concert the night before, Friday morning absenteeism, the availability of a reading about the lab procedure in the campus library); consulting with the team members to develop assessment instruments that will be used to assess students' lab performance; and synthesizing the work of the professorial teaching team to develop evaluative instruments to measure not only the effectiveness of the laboratory procedure, given the academic integrity of the procedure, but also its effectiveness in terms of students' performance, given the particular circumstances in which it was used. A stable professorial team will allow the assessor to conduct longitudinal studies that could be of immense value in evaluating teaching-learning endeavors. But it is clear that the team cannot measure every procedure, every pedagogical method, every dynamic between the classroom and extracurricular events, every relationship among all the many variables that impinge on teaching and learning during the semester; however, the team can select salient features of their teaching-learning enterprise and begin to measure the variables that impinge on those particular features.

Design Evaluations

Once the team identifies a particular feature of the teaching-learning enterprise, the assessor is primarily responsible for designing evaluations. This does not mean, of course, that the assessor does not consult the researcher, for instance, who undoubtedly has training in research methods. In fact, the assessor does not go into a corner, pour evaluative chemicals into a tube, and come forth with an instrument composed of all the right ingredients. Rather, the assessor will need to consult with other members of the team to determine whether the instrument does what the members want it to do. Such consultation will require revisions and further iterations of the instrument.

Although the involvement of team members in developing assessment instruments has an egalitarian ring that sounds sweet to the ears of those who heartily support faculty governance and academic freedom in higher education, the forging of assessment instruments from a cohesive plan agreed on by team members may in practice sound quite cacophonous. For the team to agree on appropriate assessment instruments (even given the assessor's expert guidance in such matters), the team first has to agree on learning outcomes and the most appropriate method to achieve those outcomes. Although Angelo and Cross (1993) provide useful advice, particularly their Teaching Goals Inventory, about how to identify and clarify teaching goals, consensus about those goals among team members may not be a simple task. In fact, I assume that identifying teaching-learning goals, creating (or employing existing) assessment instruments to gather data about the effectiveness of methods used to reach those goals (including assessment of students' performance), and interpreting that data will be time consuming and nerve-racking, testing team members' commitment to the professorial teaching team. Indeed, team members will undoubtedly find that agreeing on specific criteria for evaluation, articulating those criteria to students, and using those criteria as a basis for grading students' performance will be an arduous challenge demanding the team's concentrated energies. Such a challenge is multiplied tenfold when the team assesses individual students' products and performances to arrive at a summative evaluation for a course and uses that evaluation as part of the data to prepare a summative evaluation of teaching effectiveness for the course.

Because assessment is a complicated task, during the process of developing an instrument, the assessor will serve yet another function—evaluation educator, the person who gradually inducts the other team members into the language and practices of evaluation. It will not do for the lecturer, for instance, to say, "My job is to lecture. Besides, I never was much interested in statistics. I like the thrill of being in front of an audience. Someone else can crunch numbers." Although the technical aspects of "crunching numbers" is not in the domain of the lecturer, he or she does need to be able to converse with the other team members about assessment using language that the assessor provides. (Of course, a lecturer in statistics or other quantitative fields would not have the same attitude about crunching numbers.) This means that the assessor is a person who can take complex assessment concepts and explain them so that the lecturer and other uninitiated members of the team can understand them.

I have been assuming that the assessor will develop evaluative instruments, which are called *criterion-referenced tests.* Such tests, which are locally developed and based on test criteria, are generally contrasted with *norm-referenced tests,* which are developed (and packaged by agencies such as Educational Testing Service) with the presupposition that a normal distribution of scores for the test will produce a bell curve. Thus, "Norm referencing assumes a normal distribution of the skills it measures" (White, 1985, p. 64). The assessor will need to explain the differences between criterion-referenced and norm-referenced tests to the team, particularly because many people consider norm-referenced tests as true indicators of where a person stands on the intellectual ladder of life. Norming, the assessor will need to note to the team, depends on the composition of the group being normed and the supposed group assumed by the test questions. Most of the assessor's testing will be based on the philosophy undergirding criterion-referenced tests—that is, a locally developed test attempts to measure what students learned given a particular classroom setting.

However, the assessor may have to forge links between criterion-referenced and norm-referenced tests when a course is designed to help students prepare to pass licensure tests, such as certain courses in nursing, education, law, and engineering. In such cases, the team may decide to adopt a version of the norm-referenced test for some aspect of class testing. In addition, the assessor may be called on to measure individual classroom performance in relation to a norm-referenced standard. For instance, increasing concerns about the need for accountability in higher education could result in legislative mandates requiring that both student and teacher performance be measured against a state or national standard. Although such a prospect sends chills down the spines of most academics (and one would hope most administrators), the assessor would have the skill needed to measure teacher and student performance in the team in relation to teacher and student performance in another team or in a classroom setting with only one teacher.

Once the team has approved of an assessment instrument, the assessor must user-test the instrument. Such user testing requires time, another reason that during any one semester, the number of features the team investigates will necessarily have to be carefully selected and diligently investigated. The assessor will modify the instrument based on results from user testing and will prepare final copy for the team to examine before producing the instrument for the actual assessment.

Manage the Evaluation Process

The potential assessment instruments that an assessor can create are quite varied, ranging from "objective" tests to writing prompts to questionnaires and ethnographic studies. If, for example, the team chooses to use a questionnaire (most probably in conjunction with other data-collecting instruments), the assessor must manage the assessment process for that instrument. Thus, the instrument chosen for an assessment must be administered according to a legitimate research protocol. For instance, if certain members of a class are going to be asked to participate in an interview, then those members must be selected based on clearly defined criteria. Members may, for example, be selected because of their extracurricular activities (as determined by the integrator), or they may be selected randomly; but the selection criteria must be defensible in light of the research goal. In any case, the administration of the instrument is based on clear-cut criteria that can be managed easily enough.

But suppose that the assessor, in consultation with the professorial teaching team, determines that an ethnographic study is the most appropriate method to gather data. Then the management of data collection becomes a much more labor-intensive task and more complicated in some ways. The assessor may work with the lecturer to ensure that videotapes of the lectures are produced effectively. (This may mean that the assessor explains to the lecturer what color clothes to wear, what type of jewelry to avoid wearing because it can create noise during the videotaping, how to speak so that the microphone picks up the entire lecture, and so on.) The assessor may need to subcontract an agency on campus to do the videotaping. Or perhaps the professorial teaching team decides that a study of group interaction is needed. The assessor will work with the discussion leader to determine how to audiotape group interaction, will work with a secretary to explain how to transcribe the tapes so that features such as silence or interruptions are noted, will work with the researcher to ensure that other data from ethnographic research (the discussion leader's journal, the researcher's field notes, the students' products) can be systematically collected and preserved.

The assessor's managerial role also pertains to the assessments used to grade students' performance. For instance, after managing the test construction phase of an assessment, the assessor must ensure that sufficient copies of an instrument are available when they are administered, that administration of the instrument preserves the integrity of the assessment (for example, ensuring that students are not cheating or plagiarizing), that the data are evaluated, and that reports of the evaluation are disseminated to the team and others that the team specifies.

Evaluate the Data Derived from the Process

The raw data must be coded, counted, and codified, whether the data are derived from a questionnaire, an ethnographic study, an essay examination, or an objective examination. In all likelihood, the assessor will work closely with the researcher during this phase of the assessment because the researcher will need to know how the data were analyzed to write the methods section of the report or article or monograph based on the assessment. Depending on the size of the project, the assessor may need to enlist coders who are not part of the professorial teaching team. This means that the assessor may have to train coders—perhaps students who want to be initiated into the grunt work of the research community—and ensure that they do their coding well. The assessor may or may not have access to statistical packages to analyze the data, but either way, the assessor must ensure that the appropriate statistical procedures are used to analyze the data.

The assessor's evaluation of data regarding students' performance will necessarily require judgments about quality. This means that the assessor will need to explain why a 25 percent failure rate on a quiz is an indication that the quiz and lecture were not in sync, or that something in the sequence of course material explains failure rate, or that the failure rate can be explained by other variables (homecoming, lack of student motivation, and so forth). The assessor's analysis is based on the particular classroom context, and therefore generalizability is a potential problem. However, among the important features of the professorial teaching team is the natural use of holistic scoring when an assignment calls for multiple evaluations. Holistic scoring provides multiple professional judgments of students' performance and can be a hedge against the dual threats of capricious subjective judgments and inability to generalize results due to the constraints of criterion-referenced assessments.

Report Those Data to the Team and to the Wider Academic Community

Along with the researcher, the assessor will provide the team with an analysis of the data. This analysis will not necessarily be in the form of a written report, and the analysis may be presented in stages. For instance, once a particular question about the data can be answered, the assessor may write a memo to the professorial teaching team explaining what progress has been made in answering that question. If the data are judged to be significant in terms of publication, the assessor might collaborate with the researcher to produce a publishable document. This does not mean that the rest of the team should not be involved in writing the document. Indeed, team members should act as peer evaluators, responding to drafts of the document, offering suggestions for revision based on their participation in the project, and providing other suggestions—such as pertinent sources—that may be incorporated into the finished document.

Team involvement in producing a document that provides not only a description of data but also an analysis based on theoretical concerns should lead naturally and logically to an assessment of team performance. The analysis of the data should help the team consider the usefulness of particular pedagogical methods, the need to control for certain variables in and outside the classroom to provide the highest-quality learning environment, the recognition that further team training—either for certain team members or for the team as a whole—is merited, and so forth. (Incidentally, one natural outcome of the professorial teaching team is faculty development. Thus, continual quality control of the teaching environment necessarily entails continual development of faculty, so that they grow as professionals. However, data from the professorial teaching team's efforts also can point to ineffective teaching practices that if not changed, merit censure—primarily by the team, but also by administrators.) Figure 8.1 provides a graphic illustration of the assessor's role in the professorial teaching team.

Use the Data to Create a Body of Research About Effective Teaching and Learning

Ideally, a stable team will provide a series of significant research results that will grow into a body of research connected to other bodies of research produced by other stable teams. Such a joint research effort, much more systematic and powerful than the individual approaches often taken by educational researchers today, has the potential to provide data to examine issues that have been investigated only piecemeal until now. For instance, the literature on team teaching, an on-again, off-again phenomenon in the academy, has been bereft of a theoretical structure until recently (Anderson & Speck, 1998). One of the reasons for such a major flaw is that generally two teachers, operating without the benefit of expert advice about how to study their team teaching, produce an account of their experience that serves as an example of educational lore, not the presentation of useful data or credible analysis of that data for measuring the effectiveness of team teaching. Thus, the promise of rigorous, continual assessment by a stable team could benefit the entire research community enormously (see Figure 8.2).

Figure 8.1. Process and Outcomes of Assessor's Role in the Professorial Teaching Team.

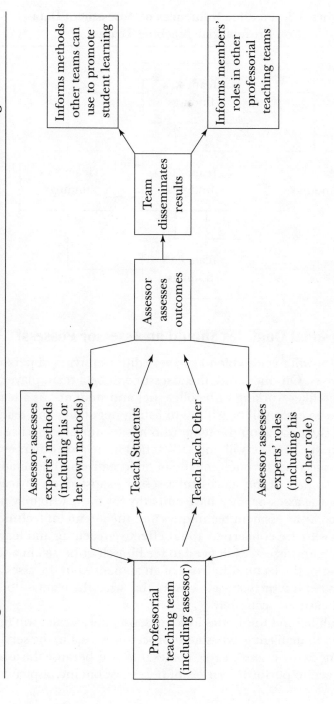

**Figure 8.2. Possible Influences of Assessment Data
on Professorial Teaching Teams.**

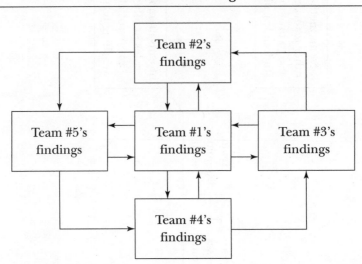

What Personal Qualities Should an Assessor Possess?

The assessor will need to blend two very different types of person-ality qualities. On one hand, the assessor will be a team player, a person who likes working with colleagues and students. As a team player, the assessor will be willing to listen, negotiate, and teach. As one of the people on the team who has technical expertise in assessment, the assessor will find satisfaction in helping others eval-uate their successes through the use of quantitative and qualitative methods, so part of the successful assessor's satisfaction is vicari-ous. Thus, the assessor must have empathy for those who may not be engaged by assessment techniques and the attendant technical issues but who are concerned about effective teaching and learn-ing. Further, the assessor will need to see himself or herself in a ser-vice role—not the lecturer in front of an audience but the assessor who works behind the scenes to ensure that what the team is doing is being measured accurately.

Though behind the scenes in some sense, the assessor will find satisfaction in managing assessment procedures. Again, the service component of the assessor's role comes into play because the asses-sor may need to perform a variety of necessary, but inconspicuous, low-profile administrative tasks—setting up equipment or ensuring that it is set up properly, training students to code data, explaining to secretaries how to transcribe interviews and group conversations, and so forth. Indeed, the assessor may need to take charge of a budget and consult with accountants and administrators about policies regulating expenditures. The assessor could very well be involved in writing grants to fund projects that the professorial teaching team wants to pursue but cannot fund without access to resources. In all these tasks, the assessor role requires a person who finds satisfaction in being a member of a team by serving the team, often backstage.

On the other hand, the assessor will have a keen interest in quantitative and qualitative methods, an interest that can be at odds with being a team player. The person interested in quantitative methods may find satisfaction working with data because data do not create the kinds of interpersonal problems associated with human relationships. Indeed, the satisfaction that the assessor finds in the technical side of the role could militate against the satisfaction that the assessor finds in teamwork, particularly the close one-on-one relationships that the assessor will engage in to evaluate team teaching efforts and learning outcomes. In fact, the technical side of the role can offer considerably more autonomy than the teamwork side, especially when teamwork entails juggling team schedules and focusing on the classroom as the arena in which a significant amount of data collection takes place. The assessor role calls for a person with a unique blend of technical and interpersonal propensities.

What Skills Should an Assessor Possess?

What kind of training is necessary to produce an effective assessor? The answer to that question is problematic, not because the components of an educational program are unavailable but because assembling the components into an acceptable doctoral program would be quite difficult as institutions of higher education now operate, including intramural theoretical clashes. I will elaborate on this problem in the next section about issues that need to be addressed regarding the establishment of a professorial teaching team, but at the outset, I think it important to note the problematic nature of educating the assessor. Broadly, however, the assessor will need education in three areas—a content area, evaluative methods, and project management.

Education in a Content Area

Although education in a content area appears at first glance to be unproblematic, it does present challenges. For instance, in these days of specialization among professors, to what extent can a content area—history, for example—be adequately represented within a subspecialty—American history, for instance? Are the methodologies of one subspecialty applicable to the study required of another subspecialty? To what extent will biologists agree with and practice the methodologies of microbiologists? Will chemical engineers understand the issues that electrical engineers are required to explore? If the subspecialties that constitute a discipline are quite diverse, the assessor might be required to take representative courses in each subspecialty, becoming a jack-of-one-discipline, a master of no subspecialty. If this is the case, core courses in each subspecialty would be appropriate as the substance of training in a content area.

A general approach to education in a content area merits consideration because although the assessor's role requires content knowledge for intradisciplinary teamwork, the assessor is not the content specialist. The question, then, of how much does the assessor need to know about a discipline to function in the assessor role can be answered by recommending core courses in various subspecialties in the discipline. If, however, the assessor envisions working with, say, a group of professors dedicated to teaching African American history courses, then the content courses should be tailored for that purpose.

Expertise in Evaluative Methods

Central to the assessor's role is expertise in evaluative methods, but immediately a problem arises that can be illustrated by the current debates over portfolio assessment. As White (1994a) notes, psychometricians have little confidence that portfolios can be effective in assessing writing ability. In fact, even advocates of portfolio assessment question its ability to provide the kind of rigor required for the reliable and valid assessments that the psychometricians call for (Elbow, 1991; Hamp-Lyons & Condon, 1993; Herman, Gearhart, & Aschbacher, 1996; Myers, 1996; Nystrand, Cohen, & Dowling, 1993; Valencia, 1991). To complicate these issues, some have questioned standard definitions of reliability and validity, suggesting that assessment should not be abstracted from professional judgment (Camp, 1993; Huot, 1996; Tyler, 1983; Williamson, 1994). Thus, two views of assessment are at odds—the psychometric view, based on traditional beliefs about the nature of knowledge, learning, and a host of other issues, and the alternative assessment view, based on different, often opposite, beliefs about the nature of knowledge, learning, and so on (Anderson, 1998). The assessor, it seems to me, could quite easily jettison either quantitative or qualitative assessment methods, particularly what are called authentic assessments, because they do not fit a single theoretical paradigm. Yet, the assessor will need training in both types of methods to provide a range of data collection possibilities to the professorial teaching team. MacNealy (1999), for example, explains the various methodologies with which the assessor should be familiar. In addition, Terenzini (1986) calls for unobtrusive measure to assess educational outcomes.

The balance between employing quantitative and qualitative methods is extremely difficult to maintain because assessment experts generally identify with either one theoretical camp or the other. White (1994b), however, identifies four groups involved in debates about assessment—teachers; researchers and theorists; testing firms and government bodies; and students, minorities, and other marginalized groups—and confirms "the inevitable nature of the conflicts that often lie concealed beneath the surface of many debates on . . . assessment" (p. 24). The assessor cannot blithely deny the force of those conflicts, and in my view cannot afford to align with a particular theoretical position and deny the value of using assessment measures derived from theoretical positions compatible with an opposing theoretical paradigm. The assessor should take White's (1994b) advice that negotiation and compromise are needed "among the interest groups involved" (p. 25). The assessor, then, will need not only training in a variety of data collection methods but also experience in using those methods, so part of the academic training in assessment should include an internship.

Training in Project Management

Academic training in a content area and assessment methods must be coupled with training in project management. Such training would include courses in personnel management, management theory, group dynamics, group psychology, interpersonal relationships, and so forth. The purposes for these courses are twofold. First, the assessor (indeed, all team members) needs to know how to function in a group and how to manage particular aspects of the group's work. Second, the assessor needs to know how classroom groups function to be able to provide insight about how to assess group functions, individual learning within groups, and professor-student interactions as they relate to learning, and so forth.

What Issues Must Be Addressed?

In the last section, I introduced some problems associated with educating the assessor. In this section, I address those problems and others.

First, the education outlined above, particularly in regard to what constitutes an acceptable curriculum for the assessor, raise issues about flexibility. For instance, the assessor may be limiting future career opportunities in a discipline by tailoring a discipline's curriculum to his or her plans to function as an assessor. Should he or she decide either during graduate education or after that the assessor role is not quite what it had seemed to be, piloting a different career course may be quite difficult. Should a graduate student be asked to make a commitment to the assessor role to the extent that tailored course work could severely limit future employment opportunities, particularly in an academic discipline?

Second, education in a content area, though ostensibly relatively easy to address, presents another difficulty. The professorial teaching team presupposes an interactive, constructivist methodology not only in interpersonal team relationships but also in the team's interactions with students. Yet, the typical model for instruction appears to be teacher centered, with the exercise of teacher authority constraining possibilities in the classroom. (For instance, student-prepared and administered tests raise questions about assessment that can send chills down the spine of a teacher married to the traditional model of teacher authority.) To what extent, then, can the assessor's education to be a member of a team be undercut by the traditional model of teaching? Can we expect an assessor raised on the traditional model to be equipped to operate in a team environment informed by a nontraditional, constructivist model?

Third, points one and two raise questions about the entire graduate education process. Will the present system of graduate education, which is focused on disciplinary concerns (read content) often to the exclusion of teaching concerns (read pedagogy), be able to produce the members of the professorial teaching team, including the assessor? There are signs that instruction in pedagogy is increasingly a concern in graduate education (Druger, 1997; Ryan, 1990; Travers, 1989; Tremmel, 1994), and the structure of higher education is based on disciplines, so the intradisciplinary team can be attractive; but the overwhelming energy devoted to building disciplinary knowledge remains an obstacle to promoting the professorial teaching team, which focuses on evaluating teaching and learning. In addition, how will potential assessors be selected? What measurement can be employed to help graduate students determine whether they might find satisfaction as an assessor?

Fourth, the problem of publication credit enters here. Generally, publications that smack of pedagogy are given short shrift in disciplines. Indeed, coauthorship in many disciplines is suspect (Calderonello, Nelson, & Simmons, 1991; Ervin & Fox, 1994; Lundgren, 1995; McNenny & Roen, 1992). Yet, I have suggested that the entire professorial teaching team should be involved in preparing written information to disseminate the team's findings. I therefore endorse team publications, recognizing that teams probably will find it extremely difficult, if not impossible, to make percentage distinctions about who did what. However, team publications represent a major obstacle in many disciplines, especially when the team members are asked to provide percentages on an annual evaluation for their efforts or when they are asked to detail individual efforts for tenure and promotion. Team publication, by the way, does not militate against individual or subgroup publications by team members.

The assessor, for instance, could help a particular team member determine how to study that individual's role in the team without being a coauthor of any publications that would issue from that team member's study.

Fifth, and following closely on the heels of number four, what is the reward structure for team efforts? Certainly, industry practices can provide models regarding team reward structure; the problem, however, is not simply models but resources. Can institutions of higher education provide the resources not only to implement a professorial teaching team approach (with some members of the team seemingly being paid not to teach, as some would perceive certain team roles) but also to reward successful teams? And what will be the measure of success? The data that the teams produce? The number of publications that the team authors? Some external evaluation by a super assessor? As higher education now functions, number of publications seems to be a standard measurement, refined by types of publications and publisher prestige. If that standard persists, how will teams survive when their goal is to explore questions related to teaching and learning, questions that may not be high on a discipline's list of concerns and may not be valued at all?

Sixth, I noted earlier that the data that teams collect and analyze are designed, in part, to inform team members about their success in meeting teaching and learning goals. Will that data be available to administrators for their evaluative purposes? If so, the possibility of overstating the positive impact of teaching is possible, thus polluting the body of research a team produces and further polluting the bodies of research other teams produce. In addition, the use of team data for administrative evaluation raises issues about consequences for incompetence. Surely, no one believes that all the professorial teaching teams would be composed of thoroughly competent professionals. What then can be done to help team members who need to develop certain competencies and after having been given every opportunity to do so, do not, for whatever reason? Indeed, what provisions are made to ensure that teams keep intact, a goal contrary, in some ways, to the goal of rigorous and equitable evaluation of the team? The nurturing of long-term teams is vital if one of the purposes of such teams is to develop longitudinal research designs.

Seventh, who will hire the assessor and the other team members? What criteria will a hiring committee use to solicit applications and to sort and evaluate candidates? What resources will institutions of higher education offer to candidates? A suite of offices for the team? Joint travel money? One, two, or three large classes per semester to support the entire team? In other words, should the academy produce an assessor and the other team members? What institution would hire the team and under what conditions of employment?

These seven issues do not exhaust the questions that would have to be addressed to train and implement professorial teaching teams, but anyone who believes in the need for and viability of the professorial teaching team, as I do, must begin to address such questions. Not to address such questions is to provide a model of teaching and learning without the hope of implementation. By raising tough issues, we can begin to consider ways to transform the academy, so that the mission of teaching, learning, and disseminating information about teaching and learning are put at the top of the academic agenda.

Conclusion

The job I have outlined is, of course, not a reality at present, but that does not mean such a job is unattainable. Indeed, the components for training assessors are part and parcel of higher education. The problem of training assessors, therefore, is not the most difficult part of realizing what is now a hypothetical position. The most difficult part of realizing such a position is a pervasive faculty attitude that the classroom constitutes a kingdom fit for a monarch who does not need a cabinet to help rule effectively. The increasing complexity of the professor's job militates against such a view of the classroom and in fact calls for a distribution of professorial classroom demands among a team of experts who work in concert to achieve a classroom that focuses on student learning, not on professorial autonomy. The assessor's job fits nicely in that team model.

References

Anderson, R. S. (1998). Why talk about different ways to grade? The shift from traditional assessment to alternative assessment. In R. S.

Anderson & B. W. Speck (Eds.), *Changing the way we grade student performance: Classroom assessment and the new learning paradigm* (pp. 5–16). San Francisco: Jossey-Bass.

Anderson, R. S., & Speck, B. W. (1998). Oh what a difference a team makes: Why team teaching makes a difference. *Teaching and Teacher Education, 14*(7), 671–686.

Angelo, T. A., & Cross, K. P. (1993). *Classroom assessment techniques: A handbook for college teachers* (2nd ed.). San Francisco: Jossey-Bass.

Astin, A. W. (1990). Educational assessment and educational equity. *American Journal of Education, 98*(4), 458–478.

Boyer, E. L. (1990). *Scholarship reconsidered: Priorities of the Professoriate.* Princeton, NJ: Carnegie Foundation for the Advancement of Teaching.

Calderonello, A. H., Nelson, D. B., & Simmons, S. C. (1991). An interview with Andrea Lunsford and Lisa Ede: Collaboration as a subversive activity. *Writing on the Edge, 2*(2), 7–18.

Camp, R. (1993). Changing the model for the direct assessment of writing. In M. M. Williamson & B. Huot (Eds.), *Validating holistic scoring for writing assessment: Theoretical and empirical foundations* (pp. 45–78). Creskill, NJ: Hampton.

Charnley, M. V. (1978). Grading standards vary considerably, experiment shows. *Journalism Educator, 33*(3), 49–50.

Druger, M. (1997). Preparing the next generation of college science teachers. *Journal of College Science Teaching, 26*(6), 424–427.

Dulek, R., & Shelby, A. (1981). Varying evaluative criteria: A factor in differential grading. *The Journal of Business Communication, 18*(2), 41–50.

Edwards, D. (1982). Project marking: Some problems and issues. *Teaching at a Distance, 21,* 28–35.

Elbow, P. (1991). Foreword. In P. Belanoff & M. Dickson (Eds.), *Portfolios: Process and product* (pp. ix–xvi). Portsmouth, NH: Boynton/Cook.

Ervin, E., & Fox, D. L. (1994). Collaboration as political action. *Journal of Advanced Composition, 14*(1), 53–71.

Gardner, D. E. (1977). Five evaluative frameworks: Implications for decision making in higher education. *Journal of Higher Education, 48,* 571–593.

Garrison, D. A. (1979). Measuring differences in the assigning of grades. *Improving College and University Teaching, 27*(2), 68–71.

Hamp-Lyons, L., & Condon, W. (1993). Questioning assumptions about portfolios-based assessment. *College Composition and Communication, 44*(2), 176–190.

Herman, J. L., Gearhart, M., & Aschbacher, P. R. (1996). Portfolios for classroom assessment: Design and implementation issues. In R.

Calfee & P. Perfumo (Eds.), *Writing portfolios in the classroom: Policy and practice, promise and peril* (pp. 27–59). Hillsdale, NJ: Erlbaum.

Huot, B. (1996). Toward a new theory of writing assessment. *College Composition and Communication, 47*(4), 549–566.

Krahenbuhl, G. S. (1998). Faculty work: Integrating responsibilities and institutional needs. *Change, 30*(6), 18–25.

Lundgren, C. A. (1995). Perceptions and evaluation of single and co-authored publications. *Delta Pi Epsilon Journal, 37*(2), 85–94.

MacNealy, M. S. (1999). *Strategies for empirical research in writing.* Needham Heights, MA: Allyn & Bacon.

Marsh, H. W., & Ware, J. E., Jr. (1982). Effects of expressiveness, content coverage, and incentive on multidimensional student rating scales: New interpretations of the Dr. Fox effect. *Journal of Educational Psychology, 74*(1), 126–134.

McNenny, G., & Roen, D. H. (1992). The case for collaborative scholarship in rhetoric and composition journals. *Rhetoric Review, 10*(2), 291–310.

Myers, M. (1996). Sailing ships: A framework for portfolios in formative and summative systems. In R. Calfee & P. Perfumo (Eds.), *Writing portfolios in the classroom: Policy and practice, promise and peril* (pp. 149–178). Hillsdale, NJ: Erlbaum.

Naftulin, D. H., Ware, J. E., & Donnelly, F. A. (1973). The Dr. Fox lecture: A paradigm of educational seduction. *Journal of Medical Education, 48*, 630–635.

Nystrand, M., Cohen, A. S., & Dowling, N. M. (1993). Addressing reliability problems in the portfolio assessment of college writing. *Educational Assessment, 1*(1), 53–70.

Ober, S. (1984). The influence of selected variables on the grading of student-written letters. *The American Business Communication Association Bulletin, 47*(1), 7–11.

Pascarella, E. T., & Terenzini, P. T. (1998). Studying college students in the 21st century: Meeting new challenges. *The Review of Higher Education, 21*(2), 151–165.

Pascarella, E. T., Whitt, E. J., & Nora, A. (1996). What have we learned from the first year of the National Study of Student Learning? *Journal of College Student Development, 37*(2), 182–192.

Paulsen, M. B., & Feldman, K. A. (1995). Toward a reconceptualization of scholarship: A human action system with functional imperatives. *Journal of Higher Education, 66*(6), 615–640.

Purves, A. C., Gorman, T. P., & Takala, S. (1988). The development of the scoring scheme and scales. In T. P. Gorman, A. C. Purves, & R. E. Degenhart (Eds.), *The IEA study of written composition I: The international writing tasks and scoring scales* (pp. 41–58). New York: Pergamon Press.

Purves, A. C., & Hawisher, G. (1990). Writers, judges, and text models. In R. Beach and S. Hynds (eds.), *Developing discourse practices in adolescence and adulthood* (pp. 183–199). Norwood, NJ: Ablex.

Quellmalz, E. S., Capell, F. J., and Chou, C. (1982). Effects of discourse and response mode on the measurement of writing competence. *Journal of Educational Measurement, 19*(4), 241–258.

Rachal, J. R. (1984). Community college and university instructor consistency in the evaluation of freshman English themes. *Community/Junior College Quarterly, 8*(1–4), 127–140.

Raymond, J. C. (1982). What we don't know about the evaluation of writing. *College Composition and Communication, 33*(4), 399–403.

Ryan, M. P. (1990). Starting with the teaching assistant: Training the professor of the 1990s. *Political Science Teacher, 3*(3), 1–3.

Sloan, G. (1975). The perils of poetry evaluation. *College English, 37*(4), 371–378.

Sneed, D. (1986). Writing teachers should be prepared for legal challenges. *The Journalism Educator, 41*(3), 26–28.

Soder, R. (Ed.). (1996). *Democracy, education, and the schools.* San Francisco: Jossey-Bass.

Speck, B. W. (1998a). *Grading student writing: An annotated bibliography.* Westport, CT: Greenwood Press.

Speck, B. W. (1998b). Unveiling some of the mystery of professional judgment in classroom assessment. In R. S. Anderson & B. W. Speck (Eds.), *Changing the way we grade student performance: Classroom assessment and the new learning paradigm* (pp. 17–31). San Francisco: Jossey-Bass.

Speck, B. W., & Jones, T. (1998). Direction in the grading of writing? What the literature on the grading of writing does and doesn't tell us. In F. Zak & C. C. Weaver (Eds.), *The theory and practice of grading writing: Problems and possibilities* (pp. 17–29). New York: State University of New York Press.

Terenzini, P. T. (1986). The case for unobtrusive measures. Paper presented at the 47th Education and Testing Service Invitational Conference, New York, October 25, 1986.

Terenzini, P. T. (1989). Assessment with open eyes: Pitfalls in studying student outcomes. *Journal of Higher Education, 60*(6), 644–664.

Terenzini, P. T. (1994). Educating for citizenship: Freeing the mind and elevating the spirit. *Innovative Higher Education, 19*(1), 7–21.

Terenzini, P. T., Springer, L., Pascarella, E. T., & Nora, A. (1995). Influences affecting the development of students' critical thinking skills. *Research in Higher Education, 36*(1), 23–39.

Travers, P. D. (1989). Better training for teaching assistants. *College Teaching, 37*(4), 147–149.

Tremmel, R. (1994). Beyond self-criticism: Reflecting on teacher research and teaching assistant education. *Composition Studies, 22*(1), 44–64.

Tyler, R. W. (1983). Testing writing: Procedures vary with purposes. In R. W. Bailey & R. M. Forsheim (Eds.), *Literacy for life: The demand for reading and writing* (pp. 197–206). New York: Modern Language Association.

Valencia, S. W. (1991). Portfolios: Panacea or Pandora's box? In F. L. Finch (Ed.), *Educational performance assessment* (pp. 33–46). Chicago: Riverside.

White, E. M. (1985). *Teaching and assessing writing.* San Francisco: Jossey-Bass.

White, E. M. (1994a). Portfolios as an assessment concept. In L. Black, D. A. Daiker, J. Sommers, & G. Stygall (Eds.), *New directions in portfolio assessment: Reflective practice, critical theory, and large-scale scoring* (pp. 25–39). Portsmouth, NH: Boynton/Cook.

White, E. M. (1994b). Issues and problems in writing assessment. *Assessing Writing, 1*(1), 11–27.

Wilkinson, D. C. (1979). Evidence that others do not agree with your grading of letters. *The American Business Communication Association Bulletin, 42*(3), 29–30.

Williamson, M. (1994). The worship of efficiency: Untangling theoretical and practical considerations in writing assessment. *Assessing Writing, 1*(2), 147–173.

Part Four

The Present and Future Organization of Teaching

Integrating Autonomous Professionals Through Team Teaching

James L. Bess

The previous chapters have depicted the tasks that would be performed by different kinds of faculty in a newly conceived, reconstituted role structure that relies on teams rather than on individuals to carry out the full range of teaching activities in a college or university. They have also identified prototypical faculty talents and personality characteristics that might predispose individuals to perform the tasks well and to find satisfactions in the performance. It remains now to take up the issues of task and interpersonal linkages through teamwork and team management that are necessary when collaboration, cooperation, sharing, and collegiality are requisite conditions for effective outcomes. This chapter relies heavily on the extensive literature on this subject that has arisen in the profit-making sector, frequently related to the organization of professionals who work in teams—for example, physicians in hospitals. There is good reason to believe that the team-based relationships among workers in academia—faculty members—will closely resemble those elsewhere. Hence, this literature is enormously valuable.

The chapter begins with a brief history of "organizations" in Western society, particularly as work roles have become more complex and knowledge based. The chapter continues with discussions of how teams in general are organized, how they operate, and how they are led. The following section addresses the question of teaching teams in particular and the group processes that might characterize the teams that are envisioned in this book. For example, the discussion considers how the special needs of faculty for autonomy and for evaluation of individual merit can be reconciled in a group setting. Because there are no extant examples of such teams in current use, this dialogue of necessity will be somewhat speculative, but also, it is hoped, provocative and informative. The next sections are concerned with an examination of the ways in which teaching teams and teaching goals are related and with the problems of matching this new form of professional activity via team structures to a supportive external academic profession, and to the question of what would constitute a faculty career under this new configuration. The final portion of the chapter takes up the question of change—the problems of moving from the present, long-standing mode of individually based organization design and evaluation of teaching to the team-based model described in this book.

The Rise of Teamwork

Prior to the industrial revolution in the last half of the nineteenth century in this country, the primary agents for the production of goods and services were large numbers of independent producers in agricultural settings and small industrial producers, craftspersons, and shopkeepers. With the advent of the revolution, much of the economy gradually moved into large-scale production modes most closely identified with assembly line operations, where the jobs of the now more highly specialized workers could be timed and programmed—sometimes in the extreme by "scientific management" techniques. Today, a century or more later, however, with the invention of increasingly sophisticated technologies, and especially as machines have increasingly been designed to do the more automatic, routine work, we have moved into a postindustrial (Bell, 1976), or postcapitalist (Drucker, 1993), society, which has created a bifurcation of the labor force. One segment is engaged primarily in repetitive, unchallenging, unskilled service sector jobs. Another is found in more complicated, multistaged work that has increasingly required discretionary decision making at lower organizational levels, where rapidly evolving technical expertise can be put to work in handling novel challenges emanating from a dynamic external environment. New technologies have shortened the time frame in which decisions must be made and have increased the amount of knowledge expected to be utilized for good decision making. Changing market forces also have compelled "learning" organizations to include many more persons in all phases of the production of a good or service (occasionally including customers and clients) in order to gather information to keep pace with competition (Edmondson & Moingeon, 1998).

Accompanying the growth in the latter labor segment has been an increase in the number of workers who are professionals or semi-professionals. More recently, there has been a change in the employment structure for both of these groups via a gradual reduction in the use of "autonomous" professionals and semiprofessionals and an increase in the use of "work teams" as the basic unit of work organizations (Blankenship, 1977; Hackman, 1990; Worchel, Wood, & Simpson, 1992).

Finally, values in today's egalitarian, democratic society seem to be calling for flatter, more participative organizational structures that recognize the importance to organizational effectiveness of input from many individuals and the value of that input as well to the sustained motivation of the worker. While in large-scale manufacturing plants "job enrichment" policies have been adopted that load single jobs with quondam responsibilities of persons above, adjacent to, and below the incumbents, in more technologically advanced industries, the opposite has taken place, as complicated individual work roles have been "unpacked" and distributed to teams (Ketchum & Trist, 1992).

These social and technological changes have forced a recognition that complex critical production decisions require input from many sources and cannot be made effectively in isolation (Sundstrom, De Meuse, & Futrell, 1995; Tornatzky, 1986; Peters, 1988). Indeed, the emergence of a "multiprofessional environment" (Abbott, 1988, p. 151) in which such decisions are made has brought about new conflicts among professionals rather than (or in addition to) the older conflicts between professionals and administrators (Bucher & Stelling, 1969). In sum, the idea of collective work and decision making in team formats has become much more salient and respectable (Senge, 1990; Osterman, 1994; Towers Perrin, 1990; Kirkman & Rosen, 1997).

In spite of these overall trends in occupations and work in society as a whole, there are countermovements that impede the institutionalization of forms of work and employment that recognize and capitalize on shifts in technology, improved education and skills, and faster communication. For example, as many have observed (see the Preface), institutions of higher education have come under fierce fire from unfriendly and unappreciative publics in recent years, who call on them to become more efficient and effective to justify the social investment in them. Trustees and administrators have found the power (for reasons whose explanations exceed the scope of this book) to make colleges and universities more and more hierarchical in authority structure, rather than flatter and more participative, and more punitively evaluative in culture. Faculty seem to have lost their will and voice as well as their authority, as decisions formerly in their control have moved into and up the administrative hierarchy.

In this book, an alternative decision-making structure (at least for teaching) is described—one that recognizes both the trend and the need for collective decision making and more properly recognizes the necessity that decision making about academic professional matters, especially teaching, be vested close to the sources of expertise; that is, in the hands of faculty. For this book, the decision-making and performing collectivity that can best represent the faculty with respect to teaching is the "team." The members of the team are those role incumbents described in the preceding chapters.

The Organization of Teams

Work that requires collective decision making can be organized in many ways. For example, there are differences among work teams, work groups, and task forces (Hackman, 1990). The first, the work team, by virtue of the collaboration among members, produces a product that is—or can be—more than the sum of the individual efforts. The second, the work group, comprises a number of individuals whose primary reason for interaction is to share information and jointly decide how each member can do his or her job better. Finally, the task force has a more short-run, limited time frame and objectives. Task forces, "by definition, start out not knowing exactly what they eventually will come up with" (Gersick & Davis-Sacks, 1990, p. 146). In this book, the focus is on work teams.

There are three major categories of teams commonly found in organizations—*problem-solving teams, self-managed work teams,* and *cross-functional teams* (Robbins, 1998). As Richard Guzzo (1996) notes, collaborating workers in teams usually manifest a combination of attributes that integrate them internally and relate them functionally to the larger organization. He says of work teams:

- They are social entities embedded in large social systems (i.e., organizations).

- They perform one or more tasks relevant to their organization's mission.

- Their task performance has consequences that affect others inside or outside the organization. They are made up of individuals whose work roles require them to be, to some appreciable degree, interdependent.

- They have membership that is identifiable not only to those in the group but also to those outside it [p. 8; see also Sundstrom, De Meuse, & Futrell, 1995].

These groups vary in the nature of their outputs and in the degree of their internal and external differentiation and work cycle-life spans. For example, some of these groups have quite diversely talented members who work without time pressure from the outside for short periods, after which they disband. Others are aggregations of similarly skilled workers who are under constraints from outside to meet production quotas, who stay together indefinitely, and who work in time frames that extend for long periods.

There is now some research evidence about the requisite characteristics of effective teams (Hackman, 1990; Dooley & Fryxell, 1999). For example, effective teams have a large role in selecting their members (Smith, 1981), stay together longer, and become more internally differentiated (Heinen & Jacobson, 1976), though at some point, because fresh blood is needed, there is a decline in commitment and productivity (Shonk & Shonk, 1988). They also have clear purposes, are less formal, and share their leadership (Parker, 1990). Effective teams usually experience extended periods of stability, punctuated by short, sometimes radical, changes (Gersick, 1988).

Teams in organizations vary in the degree to which they have control over their activities, ranging from close supervision through hierarchical methods to loosely monitored, self-directed bodies. These latter "self-managing teams" have characteristics that distinguish them from groups in general or teams in general. It is these kinds of teams that most closely resemble the teams of teachers proposed in this book. Hitchcock and Willard describe the following characteristics of self-managed teams:

1. They "include natural work group[s], meaning that team members work together full time."
2. They "include interdependent employees—those employees who must work together to complete a whole process, product, or project or to serve a set of customers."
3. The "employees share the responsibility of managing themselves."
4. The "team assumes most, if not all, the responsibilities of a traditional supervisor. That implies a spectrum of self-direction, from a little self-directed to a lot. Practically all self-directed teams assign their own work, assess their work, coordinate vacation schedules, solve technical problems and lead team meetings."
5. "Many self-directed team members are cross-trained in one another's work so that they can rotate positions or fill in during vacations and bottlenecks" [Hitchcock & Willard, 1995; see also, Mintzberg, 1983; Yeatts & Hyten, 1998].

Many observers anticipate that self-managing teams will become more and more prominent in the corporate sector in the years to come, primarily because the democratic ethos of participation is gaining force. This is because experience with group work has been shown to have positive outcomes (though see Cohen & Spreitzer, 1994; Cohen, Ledford, & Spreitzer, 1996; and Wall, Kemp, Jackson, & Clegg, 1986) and because new technology makes integration among team members more readily available (Goodman, Devadas, & Hughson, 1990). This book examines the impact of these trends in the society and workforce, especially the increasing use of teams, on the transformation of the work of teaching in colleges and universities, which, as noted earlier, seems to be moving in an opposite direction.

The New Teaching Team

A team of faculty teachers is significantly different from a football team, a basketball team (not all sports teams are alike), a surgical team, a research team, a symphony orchestra, and a road gang. Faculty in a reasonably homogeneous subject matter department, each of whom independently teaches one or two courses, often do not constitute a "team" in the conceptualization for this book, primarily because they do not collaborate, except intermittently to plan curricula or establish evaluation and credentialing criteria. Rather, the team of teachers envisioned here comprises the "experts" identified in each of the preceding chapters. The professionals in this group are continually "engaged" with one another, with their institutions, and with their clients both individually and collectively. They constitute a mini-learning community, in that they learn from outside the boundaries of their group and bring that knowledge into the group, they learn from one another, and they learn from the students they teach (Starbuck, 1996; Leithwood, 1998). As Edmondson (1999) describes group learning: "I conceptualize learning at the group level of analysis as an ongoing process of reflection and action, characterized by asking questions, seeking feedback, experimenting, reflecting on results, and discussing errors or unexpected outcomes of actions. For a team to discover gaps in its plans and make changes accordingly, team members must test assumptions and discuss differences of opinion openly rather than privately or outside of the group" (p. 353).

There are important "structural" features that are critical in the design of effective work systems. First of all, the *task* itself is the critical integrator between the social system of the group and the technical system required to produce the product, as well as between the individual and the organization (Ulich & Weber, 1996). This means that tasks both guide the design of the structure for individual productivity and generate the required and emergent activities, interactions, and sentiments (Homans, 1950).

Teams, as the primary unit for teaching in higher education, fit this description. Ulich and Weber, for example, note:

> Primary work systems consist of a social subsystem and a technical subsystem. The social subsystem is made up of "the members of the organization, with their individual and group-specific physical and psychological needs—especially the demands which they place on their work—and their knowledge and capabilities" (Alioth, 1980, p. 26). The technical subsystem consists in "the means of production, the installations and their layout, and in general terms, the technological and spatial working conditions which place demands upon the social system" (loc. cit.). The social and technical subsystems are joined in two ways by the occupational roles of the employees: first, the occupational roles establish the functions which the employees must fulfill in the production process; second, they define the necessary cooperative relationships among the employees [p. 248].

Of relevance to the concept of team teaching is the movement from the currently typical *autonomous* faculty member with a full range of varied activities to a "connected" faculty member with a more circumscribed range of tasks rendered both more complex because of the depth with which the tasks are considered and more explicitly interdependent because of their narrower range. Ulrich and Weber note further that "awareness of a common task and common task orientation substantially determines the intensity and duration of group cohesion. Work groups whose cohesion is based mainly on socio-emotional relationships are therefore less stable than groups which are characterized by common task orientation" (1996, p. 253; see also Edmondson, 1999).

These notions are important not only to the effectiveness of the group but also to the motivation and satisfaction of the individual faculty member. The necessity to substitute group effectiveness in teaching for individual effectiveness (more correctly to complement individual effectiveness) requires that the group have total control over the resources needed to reach the goals (Brodbeck, 1996), just as the individual faculty member has academic freedom (within limits) to design his or her teaching and research. "Self-" management, therefore, to some extent includes *group* as self (as, perhaps, in some Asian countries—see Bess, 1995).

This important transformation of identity is critical to the development and maintenance of motivation and commitment. *Social Identity Theory* (SIT) suggests that individuals who identify with a group tend to experience the group's success and failures as their own (Tajfel & Turner, 1979; Ashforth & Mael, 1989; see also Brief & Aldag, 1981; Ajzen, 1988). "Social *identification,* therefore, is the perception of oneness with or belongingness to some human aggregate." The development of teams and the identification with the goals and values of the team, however, does not inevitably mean the loss of the individual professional autonomy that attracted many to the profession and that is cherished as a major source of satisfaction (Giddens, 1991). In Talcott Parsons's somewhat convoluted but nonetheless valid conception of the relational aspects of worker roles and role orientations: "The key concept is that of the 'division of labor' as developed by Adam Smith and his successors in utilitarian, especially economic theory. The starting point is the conception of a given actor, ego, as instrumentally oriented to the attainment of a goal, a goal which may be of any desired degree of specificity or generality. The relational problems enter in when alter becomes significant not only passively as a means or condition of the attainment of ego's goal, but his *re*actions become a constitutive part of the system which includes ego's own goal-striving" (1951, p. 70).

Therefore, a faculty member in this conceptualization would be both a member of the team who expects satisfaction from it and a contributor to the team effort that ultimately affects his and others' satisfaction. As Yeatts and Hyten (1998) note: "The high-performing teams we studied typically made it a habit to recognize individual as well as team performance" (p. 158).

Group Processes in Team Teaching

Teaching team members must obviously be intimately connected with one another as their tasks are crucially interdependent. As noted in Chapter One, members' skills and temperaments not only must suit their tasks but also must be mutually compatible and complementary (Hinings & Greenwood, 1996). In solving problems in teaching, the team must address four critical inevitable challenges—exchanging relevant information, learning as individuals and learning as a group (see discussion below on single-, double-, and triple-loop learning), sustaining high levels of motivation, and negotiating differences.

Central to the management of these challenges is the degree of success in goal setting for the group. For the group to be successful, there must be a clear common goal or goals. Without such, the interdependent tasks will not be efficiently linked, nor will achievement of group goals be satisfactory to those for whom the goal or goals are either unreasonable or only partially acceptable.

In the *constructivist* (von Glasersfeld, 1996) and *collaborative action research* (Oja & Smulyan, 1989) models for teaching envisioned in this book, each of the seven team members must engage independently in tasks that contribute to the achievement of the goals of the team. Thus, each has one or more particular operational educational objectives that must be integrated into the overall team goal. The results of each of the tasks that faculty perform may or may not be immediately relevant to other team members. But each member must build a composite picture of his or her role and role performance that can be shared with other team members. For example, it is not necessary for the researcher to describe the particulars of the research tasks required to develop the subject matter for the course, but it is important that the synthesis of that effort be made available in a meaningful way to other team members. Each team member must, in other words, be a "teacher" of his or her peers. This process of "peer teaching" is itself a skill and an art. (Indeed, cross-*team* teaching addressed to overall institutional goals will be important to the development and maintenance of the integrity of the curriculum. Teams cannot operate in isolation, any more than individual faculty can.)

Besides sharing with others the products of individual enterprise, the team as a whole must develop a protocol for planning and executing the teaching. This requires some sequencing decisions— namely, which tasks must be started earlier than others, when particular group members need to relate their separate results, and when the whole team must be involved in discussions about next steps. Tschan and von Cranach (1986) describe this process as arranging tasks in terms of their hierarchical organization, their sequential requirements, and their cyclical regulation processes. Tasks, they say, must be ordered in terms of goals and subgoals that must be accomplished for the main goal to be achieved. They must then be sequenced so that when integrated there are none left incomplete. Finally, the entire sequence must be reviewed and revised with some regular periodicity. (One commonly used long-standing procedure for accomplishing this is PERT, or *program evaluation and review technique* [Russell & Taylor, 1998; see also Miller, Galanter, & Pribam, 1960].)

The sequencing is not necessarily fixed, however. As Bales (1950) and Bales and Strodtbeck (1951) discovered in their research on phases of group processes, there was more exploration or orientation at the beginning of the group, more evaluation in the middle, and more control in the third phase. So, teams will adopt different functioning modes as they gain experience in delivering their products and services. The assessor team member in our model will be able skillfully to monitor evolution.

For the team model described in this volume, the patterns of communication are primarily sequential, though not necessarily one way (Hirakawa, 1990). For example, although the research and pedagogy team members clearly must complete their tasks before the lecturer or discussion leader members can begin theirs, the process is not one of simply passing on completed individual member projects from the earlier to the later. There must be continual or at least frequent exchange of information in all directions about what students need and about the desired impact of the entire team's effort. Modern corporate management is now realizing that the separation of early-stage R&D personnel and market analysts from line operators has produced less-than-successful products at higher cost. Indeed, "partnering" with external stakeholders is being recognized as a significant source of innovation and higher efficiency (Harrison & St. John, 1996). Teaching teams, in other words, are not situated in some idyllic, resource-rich, constraint-free educational environment. The goals of the team must be meshed with the general education and specialization goals and with the culture of the institution and school. Further, the interface between one teaching team and another must be frequently adjudicated, particularly because small groups tend to engender group rather than organizational identification and suboptimization of goals at the group level. The goals of a team in biology, for example, and of another in English may be quite different (as they probably are between individual faculty members in these disciplines).

But the problem of communication itself is a substantial one. As Tschan and von Cranach (1986) note: "Highly skilled performance, even in originally very complex tasks, often is characterized by a declining ability to verbalize one's own action regulation processes. Indeed, highly skilled experts tend to resort to 'intuitive' strategies which they describe in words like 'playing it by ear,' 'having a feeling for it,' etc." (p. 104).

Because of the need for orchestrating the tasks of seven independent faculty members, there will, invariably, be some degree of restriction of freedom. Whereas in the present system of individual autonomy, faculty members can make their own decisions about priorities of preparation for courses and classes (some a year before, some the night before), in the case of team teaching, some concession to group timetables must be made. As noted earlier, of all the issues confronting team teaching, this may be the most difficult to overcome. Becoming a team player requires a more mature individual who believes that profound human satisfactions can be derived from at least partial identification with joint achievements and the expansion of ego to include others. American higher education, however, mirroring the society at large, is built on the principle of *individual* merit, effort, and attainment, recognized and rewarded by peers and organization. Whether group achievements and compensation by groups can be substituted for this will require more careful recruitment, selection, and socialization of different kinds of faculty members, who can thrive under these new academic cultural conditions.

Academic administration can facilitate this redirected ego identification. For example, there is some evidence that when highly collaborative teams are paid as a team, rather than individually, they come to feel that the team is both more potent and more effective (Shea & Guzzo, 1987). Ruth Wageman (1995) has found that some "hybrid" form of individual and group reward system works best.

The effectiveness of team member decisions depends importantly on the characteristics of the project goals and associated tasks. According to van Offenbeek and Koopman (1996), there are five kinds of risks that arise in certain teams—functional uncertainty, conflict potential, technical uncertainty, resistance potential, and material resources. In turn, these risks can be traced to contingencies in the context in which the work group functions.

Functional uncertainty is the risk that the project team's solution is incorrect or that the team selected the wrong problem to solve. It arises because of the complexity, continuity, and familiarity of tasks. Although in teaching, there is some continuity across successive cohorts of students, each class constitutes (or should constitute) a unique set of idiosyncratic individuals and a unique group social structure. An example of this risk for the work of a teaching team is the development of a strong mentoring component for a course in which students need neither strong cognitive nor affective assistance. Although an individual instructor is susceptible to the trap of functional uncertainty, it is less likely to occur in a teaching team, particularly one in which one or more of the team members is exceptionally well qualified to attend these risks. In the model for this book, the pedagogical expert and the assessment expert would be sensitive to this risk.

The risk of *conflict potential* in a teaching team stems from the heterogeneity of the faculty involved and the degree of their dependence on one another. By design, each member of the team is different from the others and brings personal epistemological, axiological, and ontological biases to the joint tasks at hand. Although teams will be formed partially on the basis of interpersonal compatibility, there is still some latent possibility for both cognitive and affective conflict. On the other hand, the interdependence of the members of the proposed teaching team is "pooled" (Thompson, 1967). This means that each member individually provides a unique function that contributes to the final product. Hence, if there is mutual confidence in the skills and abilities among team members and a shared commitment to a common goal, there should be relatively little territorial infringement and jealousy over improperly allocated formal or informal rewards (Yeatts & Hyten, 1998). Where work-related conflict arises, it can be and often is functional (Amason, 1996).

The third risk, *technical uncertainty,* can be traced to the complexity or newness of the technology. New teams of faculty may rely on traditional teaching methods, but it is likely that they will stretch for innovative approaches that reflect their collective wisdom and strong identification with the goals of the team. Overreaching the technological limits is a real risk. One can imagine a new team, for example, creating electronic communication links among student members of the class that go beyond their technological sophistication.

The fourth risk, *resistance potential*, comes from the heavy baggage of traditional teaching methods that each team member will bring. Though the team will want to be innovative, the usual socialization of individual faculty to strive for individual achievement and to expect individual rewards will induce some to focus on their past knowledge and skills, even at the expense of innovation on behalf of the group goal. Learning new skills means risking potential failure and the status change that may accompany the emergence of new roles and role relationships (Giacquinta, 1975). Faculty who have built strong egos on the basis of individual accomplishments may resist exposing their ignorance and ineptness in a new venture. It will surely take some time before an experimental culture with high tolerance for risk taking and occasional failure can be put in place in most institutions.

The last risk, *material resources*, has to do with budget and time contingencies. In these times of accelerated accountability, college and university administrations are looking for immediate results and are not (usually) willing to fund long-term experiments where the learning curve projections promise results in the distant future—especially if based on substantial investment. In contrast to the relative economic and budgetary powerlessness of individual faculty members under the present departmental organizational configurations, aggregates of faculty in teams may find new collective power potential for asserting themselves with respect to securing teaching resources.

Psychological Dimensions of Teaching Teams

The coalescing of individual faculty members, each with a strong ego and drive for achievement, requires some considerable personal effort on the part of each of the members. Teams do not begin in high gear, ready to engage with maximum efficiency in the tasks confronting them. Not only must they learn their tasks and the relationships between their tasks, but they must learn one another's work styles, interaction preferences, and personal idio-syncrasies. The evolution of an effective group follows rather unevenly the familiar "forming, storming, norming, and perform-ing" pattern (Tuckman, 1965; Tuckman & Jensen, 1977). The rea-son for the nonlinear character of the development is that the above-noted risks are accompanied by several streams of challenges to the group that do not necessarily appear in concert and are not (and cannot be) met simultaneously.

For example, as Bouwen and Fry (1996) note, there are three contextual contingencies that affect group development—group culture, goal achievement, and cross-boundary relationships. Key to group effectiveness are norms, cohesion, and roles. Norms pro-vide nonformal inducements and constraints on member behav-ior, the strength of each being dependent on the nature and amount of cohesion. When the cohesion is centered on work, rather than on social patterns and enjoyment, work and produc-tion norms will be strongly perceived and deviance from them severely dampened. Most groups, however, stay below the level of summed individual member productivity, let alone levels possible through synergy. Ivan Steiner (1972) calls this "process loss" or the extent to which the group is not actualizing the potential resources of the individual group members (p. 9).

The problems of mediating differences between organizational and/or group goals and individual objectives is one of the most difficult to be faced in any new configuration. Each individual and group of individuals may have divergent views from the collectiv-ity. The ever present social dilemma of attending to personal and career goals and objectives and acceding to or even attending to those of others in the group is omnipresent and must be adjudi-cated continually. Further, alignments with larger organizational structure and even with demands of those outside of the organi-zation (including family and friends) is a constant challenge.

The probability is that initially teaching teams that are self-man-aged will fit more readily into academic values and culture. The administrative side of colleges and universities, on the other hand, operates with a different set of values, norms, and expectations, which are enforced through the exercise of the common bureau-cratic hierarchical controls applied usually to each individual. A key to sustained motivation of team members, however, is the sense of control over the key ingredients in the work process (Mowday & Nam, 1997). This is not to imply that the teaching team envisioned in this book is entitled to unlimited resources and would not succeed without them. It does mean, however, that the resources allocated to the team cannot have short-term achievement strings attached to them. Further, there can be few specifications as to how resources, once allocated, are to be spent—for example, which modes of teaching are to be used. In fact, as Yeatts & Hyten (1998) note, team members are closer to the reality of performance and hence are better positioned to monitor one another. They say, "The advantage that teams have over management as the source of recognition is that they can provide recognition to themselves much faster than can upper levels of the organization. The team also has more intimate knowledge of the performance of individual team members than management, so team members are in a much better position to spot and recognize individual efforts and accomplishments, something that is risky for management to do" (p. 158).

There can (and must), of course, be assessments of the degree to which self-managed teams have accomplished their and their institution's goals. In a remodeled system of teaching such as the one proposed here, teams must still be held accountable. The pressures and constraints on team members from outside the team (memberships in other groups, formal and informal) must be reckoned with.

So also must the team recognize the inherent conflict that afflicts faculty who must newly work in teams rather than in their former independence. Faculty, especially those who have been socialized through the doctoral degree–granting process, are professionalized into thought and action modes of radical rationality in the Weberian tradition. And as Zaleznik remarks, supremely rational behavior reinforces feelings of independence rather than more vulnerability and recognition of interdependence. He notes: "To choose is to feel independent and capable of looking after self-interests in modern economic and social life, to weigh alternatives, and to compare costs and benefits. To choose rationally, the individual must learn to suppress impulse and emotion. Hence the cultivation of dispassion and the separation of thinking from feeling" (1989, p. 113).

Yet, frequent interactions in group settings evoke emotions in members that need to be openly expressed, so that the emotions do not impede the progress of the group toward the solution of group problems.

Thus, members of the team must not only have individual competencies in their areas of expertise, they must also possess *team-generic* and *team-specific* competencies. The former includes a set of ideologies and dispositions that *all* team members must possess just in order to participate in any team. These include "communication skills, interpersonal skills, leadership skills, and attitudes toward teamwork" (Austin & Baldwin, 1991, p. 53; see also Cannon-Bowers, Tannenbaum, Salas, & Volpe, 1995).

Team-specific competencies, on the other hand, are particularistic. They include knowledge of other members' likes and dislikes and modes of team cohesion. Cannon-Bowers et al. (1995) refer to this as shared "mental models." The point is that good team members must be "team players," to use the cliché. And they must be psychologically compatible with the very special nuances of the personalities of the other team members. They must learn to take the role of the "particular other," in the words of Harding and Hintikka (1983; see also Bensimon & Neumann, 1993).

The Definition of the Teaching Goal

Identifying the goals of teaching is often an elusive task. There are many different definitions, and reaching consensus constitutes a never ending, almost impossible objective on most college campuses. The usual approach is to "espouse" a very broad definition with which most or all faculty can live or to delineate somewhat narrower goals but not hold faculty accountable for them (Argyris & Schön, 1978; Argyris, 1993). From time to time, wholesale redefinitions of institutional objectives in the teaching domain are attempted—for example, the Harvard Redbook (Harvard University, 1945), Rosovsky at Harvard (Rosovsky, 1990), General Education at Columbia (A *History of Columbia*, 1954), Tussman at Berkeley (Tussman, 1969), and Hutchins at Chicago (Hutchins, 1936). These reforms sometimes, but not always, transform the curriculum; but they rarely reach down to the level of the classroom, as individual faculty members continue to teach their subject matters the same way.

To some degree, the difficulty of finding a common set of educational goals for a college or university is a reflection of the diversity of disciplinary backgrounds of the faculty. There is a correlation between faculty personalities, beliefs, and values and the disciplines in which they teach (Smart & McLaughlin, 1978). This both inhibits the forming of consensus among faculty on what knowledge, skills, attitudes, and values among students is of most worth and constrains the possibilities for collegial decision making needed for substantive changes in institutional educational philosophy.

For the team teaching suggested in this book, however, faculty will be drawn from the *same* discipline. This will most assuredly not eliminate conflict over the aims of education, but it will reduce the conflict caused by formal disciplinary diversity. However, because the knowledge bases of the disciplines of the "processes" or "crafts" represented by the team members are different (for example, the "discipline" of the craft of evaluation being different from the "discipline" of the craft of pedagogy), there is bound to be some difficulty in arriving at a consensus about team goals.

The goals of the team must be determined early in the planning phases, but then may be left unexamined for some time—until evaluation reveals lack of accomplishment or outside contingencies suggest changes. Organizations typically "recycle" the stages in problem solving and decision making as environmental contingencies demand them (Mintzberg, Raisinghani, & Theoret, 1976).

Team-Related, Rather than Task-Related, Competencies

The roles described in this book are complex and of necessity overlap somewhat. As Bouwen and Fry note: "Role ambiguity is especially present when forms of interdisciplinary work are to be executed, when multi-skilled jobs have to be performed or when non-routine work is being coordinated. In the team concept organization there is less and less reliance on formal job descriptions" (1996, p. 537). This does not mean that team members are unaware of one another's competencies, however. Cannon-Bowers, Salas, and Converse (1993) refer to this ambiguity as *interpositional uncertainty,* or a lack of accurate knowledge of what other team members do and are capable of doing—which, if excessive, can be detrimental to team performance. In the case of team teaching, however, the ambiguity of the formal roles has a positive function in that others whose competencies are informally known can readily complete tasks for which there is no clear responsible "owner." As Bouwen and Fry (1996) say, "Some, maybe only temporary, clarity of roles is desirable. The ability of the group to negotiate and reconstruct shared role definition seems critical" (p. 537).

This kind of team, then, forms a continuous base for distribution and rotation of task assignments. Team members will often have multiple memberships, and a specific team may serve as the interfacing modem at the intersection of departments or disciplines. Even when teams have a high degree of differentiation among members, it is possible to some degree for some of them to rotate their roles (Susman, 1970), contingent, of course, on the rigidity of personality and interest over the course of a life and career span.

The Relation of Teaching Teams to Academic Professions

As noted earlier, the knowledge bases of the teaching team envisioned here comprise not just subject matter knowledge but also a wide variety of process knowledge. This multidisciplinary character of the team raises important questions about the "professionalization" of faculty in higher education and about the degradation of "the" academic profession into scientifically managed satrapies comprising routine activities.

Although it is now the case that earning a doctorate in a discipline is a necessary condition for teaching in all universities and most colleges (except many community colleges), the theses proposed in this volume leave some ambiguity about what would qualify a person to teach as a member of a team in which both disciplinary knowledge and process knowledge are required. Further, as noted in Chapter One, *knowing that* is important, but for some of the roles, *knowing how* is equally important. Heretofore, faculty members have been expected to know only what constitutes their subject matter area and how to research it. The Boyer (1990) recommendations suggest a broadening of the definition of that skill, but if the team concept noted here is to be implemented, *knowing how* must be expanded beyond research skills.

For the most part, competency-based certification of capacities to teach has been accomplished in the past by disciplinary faculty who tested their protégés for knowledge. Who will now perform the assessment role to examine would-be novice teachers for their competencies to be team members with process specializations in addition to knowledge specializations? The answer lies somewhere in the future with the formation of new professional associations that feature the process skills required for each teaching team member. The professional training of team teaching members would then have to include courses and certification in the process specialization they have chosen within their knowledge domain. Eventually, a cadre of trained professionals in each discipline will evolve, but the body of process knowledge requisite to the definition of a "teaching" profession will probably be cross-disciplinary. For example, the new "profession" of lecturing need not be discipline specific. In sum, graduate education will include training in the major—the primary knowledge base—as well as in the minor—the basic skill specialization that the new faculty member wishes to bring to the team. The parallel in the medical field is the initial education and training in medicine, followed by the specialization in both theory and skill development (for example, surgery). The process would follow roughly that described by Abbott (1988):

> To investigate the relation of a profession to its work is no simple task. To be sure, the tasks of professions have certain objective qualities that resist professions' efforts to redefine them. But many basic qualities of tasks turn out to be subjective qualities assigned by the profession with current jurisdiction. These objective and subjective properties have a dynamic relation in which neither one predominates. On the one hand, a task's basis in a technology, organization, natural fact, or even cultural fact provides a strong defining core. On the other, the profession reshapes this core as it pulls the task apart into constituent problems, identifies them for clients, reasons about them, and then generates solutions shaped to client and case. Through this reshaping of objective facts by subjective means there emerges a fully defined task, irreducibly mixing the real and the constructed [p. 57].

Abbott goes on to describe the "degradation" of professions as an "essential mechanism for absorbing shifts in demand, in organizations, and in technologies that may affect a profession's jurisdictions" (p. 126). In a depiction of the history of computer programming, he remarks on the gradual differentiation of the programming "profession" into a number of sectors, which, in fact, resulted in the rise of new and different professions. In other professions—for example, British accounting and American school systems—the shift of control to external authorities resulted in a routinizing of many of the tasks of professionals, rather than a removal just of the routine tasks and the assignment of them to a secondary group of paraprofessionals. But paraprofessionals soon come to demand professional status and to compete for control of tasks with the profession from which they were split. Thus, nurses now compete with doctors for the rights to engage in certain medical practices that were formerly the exclusive province of the physician. Sometimes, the need for new professions is filled from within, sometimes through the formation of a cadre of trained workers developed outside. It is difficult to predict how the profession of teaching in higher education will evolve.

The shifts in the definition of "faculty member" raise additional questions about careers and career mobility. As teams form, allegiances develop and good working relationships sustain high productivity. Indeed, Dawis and Lofquist (1984) define "tenure" as a function of correspondence between abilities and requirements and between values and reinforcers. It is clear that the transition from individual teaching to team teaching will create major uncertainties in career opportunities and perceptions of alternative career path potentials, especially during the initial absence of the comfort of external supporting professional associations. It is likely that faculty members will increasingly come to rely on fellow team members for ego satisfactions. The intrinsic satisfaction of ego needs through teaching has heretofore been largely unrequited in part because of faculty ineptitude in discerning teaching success (Bess, 1977). The needs and satisfactions may become more salient, normative, and achievable as a result of team communication among faculty who share concerns and evidence of success. It may be that teams themselves will be the basis of career mobility. Bereiter and Scardamalia, for example, note: "In order to do justice to teamwork as a variety of expertise we would need to be able to identify expert knowledge that is the property of a group rather than the property of individuals composing it, and we would need to think of a group's having a career that might follow an expert path, continually advancing the age of its competence" (p. 21).

Though it is probable that as a profession, academia will continue to be supportive of individual creativity and of autonomous, agentic, achievement, as Cianni and Wnuck (1997) note: "In a team model, the responsibility for career development is shared among the individual employee, the team, and the organization. Individuals continue to assume primary responsibility for career planning, career goal setting, education and training" (p. 105).

How then might a faculty member move from one team to another or from one team at one university to another at a different institution? How does a faculty member earn tenure in the academic sense of the word? It may be that an expanded profession of "faculty development" and a new role for the "sabbatical" or the "educational sabbatical" will be required. As workers grow and develop and hone their competencies to higher levels, two psychological effects become salient. On the one hand, the worker relishes his or her competency, finding professional identity and pride in the demonstration of the skill. On the other hand, the work gets "tired." "Been there, done that" produces a disenchantment, a partial burnout, that in turn directs the ego to the need for new challenges and achievements.

Academic Administration and the New Teaching Team

Professionals in American society work in a variety of settings. Abbott (1988) distinguishes between *heteronomous* and *autonomous* professionals. The former work in organizations that are headed by nonprofessionals (administrators); the latter, largely as solo practitioners, sometimes in groups. We are still learning about optimum configurations of professionals and administrators from the evolving practices and debates in the health care industry. Team teaching may require a reorganization of the academic profession in a form resembling the European (Enders & Teichler, 1996) or Japanese system (Arimoto, 1996). In those systems, instead of the usual "department" comprising a broad field of study broken down into separate domains for teaching in "courses" by different faculty members, one professor heads up a small team of faculty for each narrowly circumscribed subject matter area. To be sure, these kinds of subject-organized teams do not operate collaboratively in the way envisioned in this book. Nevertheless, the conceptualization discussed in this book—of a team organization model for teaching in an institution of higher education—calls similarly for collections of small units, smaller than departments, that are responsible for teaching more circumscribed areas of study.

Finally, the structure of academic senates and representative participation in them must be reconceived in the light of the team concept. Developing a governance structure for such collectivities would admittedly be challenging, but the ultimate structure probably would not differ significantly from typical participative decision-making mechanisms in academic settings.

The Matrix Alternative

Some will say that the team organizational structure presented herein will be inefficient. If seven faculty members are required to teach a course formerly taught by one, surely colleges and universities will price themselves out of business! There is some considerable truth in this. In order for the specialization proposed here to work, the new method "specialists" must be involved with more than one course at a time. Hence, a matrix organization model may be more appropriate. Thus, within a single department with a narrow disciplinary range, there might be seven specialists arrayed, as in Exhibit 9.1 below.

Exhibit 9.1. Matrix Organization of Teaching.

Specialists	Course #1	Course #2	Course #3	Course #4	Course #5
Pedagogue					
Researcher					
Lecturer					
Discussion Leader					
Mentor					
Integrator					
Assessor					

Conceivably, these experts, all of whom have some familiarity with the discipline, would provide their expertise in the preparation and delivery of each course. It is possible that the specialization in research would be rotated, so that all of the faculty members would have at least one opportunity to deepen their knowledge of a part of the discipline.

As in all matrix organizations, there may be numerous members who specialize in the different areas and numerous sections of the particular courses. Conceivably, the teams formed in the cells of the matrix would be composed of different combinations of specialists, who not only have the knowledge and skills necessary for collaboration but also have the interpersonal compatibility that would maximize the fruitfulness of the joint venture.

Changing the System

Organizations change mostly because they have to (Dimaggio & Powell, 1983; Powell & Dimaggio, 1991). The impetus for change begins outside, but change must have its champions inside. Even though there is ample reason to believe that in many kinds of organizations, self-managed teams work more effectively than traditionally organized enterprises (Cohen & Bailey, 1997), there is still much resistance. In the case at hand, such a shift in academia would represent a radical departure from present practice and would be seen as an enormous threat by faculty themselves. Administrators would view the new arrangements as impossible to implement and manage under the present formal authority structure and informal sharing of jurisdictions.

There are also a number of myths about self-directed teams that will inhibit change. These kinds of teams are not, after all, without constraints. As Hitchcock and Willard (1995) suggest, "Self-directed teams cannot do whatever they want. Period. Nor are they leaderless groups in which no one seems to know what's going on" (p. 4). The process of building a viable and sustainable self-managed team is therefore complex and difficult, requiring knowledge, energy, commitment, and leadership toward team building. The latter, say Thamhain & Wilemon (1987), "is the process of taking a collection of individuals with different needs, backgrounds, and expertise and transforming them into an integrated, effective work unit. In this transformation process, the goals and energies of individual contributors merge and support the objectives of the team" (p. 132). The process is a dynamic one, as the external environment, the internal environment, the tasks, and the individuals are constantly changing. Each team member must make adjustments in work that account for these shifts (Dawis & Lofquist, 1984).

Barriers to and Incentives for Effectiveness

It is virtually impossible in this somewhat speculative book to anticipate both the problems of institutional change in general and the issues associated with team building. Both involve exploration of uncharted educational territory. Nevertheless, Thamhain and Wilemon (1987; see also Tannenbaum, Beard, & Salas, 1992) suggest that there are four primary issues that are relevant to performance excellence among work teams—leadership, job content, personal goals and objectives, and the work environment and organizational support. For the teams envisaged in this book to be successful, they must have clear project objectives and directions; sufficient resources; minimal interpersonal competition for power; the involvement, interest, and commitment from all parts of the administration; and personal and team security to make mistakes as the team experiments and learns. Most of these conditions address the requirements that the team process and its output be both satisfactory to external constituencies (*satisfactoriness,* according to Dawis and Lofquist) and to the workers themselves (*satisfaction*). The fields of organizational psychology and organizational development (OD) contain prodigious literature that pursues the reasons that organizational conditions produce satisfaction and motivation. Space does not permit a full explication of that literature here.

It is true, however, that because the actions of the members of the team are so intimately connected, the patterns of communication must be free and open, readily available, and consistent with member work schedules. As Kozlowski, Gully, McHugh, Salas, and Cannon-Bowers (1996) note: "The teamwork or enabling skills which facilitate congruent, synchronous, and coherent actions across team members are a critical component of team effectiveness" (p. 254). Although most faculty members can themselves develop skills related to the tasks they must perform, they are not (usually) trained in the communications needed for good team-work. Indeed, the opposite is probably true. The pattern of learning and working in graduate school and at faculty work is largely one of individual research separated from others (though in some disciplines there are different patterns). Peer-oriented communication focused on teaching is not guided by either the natural dispositions or the learned talents of most faculty members. As teams go through the phases of their development (forming, storming, norming, and performing), different communication patterns are both necessary and inevitable. If teams are to be self-managing (Fairhurst, 1993) in the tradition of academic freedom, there must be leadership from within that is attentive to potential interpersonal (but not necessarily task) problems. As the faculty teams conceived here are not leaderless but "leaderful," each member of the team must recognize the need for team process management, as well as task management. Attention must be paid to communication, coordination, and adaptation as well as to culture and climate and cohesion issues (Hackman & Morris, 1975; McGrath, 1984). The care of the team in attending to the group dynamics of the team must be a shared responsibility.

A central issue in the management of communications in a team effort is the reactions of members to challenges to their task authority. The pattern of professional authority is largely unquestioned in classroom settings and only indirectly challenged in research by rejections of or rebuttals to papers submitted to journals and books. Because the interdependent complexity of the teaching team venture requires frequent challenges to each member's domain based on its connection to other domains, the psychology of the dynamics of group behavior must be understood and attended to. As noted above, teams must be learning communities, engaged in double-loop learning—that is, correcting ineffective practices by questioning fundamental organizational beliefs and challenging long-standing perspectives, rather than relying on past routines and habits.

Teams do not become self-managing overnight. Hence, there will be a necessity for phasing in the process. Initially, faculty development personnel or consultants will need to work with teams, rather than with individual faculty members, and to function as interim leaders, gradually relinquishing their didactic or consultative roles for delegated ones, as the teams learn how to manage themselves (Dyer, 1977; Fairhurst, 1993).

Institutional Integrity

Colleges and universities currently have a somewhat schizophrenic character (Kets de Vries, 1984). The cultures of the academic professions and the administrative professions differ from each other and from the student culture. The accommodation of the differences has partially worked to date by virtue of the integration of former academics into administrative ranks, thereby improving the possibility of overlapping cultures (at least initially). Most deans, academic vice presidents, and presidents have had some teaching and research experience and can appreciate the nuances of teaching and learning. For the future, it is likely that more subcultures will develop, as teaching and research become separated from each other structurally and through education and professionalization and the emergence of outside certification agencies. Currently, we "certify" academics as qualified teachers through the earning of a single degree—the doctorate (more often the master's degree in community colleges). If this new form of team teaching is institutionalized, it is likely that the teaching side of the academic profession will be supported by separate certification associations. The multiple cultures that will emerge will certainly be seen as a threat to the integrity of our current forms of higher education institutions, where research, teaching, and service are allegedly functionally linked. Whether this change to more internally differentiated organizations will result in the loss to society of a deservedly venerated and functional institution or in the creation of new, more specialized, integrated ones that can be more responsive to contemporary social needs is impossible to predict.

References

Abbott, A. (1988). *The system of professions: An essay on the division of expert labor.* Chicago: University of Chicago Press.

Ajzen, I. (1988). *Attitudes, personality, and behavior.* Chicago: Dorsey Press.

Amason, A. C. (1996). Distinguishing the effects of functional and dysfunctional conflict on strategic decision making: Resolving a paradox for top management teams. *Academy of Management Journal, 39*(1), 123–148.

Argyris, C. (1993). *On organizational learning.* Cambridge, MA: Blackwell.

Argyris, C., & Schön, D. A. (1978). *Organizational learning: A theory of action perspectives.* Reading, MA: Addison-Wesley.

Arimoto, A. (1996). The academic profession in Japan. In P. G. Altbach (Ed.), *The international academic profession* (pp. 149–190). Princeton, NJ: Carnegie Foundation for the Advancement of Teaching.

Ashforth, B. E., & Mael, F. (1989). Social identity theory and the organization. *Academy of Management Review, 14*(1), 20–39.

Austin, A. E., & Baldwin, R. G. (1991). *Faculty collaboration: Enhancing the quality of scholarship and teaching.* ASHE-ERIC Higher Education Report No. 7. Washington, DC: School of Education and Human Development, George Washington University.

Bales, R. F. (1950). *Interaction process analysis: A method for the study of small groups.* Reading, MA: Addison-Wesley.

Bales, R. F., & Strodtbeck, F. L. (1951). Phases in group problem-solving. *The Journal of Abnormal and Social Psychology, 46,* 485–495.

Bell, D. (1976). *The coming of post-industrial society: A venture in social forecasting.* New York: Basic Books.

Bensimon, E. M., & Neumann, A. (1993). *Redesigning collegiate leadership: Teams and teamwork in higher education.* Baltimore: Johns Hopkins University Press.

Bereiter, C., & Scardamalia, M. (1993). *Surpassing ourselves: An inquiry into the nature and implications of expertise.* Chicago: Open Court.

Bess, J. L. (1977). The motivation to teach. *Journal of Higher Education, 48*(1), 243–258.

Bess, J. L. (1995). *Creative R & D leadership: Insights from Japan.* Westport, CT: Quorum/Greenwood.

Blankenship, R. L. (Ed.). (1977). Introduction: Professions, colleagues, and organizations. In *Colleagues in organization: The social construction of professional work.* New York: Wiley.

Bouwen, R., & Fry, R. (1996). Facilitating group development: Interventions for a relational and contextual construction. In M. A. West (Ed.), *Handbook of work group psychology* (pp. 531–552). New York: Wiley.

Boyer, E. L. (1990). *Scholarship reconsidered: Priorities of the professoriate.* Princeton, NJ: Carnegie Foundation for the Advancement of Teaching.

Brief, A. P., & Aldag, R. J. (1981). The "self" in work organizations: A conceptual review. *Academy of Management Review, 6,* 75–88.

Brodbeck, F. C. (1996). Criteria for the study of work group functioning. In M. A. West (Ed.), *Handbook of work group psychology* (pp. 285–315). New York: Wiley.

Bucher, R., & Stelling, J. (1969). Characteristics of professional organizations. *Journal of Health and Social Behavior, 10,* 3–15.

Cannon-Bowers, J. A., Salas, E., and Converse, S. A. (1993). Shared mental models in expert team decision making. In N. J. Castellan, Jr. (Ed.), *Current issues in individual and group decision making* (pp. 221–246). Hillsdale, NJ: Erlbaum.

Cannon-Bowers, J. A., Tannenbaum, S. I., Salas, E., and Volpe, C. E. (1995). Defining competencies and establishing team training requirements. In R. A. Guzzo, E. Salas, & Associates, *Team effectiveness and decision making in organizations* (pp. 333–380). San Francisco: Jossey-Bass.

Cianni, M., & Wnuck, D. (1997). Individual growth and team enhancement: Moving toward a new model of career development. *Academy of Management Executive, XI*(1), 105–115.

Cohen, S. G., & Bailey, D. E. (1997). What makes teams work: Group effectiveness research from the shop floor to the executive suite. *Journal of Management, 23*(3), 239–290.

Cohen, S. G., Ledford, G. E., Jr., & Spreitzer, G. M. (1996). A predictive model of self-managing work team effectiveness. *Human Relations, 49*(5), 643– 676.

Cohen, S. G., & Spreitzer, G. M. (1994, Aug.). Employee involvement: The impact of self-managing teams on productivity, customer satisfaction, and employee quality of work life. Paper presented at the annual meeting of the Academy of Management, Dallas.

Dawis, R. V., & Lofquist, L. H. (1984). *A psychological theory of work adjustment: An individual-differences model and its applications.* Minneapolis: University of Minnesota Press.

Dimaggio, P. J., & Powell, W. W. (1983). The iron cage revisited: Institutional isomorphism and collective rationality in organizational fields. *American Sociological Review, 48,* 147–160.

Dooley, R. S., & Fryxell, G. E. (1999). Attaining decision quality and commitment from dissent: The moderating effects of loyalty and competence in strategic decision-making teams. *Academy of Management Journal, 42*(4), 389–402.

Drucker, P. (1993). *The post-capitalist society.* New York: HarperCollins.

Dyer, W. G. (1977). *Team building: Issues and alternatives.* Reading, MA: Addison-Wesley.

Edmondson, A. (1999). Psychological safety and learning behavior in work teams. *Administrative Science Quarterly, 44,* 2, 350–383.

Edmondson, A., & Moingeon, B. (1998). From organizational learning to the learning organization. *Management Learning, 29,* 499–517.

Enders, J., & Teichler, U. (1996). The academic profession in Germany. In P. G. Altbach (Ed.), *The international academic profession* (pp. 439–492). Princeton, NJ: Carnegie Foundation for the Advancement of Teaching.

Fairhurst, G. (1993, August). The language of self-managing teams. Paper presented at the annual meeting of the Academy of Management, Atlanta.

Gersick, C.J.G. (1988). Time and transition in work teams: Toward a new model of group development. *Academy of Management Journal, 31*(1), 9–41.

Gersick, C.J.G., & Davis-Sacks, M. L. (1990). Summary: Task forces. In J. R. Hackman (Ed.), *Groups that work (and those that don't): Creating conditions for effective teamwork* (pp. 146–153). San Francisco: Jossey-Bass.

Giacquinta, J. (1975). Status risk-taking: A central issue in the initiation and implementation of public school innovations. *Journal of Research and Development in Education, 9*(1), 102–114.

Giddens, A. (1991). *Modernity and self-identity: Self and society in the late modern age.* Palo Alto, CA: Stanford University Press.

Goodman, P. S., Devadas, R., & Hughson, T. L. (1990). Groups and productivity: Analyzing the effectiveness of self-managing teams. In J. P. Campbell & R. J. Campbell (Eds.), *Productivity in organizations* (pp. 295–327). San Francisco: Jossey-Bass.

Guzzo, R. A. (1996). Fundamental considerations about work groups. In M. A. West (Ed.), *Handbook of work group psychology* (pp. 3–21). New York: Wiley.

Hackman, J. R. (1990). Work teams in organizations: An orienting framework. In J. R. Hackman (Ed.), *Groups that work (and those that don't): Creating conditions for effective teamwork* (pp. 1–14). San Francisco: Jossey-Bass.

Hackman, J. R. & Morris, C. G. (1975). Group tasks, group interaction process, and group performance effectiveness: A review and proposed integration. In L. Burkowitz (Ed.), *Advances in Experimental Social Psychology.* New York: Academic Press.

Harding, S., & Hintikka, M. (Eds.). (1983). *Discovering reality: Feminist perspectives on epistemology, methodology and philosophy of science.* Dordrecht, The Netherlands: Reidel.

Harrison, J. S., & St. John, C. H. (1996). Managing and partnering with external stakeholders. *Academy of Management Executive, 10*(2), 46–60.

Harvard University. (1945). *General education in a free society: Report of the Harvard committee.* Cambridge, MA: Harvard University.

Heinen, J. S., & Jacobson, E. J. (1976). A model of task group development in complex organizations and a strategy of implementation. *Academy of Management Review, 1*, 98–111.

Hinings, C. R., & Greenwood, R. (1996). Working together. In P. J. Frost & M. S. Taylor (Eds.), *Rhythms of academic life: Personal accounts of careers in academia* (pp. 227–232). Thousand Oaks, CA: Sage.

Hirakawa, R. Y. (1990). The role of communication in group decision-making efficacy: A task-contingency perspective. *Small Group Research, 21,* 190–204.

A history of Columbia College on Morningside. (1954). New York: Columbia University Press.

Hitchcock, D., & Willard, M. (1995). *Why teams can fail and what to do about it: Essential tools for anyone implementing self-directed work teams.* Burr Ridge, IL: Irwin.

Homans, G. (1950). *The human group.* Orlando: Harcourt, Brace.

Hutchins, R. M. (1936). *The higher learning in America.* New Haven, CT: Yale University Press.

Ketchum, L. D., & Trist, E. (1992). *All teams are not created equal: How employee empowerment really works.* Thousand Oaks, CA: Sage.

Kets de Vries, M.F.R. (1984). *The neurotic organization: Diagnosing and changing counterproductive styles of management.* San Francisco: Jossey-Bass.

Kirkman, B. L., & Rosen, B. (1997). A model of work team empowerment. *Research in Organizational Change and Development, 10,* 131–167.

Kozlowski, S.W.J., Gully, S. M., McHugh, P. P., Salas, E., & Cannon-Bowers, J. A. (1996). A dynamic theory of leadership and team effectiveness: Developmental and task contingent leader roles. *Research in Personnel and Human Resources Management, 14,* 253–305.

Leithwood, K. (1998). Team learning processes. In K. Leithwood & K. S. Louis (Eds.), *Organizational learning in schools* (pp. 203–217). Lisse, The Netherlands: Swets & Zeitlinger.

McGrath, J. E. (1984). *Groups: Interaction and performance.* Englewood Cliffs, NJ: Prentice-Hall.

Miller, G. A., Galanter, E., & Pribam, K. H. (1960). *Plans and the structure of behavior.* New York: Holt.

Mintzberg, H. (1983). *Power in and around organizations.* Englewood Cliffs, NJ: Prentice Hall.

Mintzberg, H., Raisinghani, D., & Theoret, A. (1976). The structure of "unstructured" decision processes. *Administrative Science Quarterly, 21,* 246–275.

Mowday, R. T., & Nam, S. H. (1997). Expectancy theory approaches to faculty motivation. In J. L. Bess (Ed.), *Teaching well and liking it: Motivating faculty to teach effectively* (pp. 110–124). Baltimore: Johns Hopkins University Press.

Oja, S. N., & Smulyan, L. (1989). *Collaborative action research: A developmental approach.* Social research and educational studies series (Vol. 7). Bristol, PA: Falmer Press.

Osterman, P. (1994). How common is workplace transformation and who adopts it? *Industrial and Labor Relations Review, 47,* 173–188.

Parker, G. M. (1990). *Team players and teamwork.* San Francisco: Jossey-Bass.

Parsons, T. (1951). *The social system.* New York: Free Press.

Peters, T. J. (1988). *Thriving on chaos.* New York: Knopf.

Powell, W., & Dimaggio, P. J. (1991). *The new institutionalism in organizational analysis.* Chicago: University of Chicago Press.

Robbins, S. P. (1998). *Organizational behavior: Concepts, controversies, applications.* Upper Saddle River, NJ: Prentice Hall.

Rosovsky, H. (1990). *The university: An owner's manual.* New York: Norton.

Russell, R. S., & Taylor, B. W., III. (1998). *Production and operations management* (2nd ed.) Englewood Cliffs, NJ: Prentice Hall.

Senge, P. N. (1990). *The fifth discipline: The art and practice of the learning organization.* New York: Doubleday.

Shea, G. P., & Guzzo, R. A. (1987). Groups as human resources. In K. M. Rowland & G. R. Ferris (Eds.), *Research in personnel and human resources management* (Vol. 5, pp. 323–356). Greenwich, CT: JAI Press.

Shonk, W., & Shonk, J. H. (1988). What business teams can learn from athletic teams. *Personnel, 65,* 76–80.

Smart, J. C., & McLaughlin, G. W. (1978). Reward structures of academic disciplines. *Research in Higher Education, 8,* 39–55.

Smith, R. (1981). Let your employees choose their co-workers. *Society for Advancement of Management, Advanced Management Journal, 46,* 27–36.

Starbuck, W. H. (1996). Learning by knowledge-intensive firms. In M. D. Cohen & L. S. Sproull (Eds.), *Organizational learning* (pp. 484–515). Thousand Oaks, CA: Sage.

Steiner, I. D. (1972). *Group process and productivity.* Orlando: Academic Press.

Sundstrom, E. K., De Meuse, P., & Futrell, D. (1995). Work teams, applications and effectiveness. In D. A. Kolb, J. S. Osland, & I. M. Rubin (Eds.), *The organizational behavior reader* (pp. 268–289). Englewood Cliffs, NJ: Prentice Hall.

Susman, G. I. (1970). The impact of automation on work group autonomy and task specialization. *Human Relations, 23,* 565–577.

Tajfel, H., & Turner, J. C. (1979). An integrative theory of intergroup conflict. In W. G. Austin & S. Worchel (Eds.), *The social psychology of intergroup relations.* Pacific Grove, CA: Brooks/Cole.

Tannenbaum, S. I., Beard, R. L., & Salas, E. (1992). Team building and its influence on team effectiveness: An examination of conceptual and empirical developments. In K. Kelly (Ed.), *Issues, theory, and research in industrial/organizational psychology.* New York: Elsevier.

Thamhain, H. J., & Wilemon, D. L. (1987). Issues in managing technical teams and group process. *IEEE Transactions on Engineering Manage-*

ment, EM-34(3), 130–137.

Thompson, J. D. (1967). *Organizations in action.* New York: McGraw-Hill.

Tornatzky, L. G. (1986). Technological change and the structure of work. In M. S. Pallak & R. Perloff (Eds.), *Psychology and work* (pp. 89–136). Washington, DC: American Psychological Association.

Towers Perrin. (1990). *Workforce 2000 today: A bottom-line concern.* Valhalla, NY: Towers Perrin.

Tschan, F., & von Cranach, M. (1986). Group task structure, processes, and outcomes (pp. 95–121). In M. A. West (Ed.), *Handbook of Work Group Psychology.* New York: Wiley.

Tuckman, B. W. (1965). Developmental sequences in small groups. *Psychological Bulletin, 63,* 384–399.

Tuckman, B. W., & Jensen, M. C. (1977). Stages of small group development revisited. *Group and Organizational Studies, 2,* 419–427.

Tussman, J. (1969). *Experiment at Berkeley.* New York: Oxford University Press.

Ulich, E., & Weber, W. G. (1996). Dimensions, criteria and evaluation of work group autonomy. In M. A. West (Ed.), *Handbook of work group psychology* (pp. 247–282). New York: Wiley.

van Offenbeek, M., & Koopman, P. (1996). Interaction and decision-making in project teams. In M. A. West (Ed.), *Handbook of work group psychology* (pp. 159–187). New York: Wiley.

von Glasersfeld, E. (1996). Introduction: Aspects of constructivism. In C. T. Fosnot (Ed.), *Constructivism: Theory, perspectives, and practice* (pp. 3–7). New York: Teachers College Press.

Wageman, R. (1995). Interdependence and group effectiveness. *Administrative Science Quarterly, 40,* 145–180.

Wall, T. D., Kemp, N. J., Jackson, P. R., & Clegg, C. W. (1986). Outcomes of autonomous workgroups: A long-term field experiment. *Academy of Management Journal, 29,* 280–304.

Worchel, S., Wood, W., & Simpson, J. A. (Eds.). (1992). *Group process and productivity.* Thousand Oaks, CA: Sage.

Yeatts, D. E., & Hyten, C. (1998). *High-Performing self-managed work teams: A comparison of theory and practice.* Thousand Oaks, CA: Sage.

Zaleznik, A. (1989). *The managerial mystique: Restoring leadership in business.* New York: HarperCollins.

Chapter Ten

The Future of Teaching
Creating a New Academic Identity
James L. Bess

The preceding chapters address key issues in the conduct of teaching in colleges and universities. Drawing on theoretical underpinnings that are essentially from the social and behavioral sciences, the authors describe possible future modes of teaching that take into account the contemporary, if not ageless, problems of the communication of the wisdom and values of one generation to the next. As Margaret Mead (1970) notes, however, the direction of this transference is not always from the old to the young. Hence, the more proper context for the conceptualization of teaching is a *total learning environment,* in which mixes of generations learn from and teach one another. More than double-loop learning, in Argyris's (1993) terms, this framework for conducting the work of teaching embodies a collective, reflexive imagination that allows information and affect to flow in many directions, yet ultimately be coherent, forward moving, and cumulative (very much in the modern, not postmodern, tradition). There is, further, a considered assumption in this book of the possibility and probability of making meaning out of the mix of ideas, facts, and people that comprise a team with appropriately permeable boundaries.

Because the proposals here involve rather radical changes in the structure of teaching in higher education, however, there are a number of unresolved issues that need at least to be recognized in this final chapter. The first has to do with personal satisfactions that faculty derive from teaching. Readers of this proposal who conceive of teaching in traditional terms may lament the loss for some team members of structured direct classroom contact with students. They will suggest that these team members will miss the teacher's perception and apprehension of the understanding that suffuses an enlightened student who grows in maturity due partly at least to the teacher's imagination and initiative. Such worries, however, beg the question by generalizing to all faculty the motivation and pleasures of the direct-contact person. In this book, we recognize and capitalize on the principle that many faculty find their critical intrinsic satisfactions elsewhere, in other pursuits that do not depend on the immediacy of student responses. This is not to say that some faculty are less altruistic in their specialized teaching motivation—only that their gratification can be realized through indirect modes of appreciation of their achievements. When the accomplishments of the team are adequately communicated and rewarded, especially as "team ego" partially replaces individual ego, all faculty members on the team will find personal satisfaction through the exercise of their craft and the manifest meaningfulness and significance of their work (Hackman & Oldham, 1980; Hackman, 1985).

Ethnicity, Gender, and Age in Team Composition

Another unresolved issue is the question of the composition of the team. Some would argue that teams must be diverse in race, ethnicity, gender, and age (and other characteristics of diversity). The authors of this volume unequivocally endorse vigorous affirmative action efforts to afford equal opportunity to all, especially those who have been denied it in the past. The argument here, however, is that no special diversity characteristic *must* necessarily be represented on a teaching team as we have described it. Team composition need not reflect the ethnicity, gender, age, or other minority distributions in the population. In our view, any of the roles can be played equally well by members of any race or religion, people of any sexual orientation, or any age. In the light of the sociotechnical approach outlined in earlier chapters, the only constraint is compatibility of the work-task-occupational preferences of team members, the congruence of their ideological persuasions, and the affinities of their social relationships. That is, preferences for tasks and individual talents, temperaments, and social skills fit faculty members to work roles in teaching teams. This is not by any means to suggest that sensitivity to diversity is irrelevant to teaching. Indeed, every team member must recognize and give attention to the unique backgrounds and orientations of the students being taught. Conscientious discernment of diversity issues may in some cases require collaboration by each of the team members with knowledgeable others outside of the team whose own backgrounds are more closely matched to student body diversity.

The Matter of Diverse Student Learning Styles

Central to the theses of this book is the interplay of learning styles, the sociology of knowledge, the associated tasks of teaching, and the requisite characteristics and skills of teachers. The next open question to be considered is how the team addresses the idiosyncratic needs and associated learning styles preferred by students. This challenge of learner diversity in the classroom has plagued teachers forever, with the proposed solutions restricted largely to the Hopkins-and-his-log metaphor noted in Chapter One. The issue has implications for each of the roles discussed in earlier chapters. Even mentoring, where the usual interactive mode is one-on-one, can take place in other multiple-person settings in which there may be no common student learning style preferences.

Most teachers are forced to make assumptions that their institution has attempted to recruit a relatively homogeneous student body (compared with the heterogeneity in the college student population at large nationally). That means that students at, say, Harvard, can be assumed to learn best in fairly similar ways. The same can be thought to be true of students at Montana State University or Northeastern Oklahoma Agricultural and Mechanical College. (Within-group variance is smaller than between-group variance, to adopt another familiar terminology.) Though to be sure (and thankfully) at each of these institutions, there is a rich diversity of student types, instructors of class size greater than one (in our case, with team members as the instructional faculty) must make simplifying assumptions that allow them to address the needs of different kinds of students simultaneously, rather those of one student at a time. This is not to say, of course, that the team cannot work with individual students to accommodate them when their learning style preferences deviate from the majority of the class. But it recognizes the practical reality of limitations on faculty time. One of the strengths of the team concept proposed in this book is that collaboration between the assessor team member and the pedagogy expert will result in the design of instructional methods that do, in fact, take into account student learning style preferences.

Issues of the Structure of Knowledge

A similar problem occurs with respect to the structure of knowledge. The work of the team (that is, of each team specialist) changes depending on the structure of knowledge in the course being taught. For example, not only is English different from physics, but the philosophical assumptions, sociological characteristics, and stage of paradigmatic development of each discipline vary (Hativa & Marincovich, 1995). One department may see truth as "meaning," another as "facts," and so forth. What is taught and how it is taught and what kinds of teachers are necessary to teach it are also different. Again, a simplifying assumption is made here. For our purposes, the team is conceived as comprising members from the same discipline. Obviously, this is not the usual conception of team teaching, which crosses disciplines (certainly not a bad idea, but something outside the limits of this book). Controlling for the sample of team members by preselecting more homogeneous faculty by discipline aids in the assumptions that can be made about the sociology of knowledge. Nevertheless, insofar as each team member represents a process discipline as well as a cognitive one centered in the college curriculum, the philosophical underpinnings of the structure of knowledge to be taught may be subject to continuing controversy.

Teams and the Division of Labor

How much individual specialization on a team is possible? How, for example, Tiberius and Tipping ask in their chapter on teaching in small discussion sections (Chapter Five), can pedagogy or research be ignored by the instructor and attention paid just to classroom dynamics? The same question applies to Saroyan's chapter (Four) about lecturing. Does not the behavior of the teacher *depend* on the pedagogy and the research that informs the content of the class? Or finally, is it reasonable for Grace in Chapter Seven to propose integrating the classroom and residence hall or student organizations without taking into account both the knowledge transmitted or evoked in class as well as the mentoring that may take place out of class?

This subject is discussed at length and more theoretically in Chapter Nine. As was noted, there are potential and real overlaps across the team members. It seems necessary to be somewhat general about these overlaps. Team members are "loosely coupled," in the jargon of Karl Weick (1976, p. 1). Though the tasks that each of these role players takes on are specialized, it is expected that the connections across roles will be articulated through close teamwork. Indeed, this is the essence of good teamwork. The lecturer must, of necessity, work closely with the researcher and the pedagogue. Note that in the individual chapters, by intention, just those skills and knowledge domains that are needed for the particular role are identified. As team dynamics evolve, however, it may be that each member increasingly becomes a generalist and integrates other members' knowledge and skills without needing as much communication as when the team collaboration began.

Goals and Objectives of Institutions of Higher Education

There is yet another critical area that remains problematic for teams. All of the chapters are based on assumptions about goals to be achieved by the institution, course, or teacher. So also are the learning-teaching objectives derived from them. Didactic objectives obviously can vary (for example, acquisition of vocational knowledge and skills versus the "owning" of the values and attitudes of a liberal education). Cognitive objectives also are quite different from teaching goals, which include personality growth and value change—for example, development of identity and tolerance for ambiguity. Objectives vary too by discipline, by type of course (for example, required or elective), by student year in school, and so on. Equally important is the time dimension, as Bruce Speck, writing in Chapter Eight about assessment, is quick to point out. Different types of institutions and different institutions within those types place different emphases on these alternatives. For the purposes of this book, we have adopted a rather unexceptional, though nonetheless valuable, set of aims of education—namely, that instruction in college education is *primarily* intended to expand minds, develop critical thinking skills and habits, encourage divergent thinking, engender exploration of alternative ranges and manifestations of personality, and foster relativistic thinking, especially about values. No mean feat! This list obviously constitutes a simplification but has permitted each chapter author to develop his or her ideas along a reasonably common front. The team approach to teaching advocated in this book hypothetically will be more effective in achieving all of these goals.

The Issue of Expertise

Finally, the meaning of the concept of *expertise* in any professional endeavor is a critical theme throughout this volume. Essentially it marks the difference between a logical-empiricist philosophy versus an emancipatory one. Certainly, if the idea of expertise in teaching were abandoned, it would be necessary to reconsider the ideas of authority and leadership in the classroom, not to speak of ontology and epistemology! In this book, consequently, the authors tend to side with Socrates (in *Charmides*), who argues that people with specialized knowledge and skills are the best sources of "opinion" about a particular domain, and lay people (for example, students) can learn by questioning them to test their wisdom. Indeed, as Parker Palmer (1998) notes: "In the community of truth, as in real life, there are no pristine objects of knowledge and no ultimate authorities. In the community of truth, as in real life, truth does not reside primarily in propositions, and education is more than delivering propositions about objects to passive auditors" (p. 101).

Further, Palmer goes on to say: *"Truth is an eternal conversation about things that matter, conducted with passion and discipline.* Unlike the objectivist, I do not understand truth to be lodged in the conclusions we reach about objects of knowledge. How could it be, since the conclusions keep changing? I understand truth as the passionate and disciplined process of inquiry and dialogue itself, as the dynamic conversation of a community that keeps testing old conclusions and coming to new ones" (p. 104, emphasis in original).

In the separate chapters, the idea of having students contribute ideas to help articulate and define each of the teacher roles makes sense in terms of many of the objectives noted earlier. Nevertheless, there are certain kinds of expertise that each team member must have regardless of the conception of who has final "authority" either over truth or the teaching process. (See the discussion of Margaret Mead above.) These various expertise domains are brought to the table of teaching and learning by the members of the team.

A final word for the future: consider how teams might be assembled in institutions of the future whose electronic communications mechanisms become more sophisticated (Townsend, DeMarie, & Hendrickson, 1998). Might it be possible to assemble teams across institutions, indeed, even across nations, in which the members of the teams represent expertise that can create unique products and services for given student bodies? Going one step further, is it not possible that information technology may some day be able to produce class profiles of students with optimally mixed learning style preferences and other personal characteristics and that these can be matched with a team of appropriately skilled faculty drawn from a national or international pool—all combined in an interactive virtual classroom?

The Coming Shape of the Academic Profession

Academic pundits for a number of recent years have been portraying with alarm the new trends toward hierarchical, centralized decision making in organizations. Demands for accountability, contracts, and increased job and role specification by "higher" administrative authorities portend a future in which the traditions of academic freedom that underpin teaching and research creativity will diminish. Clark (1997) depicts this faculty as a relatively "powerless proletariat" (p. 35) in a system in which many more part-time faculty participate in colleges and universities as migrant workers under the control of administrative power brokers. An alternative scenario, however, sees the rise of migrant faculty workers seeking work in a variety of institutional settings as a source of new vitality, as new teams of affiliated and unaffiliated faculty are formed. The team would integrate the outside players far more meaningfully than the typical mode for adjunct faculty today. Such itinerant faculty, as part of an interdependent team, would be welcomed and rewarded for their contributions in ways that extant minuscule adjunct faculty salaries cannot possibly do.

The Promise of Instructional Teams

Harold Leavitt (1996) describes a possible future for teams that recognizes how a downsizing organization can reshape its internal structure and capitalize on the use of decentralized small groups of workers. Describing two *hot groups* in which he participated in his younger days, he portrays them in general as "totally consuming places," where "excitement, ideas, and innovative research bubbled all over the place" (p. 289). Hot groups, he goes on to say, are democratic, competitive, ambitious and aspiring, visionary, unpretentious, somewhat chaotic, and all involving. Although there are personal psychological risks in participating in hot groups, Leavitt suggests that "hot groups must surely be good for human beings, too."

The teams described in this book may not and probably will not be paragons of "touchy-feely," "good" human relations, in perpetual comity, if for no other reason than the *required* diversity of interests, talents, and temperaments of the faculty membership. There are bound to be conflicts, occasional losses of trust, and diversions of attention (Dooley & Fryxell, 1999). Yet, imagine what an exciting environment for teaching can be created by virtue of that very diversity! Imagine the challenges to habitual thinking about teaching, the stretching of faculty vision, the growth and development of each person, and the new sources of rewards for teaching—and, of course, the increased sustained strength of motivation to teach. Surely this is a model of teaching that can result in ever higher achievements for students.

References
Argyris, C. (1993). *On organizational learning.* Cambridge, MA: Blackwell.
Boice, R. (1992). *The new faculty member: Support and fostering professional development.* San Francisco: Jossey-Bass.
Clark, B. R. (1997). Academic professions. *Daedalus, 126*(4), 21–42.
Dooley, R. S., & Fryxell, G. E. (1999). Attaining decision quality and commitment from dissent: The moderating effects of loyalty and

competence in strategic decision-making teams. *Academy of Management Journal, 42*(4), 389–402.

Hackman, J. R. (1985). Doing research that makes a difference. In E. E. Lawler III & others, *Doing research that is useful for theory and practice* (pp. 126–149). San Francisco: Jossey-Bass.

Hackman, J. R., & Oldham, G. (1980). *Work redesign.* Reading, MA: Addison-Wesley.

Hativa, N., & Marincovich, M. (Eds.). (1995). *Disciplinary differences in teaching and learning: Implications for practice.* New Directions for Teaching and Learning, no. 64. San Francisco: Jossey-Bass.

Leavitt, H. J. (1996). The old days, hot groups, and managers' lib. *Administrative Science Quarterly, 41*(2), 288–300.

Mead, M. (1970). *Culture and commitment: A study of the generation gap.* Garden City, NY: Natural History Press/Doubleday.

Palmer, P. J. (1998). The courage to teach: Exploring the inner landscape of a teacher's life. San Francisco: Jossey-Bass.

Townsend, A. M., DeMarie, S. M., & Hendrickson, A. R. (1998). Virtual teams: Technology and the workplace of the future. *Academy of Management Executive, 12*(3), 17–29.

Weick, K. E. (1976). Educational organizations as loosely coupled systems. *Administrative Science Quarterly, 21*(1), 1–19.

Name Index

Oldham, G., 237
Orsburn, J. D., 21, 23
Osterman, P., 206
Ostroff, C., 18

P

Pace, C. R., 41, 165
Pajares, F., 121
Palmer, P. J., 115, 241
Park, J., 109
Parker, G. M., 208
Parsons, T., 4, 62, 211
Pascarella, E. T., 47, 119, 154, 158, 165, 177, 178
Paulsen, M. B., 176
Paunonen, S. V., 74, 95, 96
Pazandak, C. H., 167
Penner, K. S., 92
Perrow, C., 9
Perry, R. P., 92
Perry, W. G., 46, 48, 164
Pervin, L. A., 18
Peters, T. J., 205
Pintrich, P. R., 50, 54
Platt, G. M., 62
Playko, M. A., 144
Polanyi, M., 113
Poston, W.S.C., 164
Pougiales, R., 56
Powell, W. W., 226
Pratt, D. D., 100, 135, 136
Pribam, K. H., 213
Puett, P., 90
Purves, A. C., 174
Putnam, R. T., 109, 120

Q

Quellmalz, E. S., 174

R

Rachal, J. R., 174
Rahilly, T., 93
Raisinghani, D., 220
Ramin-Gyurnek, J., 156
Ramirez, B. C., 159
Raymond, J. C., 174

Reader, G. G., 64
Reisman, D., 65
Reisser, L., 153, 154, 164
Rentz, A. L., 153
Reskin, B., 65
Rhoads, R. M., 156
Robbins, S. P., 207
Roe, R. A., 16
Roen, D. H., 193
Rosen, B., 206
Rosovsky, H., 219
Rudduck, J., 109
Rushton, J. P., 74, 75, 95, 96
Russell, R. S., 213
Ryan, M. P., 193

S

St. Clair, K. L., 134
St. John, C. H., 213
Salas, E., 8, 219, 220, 227
Salovey, P., 119, 123
Saroyan, A., 87, 93, 99
Scardamalia, M., 15, 93, 112, 114, 115, 117, 126, 223
Schinka, J. A., 17
Schiralli, M., 43
Schlossberg, N., 165
Schmitz, C. C., 75, 76
Schön, D. A., 109, 219
Schonwetter, D., 91, 92
Schroeder, C. C., 159
Segebarth, K., 118
Seldin, P., 5
Seligman, M., 118
Senge, R. N., 206
Shaman, S., 7
Shaw, K. M., 46
Shea, G. F., 144, 214
Shelby, A., 174
Shonk, J. H., 207
Shonk, W., 207
Shulman, L. S., 36, 37, 43, 52, 53, 62, 87, 93, 94, 102, 120
Silberman, M., 53
Simmons, A., 119
Simmons, S. C., 193

Subject Index

A

Academic performance: and curriculum-cocurriculum integration, 158–161; feedback, 119

Action research, 109, 212

Active learning: defined, 122; in discussion groups, 110; and social constructivism, 122–123; techniques, 53–54

Administrative culture: hierarchy in, 206; team alignment with, 217–218

Administrative evaluation, team data in, 194

Apprenticeship concept of teaching, 100

Assessment: and classroom practices, 173–175; criterion- versus norm-referenced, 182–183; definitional and methodological problems in, 175–177; generalizability of, 176; holistic scoring in, 185; and joint research efforts, 186; psychometric versus alternative views of, 191; of teaching outcomes, 177–178; of team performance, 186, 218; theory, 175–178

Assessment measures: development of, 181; and evaluative frameworks, 176, 190–192; team consensus on, 181; user testing of, 183

Assessor: and content area education, 190, 192–193; curriculum for, 190–193; data evaluation by, 184–185; managerial role of, 183–184; methodology expertise of, 190–192; pedagogical tasks of, 55–56; personal qualities of, 188–189; project management training of, 192; requisite skills of, 189–192; tasks, 178–187; theoretical paradigms and, 191

Attribution theory, and interactive teaching, 118–120

C

Career development: faculty, 26, 222, 223–224; student, facilitation of, 156–158

Class size, 39, 93, 94

Cocurricular domain: in segregated academy, 152–154; and student outcomes, 154–155. *See also* Curriculum-cocurriculum integrator

Cognitive competencies, classification of, 112–113

Collaborative action research, 212

Communication, team: management of, 228; patterns in, 213, 227–228; sequential, 213

Competencies: research on, 65, 69; and role ambiguity, 220–221; team-generic versus team-specific, 219

Conflict, team, 215

Constructivist learning theory: and group goals, 212; and social constructivism, 122–123

Cooperative learning strategies, 156

Course ratings, contextual variables in, 97–98

Curriculum: innovative, 2; knowledge, defined, 37; and organizational theory, 4–5; and pedagogical locus of control, 42; traditional, 3–4

Student learning: attribution theory and, 118–120; classroom size and, 39; difficulties, and pedagogical strategies, 54–55; disciplinary area and, 48–49, 120; in discussion group, 108–127; diverse styles of, 238–239; educational/institutional goals and, 43–47; individualized strategies for, 155–156; instructor's estimation of, 51; low-inference teaching behaviors and, 92; monitoring and evaluation of, 54–57; process of representation in, 52–53; self-concept and self-efficacy in, 101, 135; as student responsibility, 41, 50; teaching strategies and, 53–54, 159

Student outcomes: cocurricular domain and, 154–155; teachers' feedback on, 119. *See also* Assessment

Student-faculty relationship: disparate learning and teaching styles in, 159; limited context of, 154; teacher-learner alliance in, 119, 123; technology's impact on, 160

Subject matter content knowledge, 37, 38

T

Task assignments, rotation of, 221

Task sequencing, 212–213

Tasks, in organizational theory, 9–10. *See also* Teaching tasks

Teacher knowledge, categories of, 36–37

Teacher preparation. *See* Graduate education; Professional development and training

Teacher-learner alliance, 119, 123

Teaching: goal identification in, 219–220; interactive, learning theory and, 117–124; matching of tasks, talents, and temperaments in, 8–9; need for role reclassification in, 21; nurturing perspective in,

135–136; rewards, 2, 26, 194, 214; and role rotation, 24; self-efficacy theory and, 118–120; sensitivity in, 15; strategy, selection of, 53–54; style, versus teaching perspective, 135; subroles, 5, 15, 21; total learning environment and, 236; two-level categorization model, 99–101

Teaching Goals Inventory, 181

Teaching skills: concept of expertise and, 14–16; constituents' expectations and, 12; curricular redesign and, 13; knowledge structure across disciplines and, 10–12

Teaching tasks, 10–13; axes of separation in, 102; and constituent educational goals, 10–13; and disciplinary differences, 12; teacher- versus learner-centered, 99–101

Teaching team: academic administration and, 217–218, 224–225; assessment of, 218; budget and time constraints on, 216, 218; communication in, 213, 227–228; conflict in, 215; cross-departmental, 4; diversity, 237–238; division of labor in, 239–240; ego identification and individual accomplishment in, 214, 216, 223; functional uncertainty in, 215; goal setting, 212, 220; group processes in, 211–216; hiring issues, 195; individual recognition in, 211; implementation, 22–23; intradiscipline, 4; matrix model, 225–226; migrant adjunct faculty and, 242–243; peer teaching in, 212; personality traits of, 98; planning process, 26; professional development and training of, 26, 186, 222, 223–224; promotion in, 193; psychological dimensions of, 216–219; publication credit and, 193; research findings, administrative use of, 194; resistance to, 226–227; rewards, 26, 194, 214; risks, 214–216; structural features of, 209–211; subject-oriented models in, 224–225; task sequencing in, 212–213; team-related competencies in, 219–221; technological-pedagogical integration and, 20–21. *See also* Curriculum-cocurriculum integrator; Discussion leader; Lecturer; Mentor; Pedagogical expert; Researcher

Teaching-learning relationship, evaluation of, 178–180. *See also* Student learning

Teams: business sector development of, 204–206; common task orientation and identity transformation in, 210–211; organization and characteristics, 206–209; self-managed, 208, 210; social and technical subsystems in, 210. *See also* Teaching team

Technology: and future teaching teams, 242; and team innovation, 215–216

Temperament: defined, 16; and person-environment fit, 17–19

V

Virtual classroom, 159–160